POPULAR CULTURE IN THE FIFTIES

Frank A. Salamone

University Press of America,® Inc.
Lanham · New York · Oxford

Copyright © 2001 by
University Press of America,® Inc.
4720 Boston Way
Lanham, Maryland 20706
UPA Acquisitions Department (301) 459-3366

12 Hid's Copse Rd.
Cumnor Hill, Oxford OX2 9JJ

Library of Congress Cataloging-in-Publication Data

Salamone, Frank A.
Popular culture in the fifties / Frank A. Salamone.
p.   cm
Includes bibliographical references and index.
1. United States—Civilization—1945- 2. Popular culture—United
States—History—20th century. 3. United States—Social life and
customs—1945-1970. 4. Nineteen fifties. I. Title.
E169.12 .S233 2001   973.921—dc21   2001043084 CIP

ISBN 0-7618-2103-1 (pbk. : alk. paper)

047696536

⊖™The paper used in this publication meets the minimum
requirements of American National Standard for Information
Sciences—Permanence of Paper for Printed Library Materials,
ANSI Z39.48—1984

Contents

Preface

The 1950s were an exciting, complicated time. In general, Americans like exciting times but are not too keen on complicated ones. The urge to simplify burns deep within the American soul. Thus, the fifties have often been presented as a rather homogeneous period in which everyone lived in Suburbia or was on the way there. Additionally, everyone saw the same TV shows, read the same magazines and books, and viewed the same movies.

The reality was more complex, of course, and much more exciting. There was dissent among those whom wags designated the silent generation. In retrospect, people in the fifties sowed the seeds that blossomed into the movements for which the sixties are so famous. The presumably buttoned down generation of the fifties provided the leaders for the swinging sixties.

This book examines the complexities of the fifties through its popular culture. It looks into the sorts of things that "everyone" was talking about. The popular issues of the day, movies, TV, lives of celebrities, the songs that filled the air – these things were the stuff of everyday life. Beneath them were basic assumptions that seemed to be accepted but were often questioned.

Popular culture provides a way into the minds of people of the age. The fads that whiled away the time, the clothes people wore allow the student of popular culture to discern deeper patterns of what life was llike and, more importantly, what it meant to people living that life.

I hope that this book entertains while it corrects some misconceptions about the fifties. The fifties was an entertaining period. It was anything but homogeneous and bland. Serious issues were certainly present, and people took them seriously, but there was also a sense of fun that seems to be missing today in so much of American life. I want this book to capture that fun as well as the seriousness. So, as Dickens said about an earlier age, "It was the best of times. It was the worst of times."

Acknowledgements

This book is dedicated to my wife, Virginia, for all her encouragement and patience. She has had to hear more about the fifties than anyone should have to. My children are always in my heart if not on my lips and I want to leave them something about me that is so much a part of the fifties. My sister, Jo, was always there for me in the fifties. Unfortunately, I didn't always listen to her. My friends of the fifties were frequently in my mind as I wrote. My neighbor, Mario Bonfiglio, shared many great times with me and still keeps the secrets. My cousins, Jack and Ron Di Polito, shared common ancestors and a common culture with me. They were a major part of the fifties for me. My cousin Marion Salamone and my Aunt Antoinette were additional sources of secutiry. The biggest part of the fifties for me, however, was my parents, Angelo and Frances. They still dominate my thoughts. Their lives and ideals made mine possible. They provided strong models for me to follow and define myself against. I miss them and love them very much. Dan Smith of Iona College's History and Political Science Department offered me many valuable suggestions and helped shape the first chapter. All errors are, of course, my own.

Chapter 1

Everyday America

The fifties were a period in transition from the depths of the Great Depression and the fervor of the Second World War to the peacetime prosperity and togetherness of the "Golden Age." In 1952, for example, despite heavy taxes, with only 7% of the world's people, the U.S. produced 52% of the world's mechanical energy. More importantly, the United States used that energy so well that it made 65% of the world's manufactured goods. In that year its gross national product was $350 billion, the greatest material outpouring in its history. And as those who were alive in the fifties like to say, that's when a billion was worth something. In this chapter, I am presenting an overview. Many of the topics that I mention receive more detailed treatment in later chapters.

The population of the United States in 1950 was 149,1888,000 compared with over 280,000,000 in 2000. There were 3,288,000 unemployed workers in 1950 and about 6,000,000 in 2000.[1] As the decade began, the life expectancy for women was 71.1, and for men 65.6 years. In 1997 the overall life expectancy was 75 years. For women it was 79 years and for men 73 years. 6, 665, 800 cars were sold. The average American worker earned $2, 992. In 2000 the figure was $29, 120.The male to female ratio of workers, 5/2, reflects the influence of gender ideology of the period. The ratio for January 2001 was 10/7. [2]On the other hand, the cost of a loaf of bread was fourteen cents, easily affordable for most people on one paycheck. [3] For comparison, a loaf of bread cost $.98 in January 2001.[4]

The last year of the Truman administration and the last full year of the Korean War, 1952, is sometimes considered the first real year of the fifties. It was the first year in which business expanded not to catch up with demand but to meet future demand. To their surprise, businessmen could see no limit to expansion. Additionally, American population kept expanding, providing further stimulus to the economy. America, for example, added 3,000,000 citizens in 1952, exceeding demographic estimates by more than half. The population reached an unbelievable 157 million. Business rooted for a continued population explosion. It became part of the accepted wisdom of the period that the baby boom was good for business.

Truman emphasized peacetime production at the expense of military, a reflection of the mood of the times. The Korean War (1950-1953) was not a popular one and Harry S. Truman knew that the American public would not support a war that drained the civilian economy and its cornucopia of goods. Eisenhower, in fact, generally kept that fact in mind and rarely sacrificed civilian needs for the military while actually cutting the military budget and proposing to unify the armed forces for the sake of economy.

The period was marked by a love for speed that came to define it. There was a sense of urgency, of a people in a hurry to get somewhere. The image of "the rat race" or of people on a treadmill captures the spirit of the age. When Chuck Yaeger broke the sound barrier on October 14, 1947, he set the pattern for the age, helping speed become the dominant motif for the period. Cars, for example, began to have powerful overhead-valve high-octane engines. Tubeless tires, moreover, enabled cars to reach higher speed on safer tires. Cars became more streamlined to deliver the illusion as well as the reality of speed. Tail fins, the great icons of the decade, signified sleekness, and speed.

The first tailfin, in fact, made its appearance in the forties on the 1948 Cadillac. Contrary to popular belief, the fin did have a purpose, namely, to provide high-speed stability. It was based, symbolically, on the P-38, a World War II fighter plane. The fins, of course, also symbolized the desire of many people to get from one place to another as quickly as possible. By 1956, for example, passenger air travel matched rail traffic. It had grown from 2% of all passenger travel in 1950 to 50% of all such travel in six years.

The fifties were also marked by a great expansion of the suburbs and their concomitant home ownership. In the fifties, most suburban residences were owned, or at least mortgaged. Owning a home, after all, was the purpose of the suburbs. The late forties also set the pattern for this fifties characteristic, good, affordable housing. In 1947, the first Levittown, Long Island, home was occupied. The first Levitt homes set the standard for those "little boxes on the hillside, all made out of ticky-tack" that all looked alike, at least at first. It cost $7500 and the down payment was $58. The buyer even received a free TV set. [5]Capitalizing on the desire for new homes outside the urban environment with space for their kids and a clean white picket fence, developers followed Levitt's lead and built low-cost tract housing that marked the suburban explosion.

As new housing developments matched the desire of middle-class families to migrate to the suburbs, the government began to build high-speed roads (turnpikes, expressways and freeways) to get commuters into their urban workplaces and home again. The Fifties love affair with cars was so great that instead of building better public transportation, the government actually helped kill public transportation systems as many cities dismantled subways (Rochester, NY) or trolleys (New York City) in favor of roads and highways. Los Angeles, for example, began the decade with one of the better public transportation systems in the world and spent the decade replacing it with the freeway system that, tragically, not only failed to live up to its billing but helped spread urban blight and pollution.

Women found that new convenience foods freed them from daily drudgery, or at least lessened the monotony of "housework." This trend accelerated as the fifties witnessed the mass production of laborsaving home appliances and convenience foods that fit in well with the pursuit of "leisure" that marked the fifties.

The Fifties saw a tremendous improvement in the American standard of living. Americans sought to make up for lost time, seeking to put the nightmares of the Depression and World War II far behind. The Korean War (1950-1953) only further strengthened their resolve. There were, certainly, those essential improvements in American life, such as flush toilets and telephones in a majority of American homes in all parts of the country, including rural areas. Surprisingly, there was a dramatic decrease in the automobile fatality rate, a drop of more than 40%. The murder rate also dropped 32%. By the end of the fifties almost 50% of adults were high school graduates, a sharp increase from the approximately 33% in the forties. New technology was also changing the American way of life.

Television came into its own in the fifties, but there were many other technological advances. [6] The transistor, a forties invention, led to the miniaturization that bloomed in the fifties. Jet planes also expanded in the decade. Other everyday items that were invented or developed in the fifties include Adidas athletic shoes, the. PaperMate leak-proof ballpoint pen, Haloid Corporation's (later renamed Xerox) first xerographic copy machine, the first credit card (the Diners Club card), and the classic, award-winning, ubiquitous Eames shell chair, made from fiberglass-reinforced polyester plastic. Fiberglass eventually made its fortune in car bodies when the 1953 Chevrolet Corvette (cost $3513) was the first production car to have an all-fiberglass body. Solar batteries, Con-Tact paper, at 59 cents per yard, and more and more plastics became hallmarks of the period.[7]

Medical advances matched technological gains. In 1955, for example, Jonas Salk developed a polio vaccine. Seven million American schoolchildren received it and polio was basically ended. Miltown introduced its tranquilizer, starting a trend of "happy pills" that would end "depression." Battery powered watches aided those too hurried to wind their watches when Hamilton introduced the first battery-powered electric wristwatch in 1956. Other familiar things that came from the fifties, meant to improve life, were Midas Muffler Shops, Comet cleanser and Pampers disposable diapers.

America was shocked out of its complacency, however, in 1957 when the Russians launched a 184-pound satellite, Sputnik I. That launching marked the beginning of the space race, and an examination of America's conscience. Educators bewailed the laziness of American schoolchildren, and suddenly a number of American secondary schools and colleges offered classes in Russian and Chinese. Others critics blamed teachers and "progressive education." Such critics said that schools were too easy, and theories of "why Johnny can't read" abounded. Calls came for longer school days and even longer school years. The government poured money into science and language instruction to help Americans catch up with the Russians. Catching up was simply another aspect of America's love for speed, of getting somewhere else, even anywhere else fast. Appropriately, the passenger jet made its debut with the Boeing 707's inaugural flight in 1957.

U. S. workers were also catching up. By 1958, the average worker in manufacturing, and the US still did a great deal of manufacturing in the Fifties, averaged $83.56 per week as opposed to $54.32 in 1949. Business kept finding more ways for workers to spend their money. In 1958 the American Express Card debuted. Soon after, the Ski-Doo snowmobile made its first appearance, providing greater speed on snow and yet another way to spend excess money. The decade ended in 1960 with the launching of Echo I, the first telecommunications satellite, a way to make calls more quickly to stay in touch with people when you got from here to there in the quickest possible way. The FDA approved the first birth-control pill in 1960, which helped change the nation's sexual behavior and encouraged the sexual revolution of the sixties.

Women

The typical image of women in the fifties is that presented in various Home Economics courses and the media. One book, for example, advised students to plan ahead so that they would have meals on time for their husbands. The book also counsels "Prepare yourself; Take 15 minutes to rest so you will be refreshed when he arrives. Touch up your make-up, put a ribbon in your hair and be fresh-looking. He has just been with a lot of work-weary people. Be a little gay and a little more interesting. His boring day may need a lift." Further advice included clearing the clutter, preparing children, minimizing noise, making the male comfortable, and not complaining. Moreover, a husband expected his wife to listen to him and to "make the evening his." After all, according the book, a home is a place where husbands should be able to relax.[8]

It was against this image that feminists rebelled. One feminist, Phyllis Chesler, stated, "I was veiled: physically, psychologically, sexually, politically, intellectually. The era was like a fundamentalist country (-Wilson 12: 1)." Chesler depicts an era in which young women were greatly repressed. Although her own background may have been more restricted than many, she was a first generation American of strict Eastern European Jewish parents, the picture she paints reflects a reality many women who lived in the fifties recognize.

According to Chesler, the fifties were a period in which sexuality was a hidden subject, something to be ashamed of. Good girls used sanitary napkins and not tampons, lest they be considered "loose." Girdles and petticoats made of stiff material, like crinoline – originally a product made of horsehair - also were standard wear to hide a girl's figure. Such wear impeded any chance of girls' excelling in sports.

Additionally, according to Chesler, girls further suffered from other restrictions. Curfews were set at unreasonably early times, and parents forbade young women to date. Relatives carefully scrutinized young women on their actions and whereabouts. Although many women will relate to certain aspects of this description, it seems a bit overdrawn for most women of the period.

Many fifties women were entering or reentering the work force. About 50% of women worked outside the home by the close of the decade. The cost of paying for those new homes, shiny appliances, and food and clothes for those new Baby Boomers frequently required two incomes, even if the family had not moved to the suburbs. Although the sit-com image was of a wife staying at home - like Donna Reed or

Harriett Nelson - the reality was often far different. Often, however, working women found their work categorized as "helping out" and "subordinate" to their husband's career. They were expected to be the parent who missed worked to care for sick kids or to prepare dinner after a day's work.

Furthermore, "corporate wives," wives of men in management positions, were expected not to work or do anything else that might jeopardize their husbands' dignity. There was good reason to fear that the corporation was threatening to dominate the American family. Many corporations had active "wife programs" to teach women how corporate wives were to behave, including suggestions on dressing appropriately. Interestingly, there was little opposition from wives to these expectations Most seemed to agree that a good wife is the one who graciously fits in by hiding any trace of intellectualism or by not mixing well. Those who desired solitude were especially to be feared as almost un-American.

Fortunately, there were exceptions to the corporate model of a good wife. Fiction provided many examples of which Grace Metalious's _Peyton Place_ is but the most egregious. Sloan Wilson's _The Man in the Gray Flannel Suit_ presents a somewhat more genteel and sedate model of rebellion. _Ladies Home Journal_ presents a 1953 rebel named Michelle who in "Fireworks for Michelle" invites her husband's boss and wife to dinner. Michelle and her husband then insult them for being slaves to the system and sacrificing their family to business.

Not all liberated women, however, favored the Women's Liberation movement. Mary McCarthy, probably one of the more independent women of the fifties, a famous novelist and critic, wrote, "As for Women's Lib, it bores me. Of course I believe in equal pay and quality before the law and so on, but this whole myth about how different the world would have been if it had been female-dominated, about how there would have been no wars—and Women's Lib extremists actually believe these things--seems a complete fantasy to me. I've never noticed that women were less warlike than men. And in marriage, or for that matter between a woman and her love or between two lesbians or any other couple, an equal division of tasks is impossible--it's a judgment of Solomon. You really would have to slice the baby down the middle." (Gelderman, Mary McCarthy: A Life, p. 307.)

Like it or not, the time was ripe for change in the way in which the culture viewed women. The old attitudes had to change along with the ever-increasing public presence of women in government, the job market, education, and elsewhere. The coming of "The Pill" in 1960 gave women greater freedom in control of their own reproductive powers and sexuality.[9]   Although still at a power disadvantage compared with men politically, economically, and in other ways, women were becoming more assertive and aware of their problems. There was still a long way to go.

At the decade's end, however, _Newsweek_ wrote "Who could ask for anything more? The educated American woman has her brains, her good looks, her car, her freedom... freedom to choose a straight-from-Paris dress (original or copy), or to attend a class in ceramics or calculus; freedom to determine the timing of her next baby or who shall be the next President of the United States."

Business

American business certainly prospered in the 1950s. It had recovered from the effects of the Great Depression and rebuilt itself on the profits made during World War II. The postwar period provided many opportunities for further profit through the rebuilding of Europe, which the Marshall Plan facilitated.[10] The business boom, moreover, was aided by the Baby Boom. Building new homes to house these new citizens further spurred the economy. The growth of the suburbs, new roads, and all that went with providing for expanding young families served to increase economic growth.

Although many Americans, Democrats and Republicans alike, remained skeptical of a political role for big business, the good times permitted business to play an increasing part in government, especially during the Eisenhower administration. That partnership between business and government had been an outgrowth of World War II. As business continued to expand, moreover, business began to exert great influence on education. Certainly, graduates wanted jobs. While business executives spoke of the need for liberal arts graduates, business recruiters sought more specialized graduates, especially those in engineering. As the decade progressed, business began to exert greater control over education through its donations, often tied to programs to advance its interests.

The fifties marked the beginning of the computer age the beginning of consumer computers. Remington Rand introduced UNIVAC on the market in 1951, and IBM entered with its product, funded largely with money from the Atomic Energy Commission, shortly thereafter. Many of its computer products were first found with the military before being introduced to the general public. IBM was the first to introduce a family of computers, the 360. This meant that the same software could run in any model of that family. Additionally, Big Blue, as people came to term IBM, set as a policy commitment to aiding each customer in implementing an IBM system so that no one would fail in using its computer products. IBM, however, so dominated the market that it lost an antitrust suit in 1956 and agreed to sale rather than lease its tabulating machines to customers.

In general, then, business was good during the fifties. The Gross National Product (GNP) grew greatly in the fifties, almost doubling in that decade. At the same time inflation remained under 2% per year, a phenomenal accomplishment. Chemicals, electronics, and aviation, stimulated by defense spending, emerged as leaders in the economy. Indeed, defense spending generally aided the growth of the economy. The United States dominated world trade since it was virtually the only country to survive the war with a good economy.[11]

That economy contributed to and was in turn aided by the rise in new home construction, a growth rate of about 50% in the 1950s, and a population increase of 35%. Consumer credit rose a remarkable 800% while savings dropped to about 5% of income. Shopping centers, however, rose form eight in 1945 to 3, 840 in 1960. The youth market came to wield real power, turning, for example, rock 'n roll into big business.

Technology

American faith in the goodness of technology reached its apex in the fifties. There was almost a touching naiveté to the manner in which Americans resisted any limits on technology and in the trust they put on its ability to solve any problem. The fifties, indeed, demonstrated a burst in technological advances. In addition to Rand's and IBM's introduction of commercially available computers, there were breakthrough in electronics and chemicals. The period seemed one of ever-increasing breakthroughs in transportation as well. There were voices, however, which warned about the dangers of such blind faith. John Kenneth Galbraith in *The Affluent Society*, for example, cautioned that private luxury led to public squalor. Galbraith was an economist who became President Kennedy's ambassador to India.

Nonetheless, American trust in technology continued throughout the decade. The Interstate Highway System and St. Lawrence Seaway were but two of the more spectacular transportation networks begun in the period. In addition to these Federal projects, there were numerous state initiatives to match. The fifties was a period in which much building had to be done to make up for the neglect of the Depression and war years. It often appeared as if the entire country were being rebuilt. New chemical materials aided that rebuilding, none more than plastic. Plastics seemed to be found everywhere from cars, through paint, to houses and in building materials and clothing.

Changes in communication were equally astounding. As early as 1950, for example, regular color television transmission was in place.

The percentage of people who actually had sets was near zero because the transmission was experimental. Technological improvements in television came quickly. Soon there were changes in the camera tube to improve the picture. The coaxial cable was completed in 1951, allowing live programs from coast to coast. Within a few years microwaves were used for early cable TV, Zenith proposed pay TV, the industry accepted a uniform system of color for TV, in 1954 commercial color programs, as opposed to 1950s experimental ones, was available, color TV tapes were in use by decade's end, and further changes were expected, including the TV-phone.

Older technologies also witnessed improvements. In 1950, for example, changeable typeface was available. Typists could shift from elite to pica or other types of type with ease. Movies sought to compete with TV through technological innovations. In 1951 Cinerama and its three projectors came on the scene, followed in 1952 with 3-D movies and Cinemascope. In 1952, the radio found itself made more portable with the use of transistors. The old family camera was improved with the addition of built-in flashes.

Computers witnessed vast improvements. EDVAC and UNIVAC pushed the technology forward into the commercial area. In 1952, UNIVAC startled the nation through predicting the winner of the Presidential election, a feat for which no computer was really necessary since Eisenhower won in a landslide. Computers also helped Ma Bell, ATT more formally, to establish telephone area codes as the use of phones expanded rapidly.

Interestingly, while America and the Soviet Union were engaged in a Cold War, American technology managed to produce an astonishing array of consumer products. Color TV broadcasts of sports and "The Wonderful World of Disney," fiber optics as a model for future communication as well as hi-fidelity music in 1955, and a videotape recorder from Ampex in 1956 were only part of the cornucopia of products that American technology made available to consumers. Americans could make a transatlantic cable telephone call to Europe by early as1956. The lessons of the Koran War were plain. In general, the American public would not tolerate great inconvenience to achieve abstract ends.

In 1957, however, the Soviet Union's Sputnik sends signals from space. The ensuing panic led to many changes in education. The space program, of course, received a boost as NASA kicked into high gear and proved that those German scientists whom America liberated from Nazi Germany were better than those whom the Russians freed were.[12] Coincidentally, American advances in computer technology advanced quickly to meet the threat. In 1957 FORTRAN became the first high-level computer language.

The consumer, of course, did not suffer. Stereo music hit the market in 1958 and cable TV services carried FM stations for those willing to pay the price. The laser came on the market. Phone lines carried data, anticipating and preparing the way for the cyber revolution. In 1959, the microchip became available, enabling computers to work faster and more efficiently while storing more information, and in the same year, Xerox manufactured a plain paper copier, solving its earlier problems of its machines setting fire to its copies. Bell Labs, meanwhile, began to experiment with artificial intelligence; lending weight to Sci-Fi warnings about "thinking machines" that would replace humans and take over the world.

There had been many even in the technology-loving fifties who were concerned with the advance of what they termed "technocracy," the rule of the technological specialist. Certainly, business leaders, industry officials, military trainers, and educators recognized the possibilities of computers. However, some instructors hoped and others feared that computers would replace live teachers. Business leaders, who had regained their control of American Society, hoped that computers would further the influence of business over education. Certainly, for better or worse, many of the changes we have seen in American life have flowed from the burst of technological innovation in the fifties.

Overview of the Mood of America

Americans literally could not believe their good fortune and felt that something or someone, usually communists or aliens of some kind, even those from outer space would try to take it away. World War II was not very long ago. The Nazi threat may have ended but its overtones still sounded in the American mind. The spread of the Soviet Union, the "loss" of China to the Communists, and the Korean War fueled the perception of that the Red Menace would steal our newfound bounty.

Some Americans became intensely patriotic during the fifties, returning to an isolationist position in which they feared anything that was foreign or "un-American." That patriotism was the other side of the coin that displayed our unease with international events. Many Americans saw enemies everywhere, and the FBI's J. Edgar Hoover and Senator Joseph McCarthy stirred up these emotions for their own demagogic uses. McCarthyism became the label for the Red Scare. In the name of anti-Communism innocent, and sometimes not so innocent, victims were denied due process and means for making a living. The Red-baiters decided to go after movie stars such as Paul Douglas, Zero

Mostel, Lucille Ball, and even John Wayne to gain attention. Most of the stars brought before Congressional investigating committees recanted their past involvement with so-called Communist front organization and gave the committees names of other possible "Communist sympathizers." Arthur Miller, the famous playwright, refused to bow down to McCarthyism and wrote a powerful play about the Salem witchcraft trial entitled "The Crucible." It was aimed at Senator McCarthy's own witch-hunt. Incidentally, Senator McCarthy never did find even one communist.[13]

The fear of losing American bounty led to a glorification of traditional American lifestyles and the concept of common decency. Many Americans attended church regularly.[14] Although American tended to be "conformists" in the fifties, despite opinions to the contrary, there were a number of exceptions tolerated. For example, the Beat writers, such as Jack Kerouac, received great praise from critics in established newspapers, such as the _New York Times_. However, there were limits to the amount of differences Americans tolerated, and Americans repressed "subversive behavior," often in the courts. Television, which became the dominant national medium, came under public pressure to promote the American way of life. [15]

Political events, for example, were televised for the fist time, giving Americans a civic lesson in democracy. Americans generally watched the same programs. Advertisers idealized the American family while getting its message across to millions of families. Common ideas of what was proper developed. For example, all the Rosie the Riveters from World War II got the message that they were out of place in the "traditional" nuclear family. [16]

However, there were signs of rebellion on the horizon. "The Man in the Grey Flannel Suit," was not happy with the restrictions and demand of his day. Teens began to turn to James Dean and other movie rebels. In addition, rock 'n roll became their music of rebellion. Sexual rebellion did not originate in the sixties. It was well underway in the fifties as teens chaffed at sexual and social restrictions.

Popular American culture during the Fifties was remarkably divided. Public figures and other pillars of the community along with advertisers endorsed images and ideals of mainstream God-fearing decency. However, popular music and literature began to reflect more rebellious strains. Clearly, something was going on. The fifties were not so clearly conformist and uncomplicated as many believed at the time and wrongly believe today. There were clear fault lines and gaps in American culture, as there always are.

The early 1950s featured songs that proclaimed mostly harmonious love, such as "Unforgettable" and "Little Things Mean a Lot." Jazz still was heard on popular music stations, and novelty tunes such as "The Naughty Lady of Shady Lane" and "Purple People Eater" had their place as well. Sex did not often hit the airwaves, nor was violence a characteristic of music. Popular music of the early fifties generally reflected the prevailing view of fundamental American decency. However, not everyone shared in American prosperity or adhered strictly to all its basic optimism.

Rhythm-and-blues, a product of blues and jazz, and developed in African American communities, reflected the longing, anguish and mischief fostered by centuries of deprivation in a land of plenty. Along with other black generated music and styles, R&B caught on among many white artists and fans. Eventually, it emerged on the main scene as rock-and-roll or rock 'n roll.

At first black artists, such as Little Richard, Chuck Berry, and the like dominated it. Eventually, whites dominated the charts as white promoters noted the power of the music, especially its power to make money. However, the music remained a means for rebellion. Elvis Presley and Buddy Holly became leading white stars of the music. Elvis became a white promoter's dream, a white boy who sounded black. Parents became concerned with the impact of this sexual "primitive" music. More importantly, the music marked a type of generational declaration of independence, hard to realize today when, in retrospect, it "ain't nothing but the blues," simple variations on three chords that the older generation had become familiar with in the swing era and the music of the popular Louis 'Satchmo" Armstrong.

Similarly, popular literature was fomenting its own rebellion against what it viewed as hypocrisy. Ralph Ellison, author of _The Invisible Man_, and James Baldwin, author of _Go Tell It on the Mountain_ and numerous essays, wrote against racial injustice. In England Aldous Huxley, author of _Brave New World_, began to advocate the use of drugs to expand human consciousness and perception. Grace Metalious in _Peyton Place_ mocked the hypocrisy of American small towns, the presumed bastions of American democracy while Jack Kerouac's _On the Road_ refused to accept traditional notions of success, spawning the "Beat" generation.

Politics

The fifties were in politics, as in so much else, divided. On the one hand, much about the political life of the fifties was conformist. There was a great loyalty pledged to the country itself. After all, World War II fought against the excesses of the fascist countries was still fresh in people's minds. The Korean War (1950 – 1953) ushered in the decade, and many saw it as a war that the United States had to fight to prevent the further spread of Communist aggression. The "loss" of Eastern Europe to the Soviet Union in the 1940s stung many Americans as a betrayal of their victory in World War II. Politicians, especially Republicans, played on that fear, resolving not to allow Americans to "lose" other areas to the Communists. Many of these Americans were the same ones who resisted Truman's plans to keep sufficient American troops in Europe to prevent Communist takeovers. However, no one ever accused the American people of logical consistency.

On the other hand, there were many Americans who were suspicious of the war in Korea, rabid anti-Communism and fervent patriotism. Adlai Stevenson, Governor of Illinois and twice the unsuccessful Democratic candidate for President (1952 and 1956), sought to provide a moderate questioning of these stances, and President Dwight D. Eisenhower provided the best means for silencing the extremism of McCarthyism. President Eisenhower isolated him within the Republican Party while fellow Republicans began to denounce his extreme tactics. The Army-McCarthy hearing, seen on live nationwide television, exposed the American people to his tactics. Finally, Edward R. Murrow, perhaps, the most respected news commentator of his day, dedicated a program to denouncing McCarthy.

The Beat Generation provided a focus for criticism of the status quo and an alternative to the search for power, wealth, and security that seemingly obsessed many Americans. The Beats, however, were well received by mainstream critics who championed much of their work. Criticism of American life met with remarkably little opposition, at least after the end of the McCarthy era.

Americans, who were seemingly obsessed with material well being, however, had good reason to be so focused. The Depression of the 1930s and the trauma of World War II and the Korean War together with the height of the Cold War with the Soviets demanded some haven of security. Even Adlai Stevenson, twice defeated by Eisenhower, conceded that it was probably a good thing for the country to pause from political turmoil and enjoy a few years of relative tranquility.

The Eisenhower years, more or less, provided that tranquility. There was general agreement on basic issues. Both sides of the political spectrum agreed on what they called basic issues. They were opposed to Soviet aggression, in favor of what are today called family values, for prosperity for as many Americans as possible, and wanted things done "democratically." Nevertheless, there was a great deal of political turmoil in the fifties.

The modern Civil Rights movement began. *Brown v Board of Education of Topeka, Kansas* (1954) is generally given as the convenient starting point for the movement. Of course, many events preceded that momentous decision and led up to it. [17] There were, of course, many events that led to the decision and many people who worked hard on the issue of equality. The NAACP, founded in 1909 in New York City had financed the legal efforts that led to the court case. Asa Philips Randolph, head of the all Negro Pullman Workers Union had threatened a March on Washington during World War II. Only a request from President Franklin Roosevelt that he delay that march until after the war kept him from organizing the march. Franklin Roosevelt, under the prodding of his wife Eleanor, established a Fair Employment Practices Committee in 1941 as the country prepared for war. Roosevelt used his power of executive order to place the Committee within the Office of Production Management. FEPC promoted full employment of all Americans and sought to eliminate discriminatory employment practices. President Harry S. Truman sought to establish a permanent FEPC. The Republican controlled Senate ended the FEPC in 1946. Truman also furthered the efforts for Civil Rights by running on a strong Civil Rights Platform in 1948, risking the breakup of the Democratic Party as southern Democrats formed the Dixiecrat Party, running Strom Thurmond for President. Truman won the election but discovered that he faced strong resistance to the implementation of his Civil Rights proposals. Truman was able, however, to integrate the military in 1948, threatening in his inimitable style to shoot the first person who defied his orders.

The Brown decision, nevertheless, gave tremendous impetus to the Civil Rights movement. It speeded up the integration of public accommodations. More subtle segregation was more difficult to eradicate. School segregation, which was not enforced by law but by residential housing patterns, termed de facto segregation, for example, has proved very difficult to end.

Thurgood Marshall, the man who led the legal team that opposed segregation the _Brown v Board of Education_ case had been on the legal staff of the National Association for the Advancement of Colored People since 1936. He was its chief counsel from 1938–61, arguing over 30 cases before the U.S.   Supreme Court. Marshall successfully challenged racial segregation, at first mainly in higher education before the victory of _Brown v. Board of Education of Topeka_ (1954) overturned the court's earlier Plessy v. Ferguson ruling of 1898. [18]

The Reverend Martin Luther King, Jr., the leader of the Southern Christian Leadership Council, came to prominence in the fifties leading various marches against segregation. In addition, these marches and the 1954 Supreme Court Decisions ordering "integration with all deliberate speed" helped lead to the passage of the first modern Federal Civil

Rights Bill. The Federal Government reluctantly put its force behind integration in Little Rock, Arkansas.   Governor Orville Faubus, Arkansas' Governor, had refused to integrate the school in 1957, defying a Federal Court order. Eisenhower sent Federal troops to enforce the court order and these troops helped escort the seven children into the school. Eisenhower may have been reluctant to do so but he did assert the primacy of Federal rights over states' rights. In 1957 and 1960, the United States Congress, under the guidance of Senate Majority Leader Lyndon Baines Johnson passed the first Federal Civil Rights Legislation since 1875.[19]

President Eisenhower was determined to keep the United States out of war. In order to aid him in reaching his goal, he decided to use the Central Intelligence Agency to removed governments that he deemed hostile to American interests. The Agency became involved in overthrowing governments in Central America.   Guatemala's government was the first of many that the agency helped replace. Eisenhower refused to become openly involved in Vietnam. He did, nevertheless, refuse to honor the Geneva Agreements that ended French involvement in the area. Eisenhower quietly sent in CIA agents and military advisers into Vietnam to shore up leaders friendly to American interests. Ironically, Senator Majority Leader Lyndon B. Johnson's objections helped keep the President from getting openly involved in the war.

By the end of his term, the President was using the Agency to protect "American interests" all over the globe. The arrest and murder of Patrice Lumumba, the duly elected Premier of the Congo, is laid at the door of the C. I. A., as is the rise to power of President Joseph Mobutu. The Agency had become a kind of secret army that carried out the wishes of the President while the surface of American life went quietly on.[20]

Although the majority of Americans did not seem to care about such issues in the fifties, there were many in the so-called Silent Generation of students who did indeed care and who spoke out openly against these matters. The comedians Mort Sahl and Lennie Bruce as well as the more politically involved of the Beats excoriated Ike and his minions for their actions, warning that he was a wolf in grandfather's clothing. That core of "malcontents" who gathered at coffee houses to listen to jazz and poetry helped shape the consciousness of the sixties rebels who succeeded them. In fact, many of the Beats merged with one faction or another of the sixties Movement. People like Alan Ginsberg, the poet who wrote "Howl" and Neal Cassady, the model for Jack Kerouac's character Dean Moriarity in _On the_ Road, for example, played a role in both movements.

Space Travel

In 1957, the Space Age began with the Soviet launching of Sputnik, beating the U.S. in it plans to be first in space with the Vanguard booster. Sputnik was highly polished aluminum sphere, which kept its temperature controlled. It had two radio transmitters. Sputnik means "fellow traveler" in Russian. The word caught on as the little beeping satellite stunned people as they watched its flights from October until January 4, 1958 when it reentered the Earth's atmosphere as a flaming ball.

The United States could not believe that the Russian had beaten it into space. Panic filled the country as people blamed the educational system, the softness of American life, and anything else that could explain how we had lost the race to space. Before any answers could be found, or Americans discovered that we were not really behind in any space race, the Russians launched another satellite on November 3, 1957.

This satellite was a 508-kg (1118-lb) spacecraft. Moreover, it had a passenger, Laika, a female Siberian dog. However, the Soviets had not devised a way to get Laika back from space, and, therefore, they put her to sleep. No one is sure how many days Laika lasted in space. Some say four days and others ten.

In contrast, the American Vanguard launch was done in full public view at Cape Canaveral, Florida. Thus, on December 6, 1957, the world watched as the grapefruit sized object took off and then fell back after going four feet in the air. Soon repeated public failures of the space program led American wits to term the launch site, Cape Carnival. Werhner von Braun on January 31, 1958 helped launch the United States first successful rocket, giving the United States a psychological boost.

President Eisenhower brought more structure to the American space program. Amid the quarreling giants involved in seeking to run the program, the Department of Defense or the Atomic Energy Commission, for example, there was a smaller agency that had been involved for some period in aeronautics. The National Advisory Committee on Aeronautics or NACA. had conducted work since 1915 and it had been involved in missile research throughout the 1950s. NACA conducted research for both the military and civilian spheres. It was, furthermore, comprised of engineers and scientists. Eisenhower opposed military control of space research and supported NACA to head it. In March 1958, plans were begun to establish a new civilian agency for space programs. On April 2, 1958, the Eisenhower Administration sent Congress a bill to create a civilian national aeronautics and space agency. On July 29, 1958, President Eisenhower signed Public Law 85-568, the National Aeronautics, and Space Act, which created the National Aeronautics and Space Administration (NASA) on October 1, 1958. NACA became NASA.

The End of Ideology

Daniel Bell summed up much of the fifties' attitude in his book *The End of Ideology*. Bell had been a product of the Great Depression, joining various political causes, such as the Young People's Socialist League when he was 13. He edited a number of prestigious leftist journals, including *Common Sense*, *The New Leader*, and that opposite of leftist magazines, *Fortune*. Bell had a distinguished teaching career at the University of Chicago and Columbia University, becoming a leading sociologist.

In common with many scholars of his generation he worried about what he perceived as the non-committal nature of the so-called "Silent Generation," a generation that seemed to be content with going along with the crowd, a group of conformists. He sums up his views in this passage

> [O]ne finds, at the end of the fifties, a disconcerting caesura. In the West, among the intellectuals, the old passions are spent. The new generation, with no meaningful memory of these old debates, and no secure tradition to build upon, finds itself seeking new purposes within a framework of political society that has rejected, intellectually speaking, the old apocalyptic and chiliastic visions. In the search for a "cause," there is a deep, desperate, almost pathetic anger. The theme runs through a remarkable book, *Convictions*, by a dozen of the sharpest young Left Wing intellectuals in Britain. They cannot define the content of the "cause" they seek, but the yearning is clear. In the U.S. too there is a restless search for a new intellectual radicalism.

Bell, unlike many of the glib critics, was correct. A new radicalism was to burst on the scene in but a few short years. Its leaders, interestingly, were those members of the so-called Silent Generation. Many received their training in the Civil Rights Movement under Martin Luther King and his disciples. That radicalism, planted in the fifties, blossomed during the anti-war movements of the sixties. [21]

Bell takes the usual easy shots at television, ignoring its essential role in the Civil Rights Movement and failing to anticipate its role in youthful opposition to an unpopular war that had its origins in the forties and fifties with American support first of the French and then of their Vietnamese puppets. He does point out that fifties culture had "almost completely accepted the avant-garde, particularly in art, and the older academic styles have been driven out completely." In itself, these were not mean accomplishments. He also correctly notes that "the workers, whose grievances were once the driving energy for social change, are more satisfied with the society than the intellectuals. The workers have not achieved utopia, but their expectations were less than those of the intellectuals, and the gains correspondingly larger." In sum, the fifties were a remarkably prosperous time and had achieved many of the goals of an earlier radicalism. Their "conservatism" was but the fruition of a radicalism completed. Of course, radicals were not happy. It is not their fate ever to be content.

Bell had been right about the fifties, in ways that he probably did not expect. In hindsight it is correct to note that many former radicals, workers who had manned the barricades against business oppression, were perfectly content with their wages, their suburban homes, two cars, and a meat and potatoes diet. It was, after all, what they had craved during the Depression and fought for in World War II. It is also correct to note, as Bell did, that these old battles had grown tiresome to the kids who had dim if any memories of the Depression or War. They felt vaguely discontented. They were, in fact, rebels without a cause. But they were finding their causes as the decade drew to a close and would lead the sixties revolution.

Conclusion

The fifties like our times was a decade in a hurry, and everyday life reflected that hurry. Credit cards made it possible to buy what you wanted now, and pay later in what the British termed "the never-never." New cars, new houses and new lives were the order of the day. Fast food made it possible to get the basics out of the way so luxuries and leisure could be enjoyed. Families were expected to do things together, and after the deprivations of the Depression and World War II those things included luxuries virtually undreamed of in those periods.

The economy was strong, and there was a deep faith in science and technology. Americans believed that things would continue to keep getting better, with a few dips for adjustment perhaps. The standard of living would, therefore, just keep going up. The government now had the hang of it and even Republicans like President Eisenhower used its power to keep things going.

Not even the threat of a possible hot war to replace the Cold War really dimmed the basic optimism of the American people. That optimism was displayed in the famous car styling of the time. They were big cars, filled with chrome and glass. That styling spilled over into other products, such as jukeboxes. These juke boxes were originally built of wood and plastic. Following car design, in the fifties more glass was used. People could then view the insides of the jukeboxes and see the records being spun. Chrome was increasingly used as the decade progressed. Contrary to what happened to other products, however, plastic did not come to dominate the jukebox's design.

In the Fifties, therefore, the culture of America reflected old and new influences. For example, the prosperity of the decade, perhaps, the greatest ever seen in American history, contrasted to the highest degree with the Depression and the tragedy of World War II. There was always a shadow in the sun of that prosperity and a feeling that, somehow, America would have to pay for it. The baby boom was another sign of catching up. Many Americans had deprived themselves of large families in the Depression because they could not afford children or the number of children they desired. The war took a terrible toll in casualties. Having children was both a sign of faith in the future and a way of staving off disaster. Families became worlds unto themselves, the gardens that Voltaire had advised people to cultivate at the end of _Candide_, a book which became a successful Leonard Bernstein musical.

The movement to the suburbs, however, had terrible consequences for cities. The population of the inner cities dwindled and work as well as prosperous middle and upper class people fled the urban areas for the greener grass of the suburbs.

Suggested Readings and Works Cited

Aksyonov, Vassily "Beatniks and Bolsheviks: Rebels Without (and With) a Cause," _New Republic_, 197, number 30 November (1987), 28.

Ash, Mel Beat Spirit The Way of the Beat Writers As a Living Experience New York: Putnam Publishing Group, 1997.

Baro, Gene. "Beatniks Now and Then," _Nation_ 189 September 5 (1959), 115-117.

Bell, Daniel. _The End of Ideology: On the Exhaustion of Political Ideas in the Fifties_. Cambridge: Harvard University Press, 2000.

Berger, Raoul. _The Fourteenth Amendment and the Bill of Rights_. Norman: Oklahoma University Press, 1989.

Branch, Taylor. *Pillar of Fire: America in the King Years,*
    1963-65. New York: Simon & Schuster, 1998.
Bruneer, Borgna. *Time Almanac 2000 and Information Please.*
    NY: Family Education Company, 1999.
Buechler, James. *In That Heaven There Should Be a Place for*
    Me Stories of the Mohawk Valley. Duxbury: Cranberry
    Books, 1994.
Carr, Roy, Brian Case, and Fred Dellar, *The Hip: Hipsters,*
    Jazz and the Beat Generation, New York: Faber and
    Faber, 1986.
Cohen, Daniel. *Joseph McCarthy The Misuse of Political*
    Power Brookfield: Millbrook Press, Incorporated, 1996.
Colman, Penny. *Rosie the Riveter Women Working on the*
    Homefront in World War II.   New York: Crown Publishing
    Group, Incorporated, 1998
Devans, Neal and Davison M. Douglas, Eds. *Redefining*
    Equality New York: Oxford University Press, 1998.
Ewing, William A. *America Worked: The 1950s Photographs*
    of Dan Weiner. New York: Abrams, 1989.
Gold, Herbert. *Bohemia: Digging the Roots of Cool,* New
    York: Simon and Schuster Touchstone, 1994.
Hunt, Linda. *Secret Agenda The United States Government,*
    Nazi Scientists & Project Paperclip. 1944-1990 New York: Saint
    Martin's Press, 1991
Integrated Education Associates. *The Continuing Challenge :*
    the Past and the Future of Brown v. Board of Education: A
    Symposium. Evanston, Il. Notre Dame Center for Civil Rights,
    1975.
Kessler, Ronald. *Inside the CIA/Revealing the Secrets of the*
    World's Most Powerful Spy Agency. New York: Pocket
    Books, 1994.
Levy, Leonard W., Kenneth L. Karst, and Dennis J. Mahoney,
    Editors, *Civil Rights and Equality: Selections from the*
    Encyclopedia of the American Constitution. New York:
    Macmillan, 1989.
Lukas, Catherine Rosie the Riveter No. 3 New York: Little
    Simon, Aug. 2000
Mammola, Joseph L. *Silhouettes on the Shade: Images from*
    the 50s Reexamined. Muncie, Indiana: Ball State University,
    1973.
Mailer, Norman. *The White Negro,* San Francisco: City
    Lights, 1957.
Nelson, William E. *The Fourteenth Amendment: From*

Political Principle to Judicial Doctrine. Cambridge: Harvard
    University Press, 1988.
Neufield, Michael. *The Rocket & the Reich Peenemunde & the
    Coming of the Ballistic Missile Era New* York: Free Press,   Sept.
    1994
Rawson, Hugh. *Unwritten Laws.* New York: Random House
    Value Publishing, Incorporated, Nov. 1998
Rose, Lisle A. *The Cold War Comes to Main Street America
    in 1950. Lawrence*: University Press of Kansas, Jan. 1999.
Schrecker, Ellen. *Many Are the Crimes: McCarthyism in
    America.* Princeton: Princeton University Press, Sept. 1999
Spangenburg, Ray. *The History of NASA.* Danbury: Franklin
    Watts Incorporated, 2000.
Time, "Bang, Bong, Bing," *Time,* 74 September 7(1959), 74.
Thomas, Brook, Editor. *Plessy V. Ferguson: A Brief History
    With Documents* (Bedford Series in History and Culture). New
    York: St. Martin's Press.
Valli, Chris *Enroute to the Emerald City.* Rana Press, July
    1997
Von Braun, Werner. *Mars Project. Champaign:* University of
    Illinois Press, April 1991
Wuthnow, Robert. *After Heaven Spirituality in America since
    the 1950s Berkeley* University of California Press, Oct. 1998.
Zepezauer, Mark and Arthur Naiman, Editors, *The CIA's
    Greatest Hits* (The Real Story Series). New York: Odonion Press,
    1994.

Viderecordings

A.   Philip Randolph: for jobs & freedom / WETA-TV;
    produced by Dante J. James; written by Juan Williams, Dante
    J. James. San Francisco, CA: California Newsreel, 1996,

Endnotes

1. The Bureau of Labor Statistics. http://146.142.4.24/cgi-bin/surveymost.
2. There are approximately $7.00 2000 dollars to one 1950 dollar. See *Time Almanac 2000*, p. 862.
3. Bureau of Labor Statistics. http://146.142.4.24/cgi-bin/surveymost.
4. Robert Mauro. American's and My Home Town. *http://IOS2.com*. The average price of a new home at the end of the 20th century was $200,000 according to the United States Department of Commerce. (CNN Financial News. http:// cnnfn.com/ 1999 /09/30/ economy/ homesales.)
5. There were 1, 500, 000 TV sets in 1951 compared with 150,000 in 1950 (TheMedia History Project Timeline. http://www.mediahistory.com/time/1950s.html.)
6. The Idaho Corvette Page. Corvette Trivia. http://vette.ida.net/trivia.htm.
7. Women's role : wysiwyg://Result_Doc_Content_Frame.e.html&ht=women+1950s&method=Get&reqdata.
8. The importance of "The Pill" is clearly presented in The Evolution of Oral Contraceptives http://www.jhuccp.org/pr/a9/a9chap1_1.stm.
9. After World War II and as the Cold War began, Secretary of State George Marshall, a former World War II American General, devised a plan to help reconstruct the devastated economies of Western Europe. The implementation of the plan helped European economies to boom and strengthened the United States in its conflict with the Soviet Union and its Eastern European allies.
10. "Gross National Product rose from $211 billion in1944 to $329 billion in 1951, but measured in 1960 dollars of equal purchasing power, the rise was only from $373 billion in 1944 to $391billion in 1951. Furthermore, the GNP growth rate (in constant dollars) was slower than many other industrialized areas, such as Japan and Taiwan. This difference might have been a beginning for the current large productivity gap between the US and these countries. The foreign balance of trade took its first major dive during this decade and for twelve of the thirteen years between 1950 and 1963, the US had a negative balance of trade. This was a primarily new occurrence for the US economy as it was the main economic powerhouse in the world previous to this time and did not have to rely on imports to be self-sustaining. This balance of trade led to $8 billion dollars of gold leaving the hands of the US government during this period of thirteen years and may have paved the way for our current deficit situation (1950s Economics. http://localhost:1234/?cat=Web&catpg=%2FTitles%3Fcat%3DWeb%26opt%3DAND%26qt%3D1950%2BGNP.)"
11. See Werner von Braun (1991) for details of the space program and the role of German scientists, Michael J. Neufield (1996) for details of the Nazi rocket

program in World War II, and Linda Hunt (1991) for an analysis of the United States' secret scientific project using German scientists.

[12] Lisle Rose's (1999) study of the impact of McCarthyism on everyday American life offers an insight into the importance of McCarthyism. Daniel Cohen (1997) assesses the serious consequences of McCarthyism for American political life.

[13] Robert Wuthnow (1998) discusses general patterns of religion in American history, including the 1950s. Chris Valli (1997) presents her own story of a typical American family in the suburbs and the role religion played in her family's life. James Beuchler (1994) conveys the role that upstate New Yorkers in the Mohawk Valley found for religion in their lives in the 1950s. His fictional collection conveys the feel of the period quite well.

[14] Hugh Rawson (1998) deals with the facts of conformity in daily life in America of the 1950s. The Beat Generation fascinated people in the American media, and many older adolescents admired their work. Mel Ash (1997) captures the spirit of that fascination.

[15] Rosie the Riveter was a real person who came to represent all the women who worked during World War II, freeing men to fight the war. After the war, people in power sent all the Rosies home to became housewives. Penny Coleman (1998) tells their stories in her excellent book.

[16] For a history of events leading to the Brown v Board of Education Topeka, Kansas see *The Continuing Challenge in Education : a symposium.*(1975). Neal Devans and Davidson Douglas , Eds., (1998) present a collection of material discussing events that led to the Brown vs. Board of Education decision and which place it in historical and sociological context.

[17] Brook Thomas, Editor (1996) offers documents that put Plessy v Ferguson into historical context. The Court's decision is given and documents that trace its significance presented.

[18] Some useful sources are W. E. Nelson, *The Fourteenth Amendment* (1988); R.Berger, *The Fourteenth Amendment and the Bill of Rights* (1989); L. W. Levy, *Civil Rights* (1989); and T. Branch, *Pillar of Fire* (1997).

[19] Mark Zepezauer and Arthur Naiman, Eds. (1994) describe some of the CIA's most important interventions in world history. Ronald Kessler (1994) provides an inside look at the Agency and its actions.

[20] Note that Bell is not one of the glib critics of the fifties. His analysis is a carefully detailed and worked out one of the ills of the time. Daniel Bell (2000) *The End of Ideology : On the Exhaustion of Political Ideas in the Fifties* is a paperback edition of his classic study. It clearly pinpoints the ills of the end of the road political ideology of the day.

Chapter 2 _____

World of Youth

In the 1950s, youth came into their own. The post war prosperity turned them into assets rather than liabilities, for they were potential consumers. The booming economy, in fact, both reflected and propelled major cultural changes in America, including the fifties' youth culture.

School Days and Work

Schools of the fifties did not have TV sets in every room. In fact, it was rare to have a TV set in the school at all. Schools generally held to the old-fashioned view that they were about learning. It was the job of the teacher to teach and of students to learn. There might have been some concern about counseling but schools did not feel responsible for psychological advisement of students and families. There was little thought given to curing poverty, dealing with the latest technology, character education, and other issues. Basically, reading, writing, and arithmetic formed the core. Students were expected to be able to read books by major authors, spell correctly, and learn history as well. Most classes were lecture-discussion sessions, with occasional reports and discussion of written assignments.

There were many clubs, academic and otherwise, and school spirit was shown at various sporting events. Moreover, there were numerous social events centered at school. Record hops, which when shoes were shed were termed sock hops, vied with dances with live bands. Clubs as well as classes sponsored various dances, usually held in school gyms. The exceptions to this rule were the big dances – junior proms and senior balls – for which formal or semi-formal attire was worn. Semi-formal meant that the girls wore gowns and the guys were a good suit. There were also youth-organization sponsored dances held in various dance halls with proper supervision, and no alcohol.

Although schools were the centers of much youth activity, they were not its only location. The diners that often were converted trolley cars also were centers of social action. Before and after schools these diners or, sometimes, coffee shops catered to hordes of teens. For a quarter or less teens could eat and drink while listening to the latest platters spin on the jukebox. A coke, with your choice of flavor, was a dime, and french fries were 15 cents or less. A burger was usually 15 cents. The food, however, was simply incidental to the companionship. These diners, sweet shops, and coffeehouses formed a safe meeting place for youngsters who considered them a haven in which to create their own worlds.

There was need of a haven in the bewildering period of the Cold War. There was always an awareness of the dangers of the political scene. Parents warned youngsters of just how good they had it both compared with the Depression of their parents' youth and with the poor starving children of Europe. And those teens in Europe were envious of the affluence of American youth, a fact that the press in its propaganda war with the Soviets played up on the home front.

There was a tug between the ideal norm of conformity to one's parents and the amorphous youth culture that was just being shaped. Youth were beginning to realize that times were changing. Perhaps, they reasoned, Mom and Dad did grow up in what we would consider deprivation and poverty but it is clear that there is wealth all around. The standard of living was tangibly rising all around. Jobs were plentiful and kids had plenty of pocket money. It was easy for kids to earn their own money at part time and summer jobs.

These jobs ranged from working behind a soda counter as a soda jerk, one who mixed those wonderful drinks and made the fabulous frappes, sundaes, and splits, to working in a factory at 16 moving boxes. There were plenty of jobs to be had, and most kids worked at least in summers to earn extra spending money. Many worked while in schools, either after school, weekends, or both. The holiday times, additionally, were times when employers such as stores and the post office went looking for temporary employees.

All that money and the fact that there were proportionately as well as really more teens in the fifties led many adults to fear that the country was going to hell in a hand basket. The new youth culture simply meant gangs and trouble to them. Certainly, there was an increase in teenage crime, or delinquency. Gangs were very real, and "West Side Story" struck a nerve, although no gangs that most people ever experienced sang or danced so well as those in the musical. Moreover, those teens who questioned tradition in more acceptable, or peaceful, ways often received an equally bad response from adults. Adults termed them pinkos or Commies, fellow travelers who were dupes of the Reds.

However most teens did not join gangs or join the Communist Party. Although many admired the Beats and questioned society, few really did want to give up the good life. Even fewer took part in drag racing that excites so many whose views of the fifties come from movies. At most, kids might race to the next light or on an abandoned street. The game of chicken, popularized in *Rebel without a Cause*, in which cars race head on at each other until one or the other driver swerves away was a game the vast majority of teens recognized as a fools game.

Most teens were too busy getting through schools, flirting with members of the opposite sex, and keeping up on the latest styles to bother with gangs or dragging. There were, indeed, many more enjoyable ways to pass time. Fashion and music, for example, took up a great deal of time. Combing one's hair could consume vast quantities of time for male or female. James Dean, Marlon Brando, Elvis Presley, Jane Russell, Jayne Mansfield and Marilyn Monroe modeled various teen styles in an age when kids spent a good deal of time at the movies in traditional or drive-in theaters. Both guys and gals decided that dressing like Dad or Mom was square. Tight dresses were the style for girls, including elaborate beehive hairstyle. For those who did not want to reveal too much, there was the American 'bobbysoxer' style. This style featured stiffened petticoats, skirts and a ponytail. Guys also had a choice of styles. The greaser, or hood, look characterized by a black leather jacket, jeans and a white tee shirt was one look. The collegiate look highlighted clean-cut white buck shoes instead of blue suede one and a varsity jacket.

Whatever the look, fifties kids managed to create a world that had not existed in prior times, that of "youth culture." At the time, they didn't realize how unique it was. It simply seemed the thing to do.

There were idols, styles, and ways of thinking different from their parents in some ways but in general they had no doubt that in most things they would grow up to be like their folks. It was a transitional age, one with one foot in the past and one in the future, a position that led to the youth growing up always feeling a bit uncomfortable.

Teen Idols and Rock 'n Roll

That culture has been thought of as one of rock 'n roll. It was also marked by the ascendancy of youth in controlling the popular music industry. Something that has come to be commonplace. While young people exerted influence on the charts before the fifties, there wasn't such a great gap between their tastes and their parents as the one that has emerged since. There was always room, moreover, for older styles in the midst, for example, of the Swing revolution of the thirties and forties.

In the fifties, however, the singers and musicians became as young as their audience. No longer were they older brothers or sisters. They were contemporaries, often in their young teens. Indeed, by the end of the decade seventeen was considered an advanced age for a teen heartthrob. The career of the Fabulous Fabian offers a case in point.

Fabian

Chancellor Records had one major star, Frankie Avalon. Avalon, however, was getting on in years. He was seventeen. Bob Marcucci, its owner, was frantically searching for a replacement when he helped rescue Dominic Forte, a cop, from a fire. He then met the cop's son, Fabian. It was one of those show business moments. Marcucci had to work to convince Fabian, then 14, to become a singer. Fabian's appeal was exactly what he sought; dark hair, olive skin, and a duck tail haircut.

Despite these advantages, Fabian was not an overnight smash. His initial records bombed. Marcucci got him singing lessons and sent him on the road. There Fabian did some disk jockey spots. His pleasant demeanor went far. Marcucci helped matters along. He ran ads that shouted, "Fabian is coming!" "Who is Fabian?" and finally, "Fabian is here!" The blitz paid off. Fabian became the teenybopper's dream. "Turn Me Loose" sold 750,000 copies. Fabian, to his credit, did try to improve. His voice tended to be smothered by overly busy arrangements. At 16 Fabian earned up to $12.000 a night, peanuts by later standards but very respectable for the period. He appeared on a number of major TV programs with Perry Como, Ed Sullivan and others

Fabian followed the path of other teen idols and turned to making movies. His first forgettable film was "Hound Dog Man."

Screaming hordes of bobby-soxers greeted him at the airport. That greeting, significantly, almost cost Fabian an eye when the teens broke a car window. Fabian went on to demonstrate that he could act in *Rio Bravo* and then faded into rock 'n roll oblivion after more than a few moments in the sun. He always remained a rather sweet natured person who never really wanted to become a rock star.

Social Progress: Youth and Civil Rights

In 1960, Kenneth Rexroth wrote about the burgeoning youth movement in an article entitled, *"The Students Take Over."* Rexroth noted that the Revolt of Youth is a new idea. Youth simply did not matter for most of history. Youth are, according to Rexroth, the only ones in the country who cared enough to strike back. They began to join movements seeking change in the 1950s, especially Civil Rights groups.

The NAACP had turned to the courts to attack racial discrimination, chipping away at *Plessy v. Ferguson* (1896). This infamous decision had put the Supreme Court squarely on the side of segregationist laws. In 1954 the NAACP had successfully argued was the *Brown v. Board of Education of Topeka* case. The Supreme Court ordered desegregation of schools. Many hailed the decision as a "second emancipation proclamation." In 1955 the Supreme Court's issued an implementation order, calling for the desegregation of schools "with all deliberate speed." However, compliance was slow.

In 1957, Orval Faubus, Arkansas's governor, tried to block the enrollment of nine black students into Little Rock High School. The still new medium of television demonstrated its power to shape events. Millions witnessed this blatant act of defiance and forced a reluctant President Eisenhower to take action. The President federalized the National Guard and forced the integration of the school. TV had shown its power to aid the Civil Rights movement even earlier in the decade.

In December 1955 the black community in Montgomery, Alabama, organized a bus boycott. The immediate cause of the boycott was Rosa Parks's refusal to give up her seat to a white man and her ultimate arrest. Martin Luther King, Jr., a minister in Montgomery, helped organize the boycott. King was part of the group that organized the Southern Christian Leadership Conference (SCLC) in 1957.The SCLC was a nonviolent organization, using nonviolent civil disobedience as its instrument to force reform. Under King's leadership it became the major force for change in the civil rights field.

Youth were always part of the movement. Their presence took on greater importance on February 1, 1960. Four black college students at North Carolina A&T University began protesting racial segregation in restaurants by sitting at whites-only lunch counters and waiting to be served. Soon students raised in the fifties began to join the movement. Sit-ins spread throughout the South and into the North. In 1960 college students formed another civil rights group, the Student Nonviolent Coordinating Committee (SNCC).

These students used to the new television medium began to use freedom rides—bus trips throughout the South in order to desegregate buses and bus stations and other modern techniques to capture TV's attention. Live news loved the drama of the movement and thrived on its immediacy. Many white students joined the movement. These generally middle class kids had begun to feel guilty, so the theory goes, about their middle class white prosperity in the fifties. However, many actually believed the patriotic lessons taught in fifties schools. There was more of Jefferson than Marx in their revolutionary zeal.

Sex and the Average Teenager

Worries about sex, drugs, and rock 'n roll were prevalent in the fifties. The Kinsey Reports of the late forties and early fifties provided a focus for these concerns. Although flawed, they were the first scientific studies of human sexual behavior, offering evidence that the real culture diverged rather strongly from the ideal. There was far more sex taking place than people realized, and much of it was occurring between teenagers. Parents tended to be alarmed; although the odds were that their teens' behavior didn't vary too much from their own.

The Kinsey Report on the Sexual Behavior of Males was shocking enough, but the fifties had a strong double standard concerning sex and the saying "Boys will be boys" was used to explain male sexual urges by many parents. However, adults were shocked, or pretended to be, to discover that females, too, had sexual urges. There were, however, many who defended Alfred Kinsey, arguing that the reports proved that every human being has a deep instinctual drive for close touch with others. That drive, they argued, underlies human society itself in its need for union with others. This corresponded with Dr. Benjamin Spock's theories of child raising. Sex was not something that sprang up overnight but, in conformity with Sigmund Freud's ideas, something that is at the very core of human nature. This "urge to merge" does not simply lie dormant until children are married.

In the 1950s parents took special care to discourage their daughters from premature sexual experiences. Many parents taught their daughters that sex is a nasty, dirty, and above all dangerous activity. Unmarried pregnancy and single parenthood were not commonplace events. While young ladies did become pregnant without benefit of clergy, the clergy appeared soon after the pregnancy became known. A clergyman sanctified the union and people expected it would be until death did them part.

The fifties, although very family oriented, did mark a significant turning point in thinking about human sexuality in America. Americans began to take Freud more seriously than they had. Although the family was paramount in the ideal culture, more open attitudes toward human sexuality began to filter into it. Parents began to talk more openly about sexuality with their children.

Although homosexuality was still generally regarded as "the sin that dare not speak its name." Novels and plays, if not TV and movies, began to address the issue more openly. There were movements toward greater understanding of the issue, and although these attempts seem rather sad in our more enlightened times, they were necessary first steps toward greater acceptance of what is now termed the gay lifestyle. Of course, even enlightened attitudes, for the time, reveal fifties biases against women.

Mom is blamed for junior's homosexuality. Little is said about lesbianism. The belief was that nurture shaped homosexuality, and it was Mom whose desire for a daughter turned Junior into a homosexual. Mom, of course, is unhappy with Dad who is not man enough for her. So she passes on this attitude to Junior along with her dislike for sex.

When lesbianism was recognized, it was Dad who received the blame for his daughter's perversion. After all, he wanted a son and when he didn't get one, he passed on his attitude to his daughter. No wonder, the argument went, that she didn't grow up and fulfill her proper role in life as a true woman. In other words, women who were "aggressive" and sought to get ahead were not living up to what society expected of them.

Males and females had very clear ideas presented to them by society regarding gender roles. Anyone who deviated from them quickly learned the cost. The most they could hope for was tolerance. The worst was rather grim. It was considered sport among some youth to batter those who were different. Gay bashing was more acceptable in the fifties than today.

The risks of promiscuity were of a different order. Enlightened parents regarded heterosexual sexual experimentation as more natural than homosexual experimentation. Much of the heterosexual experimentation, they believed, was due to that catch all villain, "teenage rebellion." Parents sought to keep their offspring chaste until marriage. They recognized that "modern society" delayed marriage until rather late and that "hormones were raging" during adolescence.

However, demonstrating trust in their children would go a long way toward keeping them pure.

That trust is evident in open discussions. The fifties ethos called for togetherness and the parent as chum. So – all those sitcoms that showed family conferences were mirroring the ideal, if not the real, culture. The belief was that open discussion would halt "rebellion" and all that ills that this made flesh heir to. Democracy in the home was the way to solve problems while repression led to rebellion. .

In the fifties, the petting party prevailed. Marriage forever was still a basic cultural belief. The automobile, readily attainable for most youth, became a moveable bedroom, which provided privacy for sexual experimentation even if its participants didn't "go all the way." Those who did at least believed they might marry, unless the girls were demonized as "that type" of girls. The fifties had only two categories for women, the Madonna and the Sexpot. It made life easier for males but rather complicated for females. However, a ring tended to open the door for sexual intercourse, either one for going steady or a true engagement ring. Many "premature" babies visited newlyweds.

The Mental Hygiene Film

The lowly mental hygiene film that all kids who grew up during the fifties remember suffering through provides insight into "the way things were" for fifties kids. These films made quickly and cheaply were blatantly didactic. They sought to teach kids what society expected of them. There was little time for dramatic subtlety. Bam, the message came through loud and clear.

Thus, there is a scene in a film that has a teen washing dishes in a sink, telling her Dad, "Those, those apple-polishers, I don't like them!" Dad, without missing a beat, responds to the scorn in her voice, while beginning to help with the dishes, "Punkin! All these people you don't like, aren't they happier than you?" Punkin' immediately breaks into tears, recognizing the truth of Dad's message.

Viewing the hygiene films provides a candid shot into the life of the times. A simple listing of some titles gives a good measure of the manner in which social pressure weighed on the teens of the day "Lunchroom Manners," "The Terrible Truth"(drugs),"The Last Prom"(reckless teenage driving), "Are You Popular?" (1958) and "Friendship Begins at Home" (1949), "Mind Your Manners!" (1953) and "What Makes a Good Party?" (1950) Evidently, teens couldn't be trusted to know how to behave on their own. Interestingly, many respectable social scientists aided in the making of these films, which today are quite humorous but were deadly serious at the time. After all, there was a feeling that American values were in danger. Youth was a rebellious period, and elders needed to beat back that rebellion. Training and propaganda films of World War II provided a model of just how to instill the appropriate attitude in youngsters.

These films, however, do have the virtue of a realistic portrayal of everyday life. That portrayal was part of its message. Teens could identify with the reality of the settings and characters, no matter how mundane. This identification would make it easier for them to accept the message and values of the film. Some films even ventured into areas not generally dealt with, such as, date rape ("Name Unknown"), substance abuse ("Keep Off the Grass"), and childhood death and injury ("Live and Learn"). Interestingly, these topics were handled in a straightforward and insightful fashion with little, if any, sugar coating.

The virtual lack of art in these films, for the most part, makes them more valuable as a window into fifties youth. There was a great deal more worry than many who get their history from 50s sitcoms would realize. The major worry was not whether Dad would let Junior have the car Saturday night. Worries concerned drugs, rape, abuse, identity, school, pregnancy, and all the terrible things that weren't supposed to inhabit a teen's life in the fabulous fifties – but all too often did.

Hang Outs: Drive –In Restaurants, Diners, and Drive-In Movies

In the fifties drive-ins referred to places where you parked your car to see a movie or to restaurants where you sat in your car and a car-hop, usually a teenage girl, brought you food in a tray that hooked onto your car window. Either place was a teen hangout as many films, most made after the fifties, depict. The institutions were part of the car culture, and there were other drive-ins that were less teen oriented, such as drive-in churches, banks, and dairies.

The carhops, or curb girls, were something to behold. In the fifties, it was typical to hire women for their beauty and grace. That did not necessarily mean that they were incapable of performing their jobs. Although many, if not most, carhops were seemingly rather delicate, they were able to handle heavy trays loaded with food. The food consisted primarily of the teenagers' stables, hamburgers, hot dogs, corn dogs, fries, shakes, sodas and similar food. Teens were, if anything, less health food conscious in the fifties than currently. Nor were teenage boys any more polite than they are now. The carhops may have looked delicate but they were able to fend off offensive comments and even more physical advances with ease. The work was hard, the tips were meager, but the carhops seemed to have fun. Some even did their jobs while on roller skates.

Teens loved to sit in their cars, drink cokes (lemon, cherry, vanilla or straight) and talk to their dates and friends. Generally, the overstuffed burgers would lose some of its stuffing – a pickle, some cheese, onions, lettuce, special sauces. A coke might spill. In any case, there would be a mess of some sort.

There were chains of drive-ins, A&W, Krystals, Surf Maid, and others. Kids would hang out in much the way "American Graffiti" shows. Some would shift between the sit down restaurant and their cars. Often people would cruise the streets and then return to the drive-in or go from one drive-in to another. The food was cheap, greasy, and full of fat. The car made everything all right and gave kids freedom and mobility.

There were places where kids hung out that didn't require a car. Drugstores and diners were strictly sit down eating-places. Drugstores typically had soda fountains and grills. Their usual fare was available. The omnipresent shakes, malts, sodas, cherry Cokes, vanilla cokes, lemon cokes, sundaes, hamburgers, hot dogs and almost any other sandwich you desired. You could also scan the shelves for the latest magazines, buy stamps, and even get your prescriptions filled by a druggist who often served as a substitute doctor for minor aches and pains.

Diners were a step up, but not a big one, from drugstores. Many were old trolley cars that had been converted to restaurants and featured blue-plate specials for $.25 or $.35. The food was basic fifties. That means that meatloaf, mashed or fried potatoes, pot roast and similar fare was the food of choice at these "greasy spoons." Service was fast, friendly, and efficient. There was nothing fancy, no "nouvelle cuisine," but the food stuck to one's ribs and would be called "comfort food" today. Parents who had suffered in the Depression did not want their kids to go hungry, and the lesson was often taught and learned too well. At the time, however, the kids enjoyed stuffing their faces, as the saying went.

It was expected that every date end with some food. The dates themselves could vary. Often the drive-in movie was the venue of choice. These "passion pits" also served food, and between the double or triple feature, cartoons, newsreel, trailers, and whatever else filled those long, sultry summer evenings, there were ads for food. Popcorn, corndogs, hot dogs, and the rest of the usual suspects, along with candy, the ever-present coke, candy apples, and whatever else the owner thought of were sold to hormone-crazed teens.

And teens did have hormones in the fifties. The drive-ins allowed a certain amount of privacy in a public setting. In a period when baggage and marriage were prerequisites for a man and woman to check into a motel, it was beyond the imagination of most teens to "rent a room" to conduct their "petting" and "necking." While petting parties did take place in people's homes when parents were absent, there was always the danger that Mom and Dad might come home early or that a neighbor might prove too curious about all those kids visiting when Mister and Mrs. Jones were away.

The drive-in became a site where rules could be broken within limits. Gentlemen did not go "too far," and girls were expected to rein their steadies in. "Going steady" was just a step below engagement. It meant that the couple promised not to date others. Generally, the boy gave his girls a ring. That is the ring to which Elvis refers in his "Won't You Wear My Ring Around Your Neck."   Going steady gave the couple some acknowledged sexual privileges beyond necking, prolonged kissing. But it did not, in theory, confer on them the right to engage in full sexual intercourse. There were very complicated rules regarding what was allowed and what was not. It is true that boys kept trying to evade the rules or reinterpret them, while girls usually were strict constructionists. It was all part of the mating dance and a good deal of it took place at the drive-in.

It is true that drive-ins were also family entertainment centers. That fact often served to cool down some of the lover's lane activity in the teens' cars. That and the tons of petticoats and other heavy undergarments fifties' girls wore. These were the days before panty hose and a girdle belt was the cutting edge in underwear.

There were a couple of things that kept the lovers and young kids apart. Kiddies' films tended to come on first. Therefore, the teens came later. Sometimes different drive-ins would cater to one group or the other. More often, there was a concerted effort to park in different areas of the parking lot. Later there were two or more screens showing the same, or different movies. There was a great skill at categorizing things in the fifties. It was not impossible to juggle two or three contradictory things in one's mind at the same time.

Parents loved to take the youngsters to drive-ins. The little ones went dressed in pajamas. Mom had probably cooked a picnic chicken, made sandwiches, and stuffed bags or a basket with various goodies. The kiddies ate themselves into a state of stupor, played at the drive-in's playground, and used their facilities. They then watched the first few cartoons and fell asleep. Then Mom and Dad could watch a movie, often imitating those teens parked off by themselves in the parking lot.

Conclusion

Fifties youth may seem to be a carefree lot, simpler than those who followed them. Perhaps, in some ways they were. Their clothes are just similar enough to give the illusion that the people who wore them can be easily understood. Their language is also so much like that which is spoken today that the illusion persists that their codes were the same as those in operation now. However, the fifties were not so simple and sunny as nostalgia would have it. The youth were certainly not so. James Dean was their cinematic idol and "Rebel Without a Cause" *their* movie.

Their music was rock 'n roll. The irony is that a jazz musician who still plays jazz every week in New York City, Les Paul, developed the electric guitar, the quintessential rock 'n roll instrument. Les not only developed the modern electric guitar, he also perfected the overdubbing technique still used in recording. He and his wife had a successful pop career in the early fifties ("Vaya Con Dios," "The World Is Waiting for the Sunrise," and "How High the Moon" among other hits). It is hard to imagine rock 'n roll without the electric guitar.

No one can state with certainty, which was the first rock 'n roll record. There were many rhythm and blues recordings that could have been "the first" and many artists have laid claim to having recorded the first. Jackie Brentson's 'Rocket 88' from 1951is often cited as the first rock 'n roll recording. It has the classic components -it's about a 1950 Oldsmobile 88 with a high-compression, overhead-valve Rocket V-8 engine. It has the added fillip of having Ike Turner on keyboards. Some give credit to Bill Haley's 'Shake, Rattle and Roll' done with his comets in 1954 as the first rock and roll song. Little Richard, on the other hand, claims to be the architect of the genre. Chuck Berry certainly deserves consideration as a possible founder of the music.

However, during its peak years, Elvis was King. He brought it to its fever pitch of popularity. In 1956 he captured the core of its sexuality in a string of songs, using his Holy Roller moves to ignite the teenage girls and make their boy friends jealous. Elvis made rock 'n roll the music of the period and gave it mass popularity. Beginning with 1956's 'Heartbreak Hotel' Presley had a number one hit for 25 of the next 37 weeks with seven million-seller hits. His company, RCA, literally cannot press records as fast as his fans demand them. Elvis was among the first to cash in on non-record merchandise, selling more than \$25 million in Elvis "stuff."

Like James Dean, Elvis projected a very ambiguous image. He was a good boy with a lot of bad in him. He was a Momma's boy whom many nubile young teens wished to cuddle. Conversely, many males could see themselves as Elvis, and soon Elvis-style clothing and sideburns were in style. He projected the complexity of the fifties and rock 'n roll, a respectable rebel who had good manners but was obviously subverting older values.

The beats under the banner of seeking the meaning of their own lives also captured that polite rebellion. Kerouak, Ginsberg, Burroughs, and Leroi Jones started out simply to write, live life, and ignore the old pieties. They, however, generally were mannerly, often dressed in ties and white shirts, and came from conventional families with close ties to their mothers. Kerouak, who influenced not only the Beat Generation of the fifties but also the hippies of the sixties, openly broke with the hippies and supported the Vietnam War.

In sum, fifties youth culture was transitional. It had not yet found its "cause" but it knew somehow that something was wrong. The culture had ties to the forties. The kids who were teens in the fifties had been born just shortly before or during World War II. Many could remember the end of the war and the immediate post war period. The Korean War filled their preteen or early teen years. When the fifties really hit after the Korean War ended in 1953, they were ready for changes, changes that culminated in the sixties, often led by those who had come of age in the earlier decade.

The fascination with African American culture that marked the sixties came of age in the fifties. Rock 'n roll was often condemned as "nigger music" that would lead to miscegenation. Elvis helped bring real rock 'n roll into white teen culture because he was a white boy who could sing like a Negro, as the head of Sun Records put it. Ironically, he helped push the black groups into the background as whites took over yet another element of black culture and painted it white. The yearning for the real thing, however, was there, and the Beats certainly embraced the real thing in their love for jazz. To be really cool and collegiate in the fifties was to dig jazz at coffeehouses where poetry and jazz were mixed.

The fifties, then, saw the real emergence of teens and their own culture. The forties were marked by a World War that took millions of American teens and turned them into cannon fodder. Disrupting and reshaping the domestic front, albeit for a worthy cause. The fifties, however, saw teens build on the forties teen culture and expand their own role in popular culture by their sheer growth in number and control of much of the vaunted growth in economic resources of the fifties.

Suggested Readings and Works Cited

Applebaum, Irwyn. *The World According to Beaver.* New York: Bantam Books, 1984.

Cotton, Lee. *The Elvis Catalog.* New York: Charlton Associates, 1987.

Faine, Edward Allan. *New Ventures : Teenage Life in the 1950s* New York: IM Press, 2001.

Feddeck, Fred C. *Bainbridge, Marion, and Decatur : (Not Revolutionary or 1812 War Heroes)/'the Calm of the Late Fifties / Early Sixties.* New York: Vantage Press, 1999.

Franzosa, Douglas. *Ordinary Lessons : Girlhoods of the 1950s.* Peter Lang, 1999.

Goodwin, Dorris Kearns.*Wait Till Next Year : A Memoir.* New York: Simon & Schuster. 1997

Keylin, Arlene. *The Fabulous Fifties.* New York: Ayer, 1979.

Morrow, Judy Gordon. *Boomerabilia : I Remember (Life Matters Series).*New York: Broadman & Holman Publishers,1998.

Schwartz, Richard B. *The Biggest City in America : A Fifties Boyhood in Ohio (Ohio History and Culture).* Akron. University of Akron Press, 1999.

Chapter 3

Food

The fifties delighted in food. The more casual the food and the setting, the better it seemed. Burgers, pizza, chips and dip, sandwiches of all kinds, and, of course, deserts were popular. There was little worry over cholesterol and fat. The lean years of the Depression and World War II were too painfully close to many Americans. Kids heard quite a bit about finishing their food because of the poor starving children in Europe. Consumption of food, huge quantities of food, was a sign of the burgeoning prosperity of the times. That the food consumed was largely "casual" food and became "fast food" was a sign of the more relaxed American mood of the fifties.

It was also a more prosperous decade with its wealth more evenly spread out than in any other earlier decade. Some food prices give an idea of its prosperity and why food could play such a prominent role in its everyday life. A Pot Roast, for example, was 50¢ a pound while that old standby Wonder Bread was 18¢ a loaf. Coffee, mainly from Brazil, was 93¢ a pound . Milk was 90¢ a gallon , and sugar sold for 52cents for a 5-pound bag . Russet Potatoes were 56 cents for a 10-pound bag.

There were more formal gatherings than the picnics and barbecues that marked the decade. For those occasions there were buffets that a bit fancier, although still with an American twist. Sandwiches in fanciful patterns, checkerboard, ribbon, or pinwheel, adorned many tables. These sandwiches had fillings of salmon, tuna, and cheese, egg salad or minced ham. Deviled eggs often completed these buffets.

Sunday dinners or other sit-down dinners in which the family gathered have become famous for their substantial fare. Pot roasts, meatloaf, and the seemingly omnipresent casseroles were standard fare. There seemed to be plenty of gravy and mashed potatoes as well as buttered rolls to complete the menu. Similarly, breakfasts were proverbially the most important meal of the day. Therefore, as kids learned in school, eggs, bacon, buttered toast, juice, and whole milk over cereal, and, for adults, coffee comprised a healthy meal.

The prosperity of the fifties was indeed quite real for more of the American population than had been the case in any other decade. During that period, the real weekly earnings of "the common man," the factory worker, increased about 50%. In the forties, about 9% of the population was middle class while in the fifties over 30% of the population was middle class. Education and housing certainly reflected that change, a majority of high-school aged people actually graduated from high school by the end of the decade, a "first" in American history, and owning a home became a reality as reflected in the fact that over 25% of all housing in America had been built in the fifties. However, that prosperity was also reflected in the kitchen. Convenience foods spread rapidly. Supermarkets stored over 4000 items on average. Roasts and cake mixes were more affordable than ever. And casseroles became a staple. Tuna-noodle casserole, green bean bake and hamburger stroganoff , each made with the ever-present cream soup, became staples. Cream soups were literally the glue that held those casseroles together.

A few dates help to set the scene for fifties cooking. In 1950, the *Betty Crocker's Picture Cook Book* becomes a best seller. In 1951, Duncan Hines cake mix comes on the market. In 1952 Saran Wrap becomes available, Lipton's now-famous onion soup mix is introduced, and the first sugar-free soft drink slips into the market. In 1953, Eggo joins the convenience food mix along with Cheez Whiz. Swanson's frozen TV dinner's become the rage and the first Burger King opened. 1955 saw the first McDonald's and in 1955 Tappan introduced the microwave oven for the general consumer. 1956 contributed the first electric can opener. Pam came onto the market in 1957 along with Sweet 'n Low. In 1959, Haagen-Dazs, a local ice cream from the Bronx with an exotic name, debuted.

Casual Food

The fast food industry, of course, did not begin in the fifties. However, the fifties was the essential decade in its expansion throughout the country and eventually the world. As early as the first decade of the twentieth century, there were early versions of "fast food." Cafeterias, hot dog stands and Automats paved the way for later fast food outlets.

The automobile also played a major role in the rise of the fast food industry. As Americans ventured out from cities and on the road, they needed to fill themselves as well as their autos. Often, they combined the two tasks in a roadside stop that served food as well as gasoline.

The hamburger stands, fried chicken huts, donut shops and other fast food places that have provided food for a nation on the move have grown with the country in the twentieth century. Some commentators note that these fast food outlets have become increasingly homogenized as the automobile and superhighways have dominated the country. McDonald's, Burger King, the Colonel, and other national chains have tended to obscure regional and ethnic differences in the country. Moreover, these chains have come to dominate the architecture of much of America.

Before McDonald's there was White Castle. White Castle goes back to 1916. J. Walter Anderson founded it in Wichita, Kansas. He specialized in five-cent hamburgers, french fries and colas. White Castle was the most successful of the fast food businesses until the McDonald brothers, Richard and Maurice (Mac), came along with a new plan for a hamburger restaurant in 1948. Efficiency was their primary goal. They embraced the good old American virtues of reducing expenses and maximizing production. selling burgers at a lower price. They wanted profit to come from increased volume. Moreover, they sold only a few products. Their restaurant in San Bernardino, California, was the classic hexagonal shape of early McDonald's. They had no waitresses and specialized in serving more customers faster. There were no indoor tables, encouraging customers to order their food at a window and eat in their cars. They sold only hamburgers, cheeseburgers, french fries and beverages.

To set their restaurant off from others, Richard came up with the idea of constructing "golden arches" right through the roof, which sloped, upward toward the front. The brothers began franchising their operation. Soon there were a number of McDonald's in the country, patterned on the original hut. The first franchises opened in 1953 in Phoenix, Arizona, and Downey, California. There were immediate imitators. Keith Cramer, for example, patterned his Florida restaurant after McDonald's. It became Burger King chain.

However, the fifties saw the explosion of the fast food restaurant. If the fast food movement had really begun to take off with the coming of the automobile, then the fifties in which the automobile dominated the culture was the logical time for it to explode. In 1951, for example, Robert O. Peterson, the owner of a chain of successful local restaurants on the West Coast and Southwest, turned to the concept of a drive-through restaurant. He named it Jack in the Box. Featuring a smiling clown, named Jack, the restaurants were mainly located in California, Texas and Arizona. Motorists had to order through Jack's mouth. There was a two-way speaker device encased inside Jack's head.

About the same time as Jack in the Box was getting off the ground, Ray Kroc began his own rise to prominence. He mortgaged his home and put all his money into the Multimixer, a five-spindled milk shake maker. Ray bought the rights to being its exclusive distributor. In 1954, he discovered that there was a burger stand in California that ran eight Multimixers at a time. Curious about this stand, he drove to San Bernardino, California, to discover the secret of the stand's success. The restaurant was owned by Dick and Mac McDonald and named McDonald's.

Ray Kroc was intrigued by the fact that the brothers were able to serve a large number of people so fast. He proposed opening up several restaurants to the McDonald brothers. He was primarily interested in selling eight Multimixers to each and every one. When Dick McDonald wondered who would open the restaurants, Kroc replied that he would be glad to take on the task. Kroc opened his first restaurant in Des Plaines, Illinois, in 1955. The cash register rang up $366.12. By the end of 1957, there were 37 McDonald's; by 1959, the total had reached over 100. By 1961, Kroc was so enamored of the drive-ins that he bought out the brothers and expanded his operation throughout America. In turn, Kroc's success encouraged the growth of other fast-food chains.

The rest is fast food history.

The drive in restaurant, as opposed to drive-throughs like Jack in the Box, were places where drivers parked their cars and were served, often by young girls on roller skates. Food was hooked onto the car window and passengers ate in their cars. Many Americans too young to have experienced the drive-ins for themselves have an idea of their ambience from the film American Graffiti and the TV show Happy Days, both produced some years after the fact.

The fifties were the era of franchise. Whether the fast food franchises really reflect the root of the word, meaning freedom, is problematic. However, it was the promise of freedom that attracted both those who purchased these franchises and customers who flocked to their restaurants. There was an overwhelming need for all types of products and services. In the 50's many people had a dream of owning their own business. Franchising enabled them to do so with a minimum of cash outlay. It also puts the franchisee into a business with name recognition and standard products. In a sense, much of the business is presold to the public. People know how much or how little to expect from a McDonald's, Pizza Hut, or Burger King. There should be no surprises.

Convenience Foods
The Fifties were also marked by a fascination with convenience foods. Again, the first highly artificial product, Reddi-Whip, was a late forties product. It was, and still is, sprayed out of a can, allowing speed and convenience into the American kitchen, a trend that also marked the fifties. Certainly, speed was replacing taste, but the fifties thought it was a fair exchange. Thus, fresh chicken pieces, as opposed to whole chickens, were first sold in the fifties. In 1952, additionally, a number of convenience products hit the markets: Lipton Dry Onion Soup, Saran Wrap, and Cascade Dishwasher soap, to list but a few. In 1953, the electric skillet and Eggos (Let Go my Eggos) were joined by the first portable outdoor grill, leading to millions of men burning tons of newspapers and pouring gallons of gasoline on charcoal in futile attempts to cook steaks. The trend continued and some familiar American staples joined the parade. In 1954 the first Butter Ball turkey made it to Thanksgiving and Christmas dinner along with M and M peanut based candies. In 1955 Roy Kroc, who sold his own patented milkshake mixers, convinced a couple of California fast food owners to let him franchise their product, and McDonald's joined the list of fast food stops. In that same year, microwaves helped Americans nuke their food. That other staple of the American diet, Kentucky Fried Chicken started its franchised spread across the countryside in 1956. The Colonel was still alive and active at the time with his "secret recipe." In 1957, interestingly, Sushi made its debut in America with the first Sushi Bar, in California, of course, It took a few more decades, at least, until it caught on.

The TV Dinner
By the 1950s, the frozen food market was ready for take off. Before frozen prepared food became popular in the home, hospitals and

fast food restaurants welcomed their convenience. Businesses of all kinds welcomed the opportunity to prepare foods cheaply, without chefs or large kitchen areas. Airlines, of course, saw the benefits of serving passengers warmed up food in coach class instead of gourmet delicacies.

The food industry noted that it could use techniques developed in other manufacturing industries. They could prepare food on demand. These foods could be packaged and prepared to meet the customers' needs. Moreover, they could so at a markedly reduced price, far less than any food prepared on site. In short order, "housewives" or "homemakers" soon realized the value of frozen prepared food.

The Simplot Company added to the options available by making a viable version of the french fry, packaging it for the home and business market. These popular snacks caught on the fast-growing prepared food market. Soon vegetables and fruit, guacamole, fresh potatoes, and other products came "ready prepared," making cooking less of drudgery, or in the language of the fifties, convenient.

Aluminum serving utensils and glass buffet plates became popular serving vehicles in the fifties, as settings for some of the ready made meals, as well as "home cooked" food.

Technological advances made the frozen food industry, and fifties TV dinners, possible. Basically, the idea is simple. Refrigeration enables the food storage temperature to be lowered to a point at which bacterial growth is reduces, lessening the possibility for food poisoning or spoilage. This advance allowed fresh food to be transported for long distances, opening the potential food market. Food is frozen below -10 degrees C, enabling people to eat some food years after it has been frozen.

Better refrigerators and freezers into American kitchens have allowed American consumers the option of storing food safely in their homes. Much of the frozen food is in the form of prepared dinners. The food company executive whose bright idea led to the TV dinner was Gerry Thomas. Thomas found that Swanson's had a great deal of leftover turkey, 520,000 pounds worth, in fact. . Therefore, he put this turkey on an aluminum tray and invented the "TV dinner" in 1954. Swanson' classic TV dinner tray had three-compartments.

Like many simple ideas, the TV dinner appears, in retrospect, to be a very simple idea. The union of TV, which was exploding rapidly in the fifties, with food seems a natural. Those little trays made TV watching easy while eating. It also put a crimp in the family dinner hours, and the convenience of the little packages meant that many families didn't even eat in front of the TV at the same time.. The TV dinners had their own version of fifties hearty cooking, fried chicken,

Salisbury steak and roast turkey. Those classic trays had a compartment for a brownie or cobbler desert as well as one for mashed potatoes, green beans and corn or similar vegetables.

.   Thomas notes that the whole ideas stemmed from those 520,000 pounds of turkey and the popularity of TV. In fact, Thomas had noted that airlines prepared meals in little metal trays. He stored that idea and when the turkey crisis hit him, he was ready.

We couldn't afford it. Television was the talk of the day. Television was something that if you had one, you were contemporary and were cool.

The first TV dinners cost 98 cents and was comprised of turkey, cornbread dressing and gray, buttered peas and sweet potatoes, packaged in a three-compartment tray

Another of the many fifties convenience foods was Rice-A-Roni, the San Francisco treat. Rice-A-Roni started as a family recipe. The family was the De Domenico family of San Francisco. Their recipe was an old Armenian dish made from rice, vermicelli pasta, and chicken broth. They sautéed the rice and pasta before adding liquid. The dish caught on quickly after Vince De Domenico packaged it for general distribution. He substituted a dry mix for the chicken broth. The cute

"Home Cooking" at Home and in Restaurants

Fifties food, whether casual, formal or at home, was substantial. A quick run through of some of the standard fare will give an idea of what was meant by substantial. Submarines, also known as heroes, poorboys, dagwoods, hogies, or any of a number of other regional names, were typical fifties' food. Almost anything good, and often did, go into these sandwiches. Many current chains offer pale imitations of these fifties' "snacks." Delis or independent sub shops come closer to their satisfactory size.

These subs were often washed down by flavored cokes (cherry, lemon, lime, or vanilla) and accompanied by french fries smothered in gravy. Sometimes a pink party punch served to wash down the food. Various floats, coke or root beer were the favorites, were good "fountain" drinks. These floats consisted of soda, or "pop," mixed with about two-thirds of a glass of ice cream. The ice cream was always loose so that the Coke or root beer could flow into the crevices. These drinks could be eaten with a spoon. It was, however, more fun to use two straws and sip one with your date or "steady." By the way, the Coke was routinely mixed at room temperature so that an icier crust was formed. They cost all of 15 cents.

There were a number of foods that were popular in the fifties that seem inexplicable to those who were not there. Some are still popular today. Spam, for example, is a mystery to many. It was a synthetic product introduced by Hormel in 1937 and later produced for the military during World War II. Its name comes from the fact that it is "spiced ham." In the fifties its advocates ate it on white bread, usually something like Wonder Bread. Of course, the peanut butter and banana sandwiches of the period still puzzle many, including some that were around at the time. Of course, the peanut butter and banana sandwiches of the period still puzzle many, including some that were around at the time.

Much of the popular food, however, still is appealing to those born at the time, although their diets may not allow them to partake of them very often. Disney, among others, has capitalized on the nostalgia for the fifties style dinner in places like the Prime Time Café and his Drive In at MGM. Some of the food was, of course, introduced for convenience. Thus, the fifties witnessed the introduction of chicken sold in parts; Lipton's dry onion soup mix (1952); Butterball turkeys (1954); Sweet `N Low (1957); Jif Peanut Butter (1958) and Häagen-Dazs ice cream (1959).

The 1950s were certainly a boom time for babies. The early fifties saw16 million babies born between 1950-53. It is not surprising, then, that fast-food chains, TV dinners, and backyard barbecues, with men as cooks, became popular. Mom's cooking often featured the casserole. Other of Mom's specialties included such standards as steak, more affordable for the fifties at around 50 cents per pound, roast beef, pork chops, meat loaf, and for desert various kinds of Dream Whip based delicacies, pies, fudge, or cake.

One party loaf tried to combine all the fifties favorites with fruit cocktail and Spam with gelatin, Miracle Whip and paprika. Three-Bean Salad, Tomato Aspic and Pickled Beet Salad were other favorites that were often found with a barbecue. Of course, if a family went out to dinner a full course meat loaf blue-plate special was $1.75. Root Beer Floats - Real Ice Cream Milk Shakes (15¢)

The fifties did indulge in more "exotic" foods. Travel was becoming more popular and Americans brought back a love for French cuisine. They also took to the Scandinavian smorgasbords. These smorgasbords had the advantage of being foreign and offering plentiful quantities of various foods. Similarly, Beef Stroganoff, which had been around for some time, became quite popular in the fifties. The Baked Alaska was a great favorite in the realm of "classy" deserts.

Casseroles became the rage and the tuna noodle casserole was near the top in popularity. It is relatively easy to make and feeds a number of people at a time. It is a "stretch" food, the cheese and liquid can make a little tuna go a long way. Other family treats were little spareribs with sweet and sour glazes and a dessert called Grasshopper

Pie, named after the sweet after dinner drink, The Grasshopper, for its green color. . In spite of its exotic name, a Grasshopper Pie is relatively easy to make and its ingredients are not so exotic. According to the instructions, it should take about fifteen minutes and serves eight. Its ingredients are crushed chocolate wafer cookies, cold milk, peppermint extract, Pistachio Jell-O, Cool Whip, and Baker's Semi-Sweet chocolate. The whole mix was frozen until solid.

A typical day's meals for the fifties was blended prune and grapefruit juice, Cornflakes, toast, cinnamon rolls, coffee, milk for breakfast. Lunch might be a hot baked cheese sandwich, endive salad, milk, and stuffed baked apples. Dinner, if light, could be baked salmon loaf, mashed potatoes, baked beet slices, deviled egg salad, whole-wheat bread, coffee, sliced cling peaches, and cookies.

An Ohio newspaper, *The Spectator*, noted that in 1955 major food recipes requested were for the following Buckeyes, Johnny Marzetti, Broccoli Cheese Soup, Hot Artichoke Dip, Vegetable Pizza, Maramor Fudge Sauce, Wor Sue Gai, Apples 'n' Onions, Sweet Potato Bake, Six-Week Refrigerator Bran Muffins, Seven-Layer Salad, Pimento Cheese Spread, potato soup of all kinds, anything with pumpkin in it, Peanut Butter Pie, Impossible Pie, Key Lime Pie, Heavenly Hash, Funnel Cakes and anything Amish.

Food and Gender Relations

In the fifties there was an awareness that food could be seductive and gendered, gelatin was for women while meat was for men. Simultaneously, there was recognition that food preparation could also be tedious and that women, the main food preparers often worked outside the home. The message then that all a women needed was a good pie recipe and a thick steak to keep her marriage happy was being contradicted by the changing reality of the era. Unsurprisingly, as women's roles changed, there were increasing attempts to keep women in the roles of wife, mothers, and homemaker.

Jessamyn Neuhaus sums up the general picture thus

If ever a nation needed comfort food, it was the United States in the 1950s. Weary from the strain of war-time separations, economy, and anxieties, and reeling from the new knowledge that the U.S. Possessed a weapon with unimaginable capabilities for destruction, Americans turned to abundant, rich food.

Women played a stereotypical role in providing that comfort. Although cookbooks sought to uphold the traditional norms by stating that convenience foods were merely breaks in a woman's task to prepare well-thought out and comforting meals for her family, they sought to shore up the crumbling remnants of gender stereotyping, under attack by the necessities of fifties life, such as, paying for the suburban home and two cars in the new two-car garage. Men were allowed to cook meat over the barbecue pit, wearing masculine aprons that contrasted with Mom's frilly ones. Meat, after all, defined the male hunter.

As in so many other areas, the fifties provide a picture of a society in flux. Popular culture, in this case through cookbooks, offers a glimpse into the crumbling of gender stereotypes beneath a seemingly uniform acceptance of men's roles and women's roles. Food may be the way to a man's heart. It also is a way into understanding changes in gender relationships.

Conclusions

Food in the fifties was generally based on "comfort" food. It was, however, a bit more complex than that. In addition to the meatloaf smothered in gravy and onions, the Sunday pot roast with mashed potatoes, and the delicious root beer floats, there was a willingness to experiment that marked the period. There was a fascination with French food that characterized the age. That fascination extended to other foreign food as well. This was the period when ethnic food began to spread throughout America. People began to sample Chinese, Swedish, and other "foreign" cooking beyond the "almost-American" Italian dishes.

While the fifties marked the true beginning of the "franchising of America" as fast food chains began their relentless march across the continent, following the Eisenhower Interstate Highway System, there were other aspects of fifties food that resisted homogenization. The increase in communication did bring regional specialties to areas beyond their origin. Cajun cooking began to spread beyond New Orleans and the Coney Island hot dog was found outside the New York metropolitan region. Both movements have continued their simultaneous spread.

Similarly, convenience foods have not disappeared but neither has fine cooking. Men have moved from the barbecue area to the kitchen. If not replacing their wives or significant others, some men have begun to admit their love for cooking. Many of us who came of age in the fifties remember our fathers cooking on their days off under the guise of "giving Mom a rest." While it was not macho to admit liking to cook, it was obvious that they did in fact enjoy their forays into the kitchen.

Fifties cooking, like the fifties, was more complicated than the stereotypes. It reveals the "ideal norms' of gender relationships as well as the "real norms." Those norms were in flux, a fact too often forgotten in the heat of culture wars. Those battles, however, should not obscure the fact that fifties food, although dangerous to our health, had a seductive quality that was also comforting.

References
Boas, Max and Steve Chain. *Big Mac: The Unauthorized Story of McDonald 's*. New York: A Mentor Book, The New American Library, 1977.
Heimann, Jim. *Car Hops and Curb Service : A History of American Drive-In Restaurants 1920-1960*. Chronicle Books, 1996.
Jakle, John A. and Keith A. Sculle. *Fast Food : Roadside Restaurants in the Automobile Age (The Road and American Culture)* Johns Hopkins University Press, 1999.
Kroc, Ray and Robert Anderson. *Grinding It Out : The Making of McDonald's*. St. Martin's Press, 1990.
Love, John F. *McDonald's : Behind the Arches* . Bantam Books, 1995.
Neuhaus, Jessamyn. "The Way to a Man's Heart: Gender Roles, Domestic Ideology, and Cookbooks in the 1950s." *Journal of Social History*, Spring 1999, volume 32, issue 3, pp. 529
Tennyson, Jeffrey. *Hamburger Heaven: The Illustrated History of the Hamburger*. New York: Hyperion,1993.
Witzel, Michael Karl. *The American Drive-In* .Motorbooks International, 1994.
Witzel, Michael Karl. *Drive-In Deluxe (Enthusiast Color Series)*. Motorbook International, 1997

Chapter 4

Travel and Transportation

The fifties is often remembered for its love of travel, of getting from here to there in the fastest possible time. Often the journey was more important than the destination, as depicted in numerous films from and about the time. The phenomenon of cruising, aimlessly driving up and down a street either to be seen or to pick up a member of the opposite sex, or both, typifies the period. The automobile, in fact, became the symbol of the age. It was the most common of many modes of transportation that came of age in the fifties. It had become the means for transporting families, and, often, the means for creating them.

The Rise of the Family Vacation

The fifties marked the culmination of changes in America's styles of pleasure and tourism. The increase in disposable income and new attitudes towards consumer debt saw changes in the family vacation. Consumer felt that prosperity would continue to grow so debt need not trouble them. Why not enjoy good things now and pay later? They felt that they would have even more money later. In a strange bit of logic, they believed that since their income would increase yearly, the vacation taken this year would cost less in next year's money. Indeed, for many families it marked the first time they could consider a family vacation. Trips to the shore, mountains, or to visit old friends became increasingly common throughout the fifties. The cost of a family vacation, of course, varied, depending on where the family went. With motels costing from a low of about $4.00 per night to the Holiday Inn range of $15.00 and gas costing below $.33 per gallon, many vacations for a family of four for a week were less than @200.

The vacation to end all family vacations, however, was the dreamed trip to Disneyland. In the early fifties, Walt Disney, famous for his "family" films and Mickey Mouse began to plan for an amusement park near Los Angeles. In 1955, Disneyland opened, and America had found "its" amusement park. It was a park filled with fantasy and nostalgia, Disney trademarks, but characteristics common to the American character. General admission on opening day was $1.00 and tickets ranged from a dime to $.35. The ticket books, in the early days there were no "passports," were labeled A, B, or C. Each book offered tickets for rides in a given price range. The D book came a bit later in the fifties and allowed a guest to ride the Jungle Cruise and the Mine Train. In 1959 the E tickets were issued for the Matterhorn, monorail, and submarines. In 1956, a book had seven tickets and general admission for $2.50 (adult). The tickets ranged from rides rated A, B, or C. A rides were a dime, B a quarter, and C thirty-five cents. B rides, for example, included the Phantom Boats in Tomorrowland, Mickey Mouse Theatre in Fantasyland, and Conestoga Wagons in Frontierland.

This prototypical family American Park, however, appealed to people from all over the world. Even the Soviet premier, Nikita Khrushchev, threw a tantrum when security prohibited his going to Disneyland. Disney had built a park for children of all ages, as the cliché goes. He had tapped into his store of knowledge of what the people want. Popular culture was his forte and in Disneyland, with its various lands, he had mapped out a world of his own. To the fifties kids no vacation could match that of Disney. Many parents were frustrated in trying to please their kids with "lesser" trips.

However, there were other possibilities for vacation in the fifties, ranging from jaunts in cars with stops at the omnipresent motels to luxury cruises. Air travel became an increasing attractive choice for travelers, virtually replacing both railroad passenger travel and luxury liners. In 1958, the Boeing 707 began regular flights. Soon air travel became affordable for many families.

Youngsters and some parents as well, dreamed of a future that is something like the recently revised Tomorrowland at Disneyland. Tony Baxter, its designer says: "Dreams about the future were very easy to tap into in the '50s. There were so many challenges left unrealized because of the Depression and World War II-- there was a lot left to dream about." Baxter was "betting that the public will be more excited by yesterday's heroic tomorrow than today's more jaundiced one."

In the fifties, the science fiction image of vacations on the moon seemed real. Jet cars and high tech homes were perceived as in the realm of the possible and just around the corner. Disney himself believed in those dreams, It is interesting that the vacation that kids dreamed of in the not too distant future is now only available at Disneyland.

Other families, the majority perhaps, spent their vacations going on trips in the family chariot. Often the trip was to visit friends or relatives and kids would ask frequently, "Are we there yet?" The idea of seeing your parents' friends was not an appealing one. However, parents usually did not give much choice in the matter.

These trips took place on pre-Interstate highway roads. Travel was through towns and cities, mainly on two-lane roads. Traffic lights impeded travel and chain fast food restaurants were still mainly in the future. Local culture impressed itself on the travel and regional differences were greater in a less homogenized America that was the fifties. The road really did have some romance left in it on Route 66, the famous highway that went west across the country and became the symbol of the freedom of the open road.

The American Romance with the Automobile

In brief, automobiles are so designed as to be dangerous at any speed. -Ralph Nader, "The Safe Car You Can't Buy," The Nation, April 11, 1959

Virtually since its invention, Americans have had a love affair with the automobile. Perhaps, the fifties mark the high point of that affair. During the fifties, the automobile industry experienced a huge growth, and cars become fetish symbols. They became more elaborate, much faster than they had been, and a sign of American prosperity and energy.

The Beat generation added to the myth of the automobile, depicting its driver as heroic and dangerous. The fifties witnessed a number of "road movies" that added to the myth, such as "The Wild Ones" and parts of "Rebel without a Cause." Brando and Dean personified these figures on the big screen. TV also added its own version. Programs like "Route 66," for example glorified the wonders of the open road. In itself, that open road had long been an American symbol, exploited by Mark Twain, Herman Melville, and Walt Whitman, among others.

Rock music and advertising also used the myth of the heroic driver, although advertisements for plush executive cars that presented them as heroes do appear a bit ironic in retrospect. However, the executive liked to think of himself as a potential rebel, with or without a cause, and dangerous in his own way. Furthermore, although there were some warnings about the danger of the big fifties gas guzzlers to the environment, relatively few Americans took them seriously.

Certainly, in the fifties, the automobile represented far more than mere transportation. It signified power, sex, freedom, and technology. The architect, le Corbusier, wrote in The City of the Future, for example, "Cars, cars, fast, fast! One is seized, filled with enthusiasm, joy ... in the joy of power." The Cadillac's famous tail fins bore witness to that lust for power. They had, after all, been copied from an American World War II fighter plane.

In the fifties, the car was part of the American courtship ritual, nicknamed a moving bedroom. The movie star, James Dean encapsulated the mythology of the car through his movies and his death. He died skidding off the road while racing his Porsche, "Little Bastard." The death in the "saddle" tied him to legendary figures of the American West, adding to his aura.

That the car is part of America's frontier mythology is generally acknowledged. Arthur Penn, the director of "Bonnie and Clyde," for example, notes, "In US western mythology the automobile replaced the horse in terms of the renegade figure." The Beats also grasped that the driver had taken place of the old gunslinger as the loner beyond the control of conventional ties to family, law, or women. Kerouac's On the Road, for example, gave us Dean Moriarty, modeled on Neal Cassady. Kerouac has Moriarity croon the following love word to a Caddy: "Ah man what a dreamboat. Think if you and I had a car like this what we could do. Yes, you and I, Al, we'd dig the whole world with a car like this because man, the road must eventually lead to the whole world."

For the fifties, the road was the whole world, or so it seemed to teens, at least male teens. Chuck Berry's "No Particular Place To Go" captured the mood of the times. Cruising up and down the road was an end in itself or a means to an end, finding "chicks" who would ride with you. The car indeed had become a phallic symbol, as so many of its critics exclaimed. Its supporters only shrugged in reply.

A brief overview of the fifties automotive scene puts the mythology of the fifties car in perspective. The look of the "typical" fifties car began in 1948 when the Hudson came up with a low center of gravity and the Cadillac put out a model with its famous tail fins. In the next year, Chrysler introduces ignition key starting. No separate starter was needed, either on the dash or floor. Virtually ignored is the introduction of the first Volkswagen Beetles. Two are brought to the United States. Those people who do see them laugh. In 1950 automatic transmission become available in low cost cars. The 1950, Chevrolet (the poor man's Cadillac), cost $1329 and had optional automatic transmission. Tires began to improve, and Goodyear sold puncture proof tires. Well over half of the American public had cars in their families, as 60% of American families own cars. In 1951, Chrysler began the horsepower race with its 331 cubic-inch V-8 engine. Power brakes are introduced in 1952 along with the gadget filled Cadillac (Dictaphone, phone, Plexiglas roof that closes with rain, etc.) In 1953, the dream car of many fifties youth was introduced, the Chevrolet Corvette. The triumph of the automobile is seen in the fact that motels outnumbered hotels by a two to one ratio. In 1955, the original Ford Thunderbird, the T-Bird to people in the fifties, made its debut. It was a two-seater sports car. In 1956, the Interstate (Eisenhower) Highway system gained Congressional approval, and cars became more powerful and luxurious. Some even sold for $10,000. Tail fins continued to become increasingly fantastic, with Chrysler's fins surpassing those of the Cadillac in 1957. In 1958, the remarkable flop, the Edsel made its debut. As the car industry goes into a 31% sales decline, the handwriting is clear, in retrospect as the first Toyotas and Datsuns are imported. Detroit, however, had not yet learned its lesson, and in 1959, Cadillac won the fin race with giant tail fins featuring rocket pod taillights. Studebaker was again a bit ahead of its time, it had introduced the sleek streamlined car a bit too early, when it brought out a compact car, the Lark. By 1960, other manufacturers brought out compacts. Ford had the Falcon; Chrysler the small Plymouth Valiant, Chevrolet a rear engine, air-cooled compact, the Corvair. By the end of the fifties, 80% of families owned at least one car.

It is clear that in the fifties, Americans wanted power and style more than safety and economy. Detroit was willing to offer them what they wanted. Thus, there were the horsepower and tail fin wars. Lots of chrome, choices of colors, hardtop convertibles, strange toothy grills, and all sorts of glitz were the order of the day. Basically, cars were sleeker, longer, and more stylish than they had ever been. Cars, in sum, were more than merely basic transportation.

Basic transportation was left to the imports. The company, better known as FIAT, S.P.A., or, more simply, Fiat, was one of a number of cars that slowly began to challenge Detroit's virtual monopoly on the American car. It was one of a number of "foreign" cars that either sports car enthusiasts or a minority of cost-conscious drivers sought out. For most Americans, the era of cheap gas was supposed to last forever. However, while Americans were looking elsewhere the former Axis powers of the Second World War were rebuilding. Italy was no exception. The bombed-out Fiat facilities were in Turin, Italy, were quickly restored, and modernized. Within ten years, FIAT was sixth in auto production in the world. Vittorio Valletta, the architect of FIAT's revival aided its growth through a lucrative contract with the Soviet Union, enabling the company to open a plant and manufacture automobiles for the Soviets. However, Valetta was no Communist. Detroit executives, who should have noted how he managed to combine a love for capitalism with a shrewd eye on placating workers and sharing his wealth, admired his methods. By the end of the fifties, FIAT's exports to the United States were substantial, a portent of things to come.

Air travel also had a great deal of romance. It was clear to close observers that after the Second World War, air travel would enjoy a period of growth. Advances made to aviation during the war would, everyone assumed, profit commercial airliners. Indeed immediately after the war the Stratoliner and the DC-4 began civilian service on longer routes, even crossing the Atlantic and Pacific oceans. The Lockheed Constellation provided great competition to the DC-4. TWA asked Lockhead to develop a plane that would increase the speed of the DC-3 by 100 miles, to over 275 miles per hour. Additionally, TWA wanted to provide non-stop service coast to coast.

By 1955, American airliners had witnessed an incredible growth in air traffic. Routes had been extended beyond most people's expectations, and markets had developed faster than almost anyone had expected. People switched to planes from ships and trains faster than expected.

In 1957, transatlantic air passengers finally surpassed ship passengers. When jets became common by the end of the decade, steamship service was virtually eliminated from competition. In 1958 the Boeing 707 revolutionized the industry and made relatively cheap jet travel more than a science fiction dream. The Boeing 707 was far more economical than the industry expected. Air travel actually became cheaper than it had been before its introduction. The actual cost of operating jets was considerably less per passenger mile than the cost of operating even the most efficient piston-engine planes,

Jet engines could be adapted for various size planes, enabling airlines to fly varying lengths with different numbers of passengers. Once this idea took, hold, as it began to do before the end of the fifties, the number of air routes increased, making travel by plane easier, more convenient, and cheaper. Many families, as well as businesses, began to switch their travel arrangements to air travel, capitalizing on ease and speed, the watchwords of the day.

Rail Travel

In the fifties, the United States began a long period of neglect for public transportation, including the rails. The vast improvement in the nation's highways simply encouraged America's love affair with the automobile. Trains did shift from coal to diesel to electricity as the decade progressed. However, rails became increasingly interested in freight rather than passengers and let its rolling stock and beds deteriorate. Americans generally switched to cars and buses for cheaper transportation and airlines for longer distances.

The Pullman cars, scenic rail liners, luxury dining cars and other amenities slowly disappeared as rail travel became slower, dirtier, and more uncomfortable. Commuter railroads continued but with ever increasing fares as people loved to complain about the Long Island Railroad and the Grand Central Commuter lines. These lines, often unheated or overheated, depending on the season, had a virtually captive audience who found it too expensive to park in the big cities into which they were funneled. Those who could do so turned to automobiles, further clogging up the new superhighways and turning them into vast parking lots.

Boats and Cruises

The Second World War ended passenger liner travel. After the war transatlantic travel resumed. Indeed, some new ships were built, including the American ship the United States in 1952. However, transatlantic airliners soon lured passengers away from the more luxurious but slower ships. Those ships that remained did so because of their luxury value as tourist attractions.

Cruise travel was dealt a severe blow when the SS Andrea Doria sank in 1956 in the worst liner disaster in history, surpassing even the sinking of the Titanic and the Lusitania. On July 25, 1956 the 290, 000 ton Italian passenger ship Andrea Doria collided with the Swedish cruise ship Stockholm .The Andrea Doria struggled to remain floating for 11 hours but finally sunk.

. The Andrea Doria, named for a famous Italian Admiral, had crossed the ocean 100 times . However, like the Titanic it seemed to be unsinkable, for she was the most modern as well as the most beautiful ship in the ocean. All the most modern safety equipment, nevertheless, did not keep her from sinking when she was hit broadside by the Stockholm on her last night at sea. It was an SOS that brought a flotilla of Coast Guard cutters, oil tankers and freighters to her rescue: . The largest ship of the rescue effort, was the enormous French liner Ile de France, a ship that almost did not respond because she was about two hours away and her substitute captain did not realize that the Andrea Doria was in grave danger.

Fifty-one people died and over 1600 were saved. There had been no passenger deaths or series injuries from 1919 until the Andrea Doria sinking in 1956. 27 million passengers had made the crossing safely in that period. However, Americans remembered the Titanic, Lusitania, and Andrea Doria rather the 27 million. The speed and relatively low cost of airline flights, moreover, eventually tipped the scales in favor of air traffic except for tourist luxury.

Conclusion

The fifties maintained its love affair with the automobile in the midst of startling transportation changes. As the rail passenger industry became all but extinct and the transatlantic passenger ship industry virtually disappeared, automobiles kept expanding. The Interstate Highway System, in fact, helped kill public transportation for many decades, helping eliminate trolley, cheap commuter rail, and in some cases, as in Rochester, NY, subways. Buses increasingly became the provenance of the poor and young. The automobile even managed to thrive alongside the jet plane.

American travel witnessed the continuing fascination and dominance of speed. Automobiles only resembled planes. Real speed lay in the air where planes were now able to promise transatlantic travel in a fraction of the time once required by steamers and even prop planes. The jet, indeed, made travel faster, more efficient, and so the advertisers argued, safer. Getting there, wherever **there** was, became easier.

The fifties continued and accelerated America's fascination with being somewhere else. Cruising the streets was but a pale imitation of taking to the road or hopping a jet. The desire to see over the next hill or to forage through the forest is deep within the American soul and drives even the most sedentary to seek new adventure. And the fifties had adventures aplenty, in reality and in dreams.

References
Armi, C. Edson. The Art of American Car Design: The Profession and the Personalities. University Park, PA: The Pennsylvania State University Press, 1988.

Ball, Don, Jr. *The Pennsylvania Railroad : The 1940S-1950s.* New York: W.W. Norton, 1986.

Georgano, Nick. The American Automobile: A Centenary, 1893-1993. NY: Smithmark Publishers Inc., 1992.

Godshall, Jeffrey I. Microphone Tail lights and Doughnut Decks: Chrysler Cars of the Exner Era. Automobile Quarterly, Vol. 29, No. 1 (January 1991), 70-95.

Hirsch, Jay. Great American Dream Machines, Classic Cars of the 50s and 60s. NY: Macmillan Publishing Company, 1985.

Kleiman, Jeffrey D. "Hard Times - Good Times: The Michigan Economy." In

Hathawa, Richard J.(Ed.), Michigan: Visions of Our Past. East Lansing, MI: Michigan State University Press 1989.

Ludvigson, Karl. Corvette, America's Star-spangled Sports Car: The Complete History, An Automobile Quarterly Library Series Book. Princeton, NJ:

Princeton Publishing Co., 1974.

May, George S. (Ed.). The Automobile Industry, 1896-1920, Encyclopedia of American Business History and Biography. NY: Facts on File, 1990.

Chapter 5

Advertising

The advertising icons of the fifties have become so imbedded in the American psyche that they have made reappearance in recent years. Speedy Alka-Seltzer, whose stop motion walk and "plop, plop, fizz, fizz" amused boomers, still amuses. The Anacin commercials that showed someone getting a tension headache through a diagram of the inside of a head being pounded can still cause tension headaches when recalled. Dinah Shore's slight Southern drawl graced the Chevrolet commercials, and many in the fifties did see the USA in their Chevrolets; Chevy was the number one selling car in the US. And then there were the Timex torture tests by John Cameron Swayze, a newscaster. Perhaps, the most famous of the torture tests is the one that shows an Acapulco cliff diver wearing an undamaged Timex. It took a licking and kept on ticking.

By the fifties, advertising had hit its stride and become an integral part of popular culture. It certainly reflected that culture but also helped shape it. There was an interaction between the two, if not an outright symbiotic relationship. Catchy ad slogans found their way into everyday conversations. Indeed, the commercials were often said to be more entertaining than the programs. In early TV, they were, in fact, often part of the program. Martin Kane, Private Eye, would stop during the program at a tobacco shop to buy his favorite brand while Jack Benny would segue from his comic routine into a Jell-O advertisement that had somehow become part of the act. It was often hard to tell the difference between entertainment and advertising, and not too many people really worried about the issue.

Print Advertising

Interestingly, magazines demonstrated a good deal of resistance to advertising. , for example, only allowed advertising in its American edition in 1955. Magazines held that they had a literary obligation to protect their audiences from crass commercialism. The , a British magazine, set the tone in 1853 by writing, "It is the duty of an independent journal to protect as far as possible the credulous, confiding and unwary from the wily arts of the insidious advertiser." refused advertising until the 1880s.

However, in spite of high-minded statements, as 's 1955 capitulation to the inevitable shows, advertising had become an integral part of magazine financing. Without advertising, most magazines would have to fold. Very few have sufficient circulation to survive without it. Circulation is now a means to induce advertisement to place their ads in a magazine or newspaper. By the 1950s advertising accounted for more than half of a magazine's profits.

While readers may regret the targeting of magazines to particular audiences so that publishers may deliver pre-selected audiences to advertisers, there have been some benefits. Advertising agencies, for example, became copywriters and designers. They wanted to produce work of high visual appeal to capture the attention of readers. That, in turn, forced editors to pay attention to their own design features, making the entire magazine more visually attractive. Ad agencies, for example, quickly caught on to the benefits of color. They began to use it in considerable quantity from the 1800s and by the fifties over half of all advertising pages were in multicolor format.

Women's magazines had close ties with advertisers. Women have traditionally been the largest purchasers of consumer goods. , for example, was considered a kind of trade journal for homemakers. provided romance and entertainment while gave a taste of high style. The number of women's magazines increased into the fifties, Woman's and Advertisers certainly have put pressure on editors to refrain from offense. Editors have, at times, found that articles that criticize a product may lead to the withdrawal of advertising orders. Once published an article praising the use of guitars for accompaniment only to find that it lost its piano advertisers.Even a belated apology could not get back their support. This pressure was, perhaps, at it height in the fifties when advertisers often insisted on a type of pre-censorship and a, "Don't rock the boat" approach.

Advertising Techniques

Basically, advertising consists in persuading the public to think the way advertisers want them to think. Advertisers promote a product, whether it is a candidate like Dwight D. Eisenhower or a washing machine. The fifties saw traditional advertising techniques increasingly used to promote public service, political candidates, and various causes, such as conservation.

There are eight principal media for advertising, according to conventional wisdom. The newspaper is the most basic. It offers advertisers a number of inducements, including large circulations, a readership located close to the advertiser's place of business, and the opportunity to alter their advertisements on a frequent and regular basis. Magazines offer some of the same inducements as newspapers. They are of two general types, general or special interest. Special interest magazines offer advertisers a target audience.

In the United States television and radio are the most pervasive media. In the 1950s, TV began to replace radio as the glamorous medium. The mass audience was never again so available as in the fifties, when all who watched TV viewed the same three basic networks. Radio and rock 'n roll became more of a youth market as the fifties went on.

Direct mail, outdoor billboards and posters, transit advertising, and miscellaneous media, including dealer displays and promotional items such as matchbooks or calendars, are other means of advertising. Each of these made an impact in the fifties. Various calendars have become classic collector's items and many recall the learn to draw matchbook ads. The Burma Shave road signs dotted many roads and provided amusement as well as product plugging.

The free market mentality of the fifties, shored up by Cold War fervor, left little interest in questioning the role of advertising. Good-natured fun, however, at the expense of the Madison Avenue types was encouraged. Stan Freeburg's record album was a best seller and only one of many comedy routines poking fun at the men in the gray flannel suits. Steve Allen cast of characters featured an advertising man who greeted him with the catch phrase "Hi, ho, Steverino."   The author Budd Schulberg had great fun in his based on the advertising phrase, "Let's run it up the flagpole and see if anybody salutes it."

No one disputed the power of advertising to inform consumers of what products are available. Most people agreed that in a free-market economy effective advertising is crucial in keeping a company afloat. There certainly was opposition to the power of advertising firms, mainly from Beatniks. In the fifties, however, student power was not yet understood or perceived as a powerful force even though the growing involvement of students in the Civil Rights movement was noted. Some old leftists grumbled about the editorial control that advertisers, or sponsors, exerted. But at least in print, there were alternative voices, and many "leftist" positions got by the censors either in very creative subtle writing or in a display of American fair-mindedness on late night talk or interview shows. Most American, however, felt that "I'm all right, Jack. Leave me alone!"

TV Advertising

The fifties marked the development of TV advertising. Certainly, there was little if any TV advertising before that time. In developing TV advertising, the usual path is followed by advertisers. They try to adopt wholesale techniques from the previous medium. Radio ads were developed for a listening audience, not a viewing one. But over the course of the decade, greater skill and sophistication develop as the infant medium matures.

In January 1950, magazine names Arthur Godfrey and Faye Emerson TV's most pleasing personalities. 1950 also marked the year that national sponsors realized that TV was a growing and viable medium. They abandoned radio in what described as "the greatest exhibition of mass hysteria in biz annals." The most popular commercial of 1950, according to was Lucky Strike's "Be Happy, Go Lucky." In the somewhat naïve spirit of the age, college cheerleaders prance about singing, "Yes, Luckies get our loudest cheers on campus and on dates. With college gals and college guys a Lucky really rates."

1951 marked the debut of "Omnibus." "Omnibus" was an advertising failure but a critical success. It remained on the air for five years despite collecting only $5.5 million in advertising revenues to help defray its $8.5 million costs. The new medium, however, was willing to lose money on prestigious programs at the time, making up the losses on other programs and gaining public favor in the process with intellectuals. There was no PBS at the time so the networks took their public service a bit more seriously.

1951 also marked the debut of "I Love Lucy." At the height of live TV, this half-hour filmed TV sitcom ranks number one in four of its six first full seasons. Interestingly, a cigarette company, Philip Morris, which continues to use its "Call for Philip Morris" signature advertisement while developing new "copy" for TV, sponsors it. The filmed program was a foretaste of TV's future but the cigarette ads were not.

The first color program further marked 1951. 25 sets received the program. It was a non-compatible format so the rest of the sets received a blank screen. However, it, too, marked the future of the media since sponsors liked what they saw and knew that novelty alone would not keep TV competitive with the movies. The continuing influence of sponsors was marked by the debut in December of the "Hallmark Hall of Fame" series, perhaps, the only series to maintain its identification with an advertiser. Hallmark's first program was Gian Carlo Menotti's "Amahl and the Night Visitors," a Christmas special.

By 1952, there were already concerns about the moral impact of TV and its advertising. Sponsors were sensitive to any charges that might inhibit sales and bring scandal. TV in its earliest days dealt with adult themes and had women in low-cut dresses flaunting their stuff. The famous Dagmar of "Broadway Open House" was but the most noticeable of these women. Others, like Loraine Day, made the plunging neckline notorious. Therefore, in 1952 the National Association of Radio & Television Broadcasters ratified a new Television Code establishing guidelines for content and addressing the concerns of social critics. Interestingly, about half the code was devoted to advertising.

A House of Representatives investigation into what was offensive in fifties TV is instructive. The distinguished representative found beer commercials and dramas that presented suicide offensive. Cigarette advertising, however, didn't appear to bother the good politicians.

Elsie the Cow and the chimpanzee J. Fred Muggs emerged as great advertising ploys in 1952. Elsie personally attested to the contentedness of Borden's cows while J. Fred helped garner advertisers and viewers to the show. There were 20 million TV sets in 1952, and that viewing public drew $288 million in advertising revenue, a 38.8% from 1951.

Even more money and viewers were gained when the FCC approved the RCA system of color on December 17, 1953. Castro Decorators, New York, commissioned the first color commercial televised in a local show in March on August 6, 1954, on WNBT. Even more revenue was guaranteed when CBS introduced the first network kids program, "Captain Kangaroo," in 1954. The Captain, however, fought CBS over the type of advertising he would allow on his program. High ratings and consequent high advertising revenues proved the Captain's point, and, for the fifties anyway, the Captain got his way.

Despite the fears of Congress, Hamm's Beer introduced a 1953 commercial featuring its Hamm's bear. The tagline, "From the land of sky blue waters," became popular along with the tom-tom dominated soundtrack.

In 1954, television became the leading national advertising medium. TV advertising showed its power in another fashion, for in 1954 Ronald Reagan became host of "General Electric Theater," a fact to which many attribute his future political career. Certainly, Reagan, whose Hollywood career had fizzled, looked like a President and was a great salesman for General Electric whose most important product, according to the ad, was "progress."

One of the dangers of sponsor-controlled TV was demonstrated in the Quiz Show Scandal. For advertisers, the name of the game was viewers to whom they could sell their products. There is a thin line at best between reality and entertainment. When Revlon began its "The $64,000 Question," June 1955, it started the U.S. game show craze, and the scandal that followed.

wrote that in 1956 a typical TV viewer saw five hours and eight minutes of commercials in one week, a total of 420 commercials.

Interestingly, in 1958 there were 525 cable TV systems with 450,000 subscribers in the U.S. Again, the future had its beginning in the fifties. CBS noted the threat and took out an ad in warning, "Free television as we know it cannot survive alongside pay television." The fear, of course, that if people paid for programs, they could avoid commercials. It is a fear that really hasn't materialized. CBS, however, had its eye on the fact that advertisers had spent more than $2 billion in 1958.

In 1959, Mister Magoo, the nearsighted cartoon character with Jim Backus's voice, became General Electric bulb's spokesman. It continued the trend toward identifiable advertising icons. It was certainly, however, among the first times that an ad agency did not develop its own icon but borrowed one from the movies. The use of cartoons, of course, has expanded since then. Disney, of course, had his own stable of cartoons, which he employed to advertise his own works. The Looney Tons characters were not far behind in lending their own peculiar charms to various products and ventures. But in 1959 Magoo brought instant recognition to a company that was already famous. It was an adman's version of Eden.

Billboards and Road Signs

Anyone who traveled on America's highways before the Interstates were completed remembers that billboards were once regarded as relief from the monotony of the road rather than visual pollution. Especially welcome were the humorous Burma-Shave signs that kept the kids busy and parents amused. By the 1950s Burma Shave had been around for a while.

Burma Shave was a brushless shaving cream. The product was part of a family business run by the Odells as a replacement for their original product, Burma-Vita, a liniment. The Odells discovered that there was just too limited and competitive a market for liniment. They decided to manufacture a product that had every day use. Copying the original brushless shaving cream, Lloyd's Euxesis an English product, they hired a chemist to produce a new version of the product. After about 300 attempts, Burma-Shave was born.

The product was on the verge of failure when Allan Odell suggested using roadside signs to promote the product similar to the ones he saw on his sales trips trying to sell Burma-Shave. After convincing his father to let him try the idea, not an easy task, Allan used $200 of his father's money to try out his idea. He bought used boards, cut them in 3-foot lengths, painted them, and used four to message. The first signs had none of the rhymes that people remember from later ones. One might read

SHAVE THE MODERN WAY
FINE FOR THE SKIN
DRUGGISTS HAVE IT
BURMA-SHAVE

The first Burma-Shave signs appeared on Route 35 between Albert Lea and Minneapolis. The signs brought in business, and customers began requesting the product from druggists, mentioning the signs. The signs were so successful that the Odells spent $25000 on them the next year and their business boomed. Rhymes added to their appeal Others performed public service by reminding drivers of their responsibilities:

HER CHARIOT RACED
AT EIGHTY PER
THEY HAULED AWAY
WHAT HAD BEN HUR

Other signs simply amused the passing drivers, putting a smile on their lips.

By the fifties, these signs were extraordinarily successful and much funnier than the originals. Drivers looked for them, and the signs kept their attention for a longer period than any billboard. The rhymes

A CHRISTMAS HUG
A BIRTHDAY KISS
AWAITS THE WOMAN
WHO GIVES THIS

Additionally, shoppers were warned to avoid substitutes.

The fifties proved to be the height of the Burma-Shave signs and their last full decade in use. These signs that had been found in 45 states and, during World War II in Europe thanks to the GIs, disappeared from the highways. Philip Morris, Inc., purchased the company in 1963 and deemed the signs to be silly. The company pulled them from the highways. Millions of motorists, however, disagreed, and now the Smithsonian has collected a number of signs for display and those too young to have seen the signs on the open road can read them in our national museum.

The fifties marked a turning point in highway travel. The Eisenhower Interstate Highway system began to replace state roads as the predominant form of long distance travel. What was gained in speed was lost in individuality. The old Burma-Shave signs, Mom and Pop food stands, and other signs of the old road were doomed to extinction. Roadside standardization became the rule for roadside architecture.

The fifties marked a return and advance in American car culture. The depression and production restrictions from World War II had hurt the car industry. However, in the fifties, gasoline dropped dramatically in price, the new prosperity was going full throttle, and cars were more affordable than ever. However, Americans tended to be in more of a hurry than previously. There was, therefore, a transition in American car culture. The old signs, billboards, and diners were still appreciated but travelers wanted to reach their destinations more quickly. Billboards changed as roads changed. The four and six lane superhighways permitted much faster travel. The Interstate System Act of 1956 was planned as a military system in case of and atomic attack. The roads allowed for quick evacuation and military promptness. 42,000 miles of interstate highway was the result of the act, changing the American highway system.

As the highway system expanded and government standardization kicked in, billboards boomed. Mass production of motels and restaurants for easy identification became the rule. The government also imposed standards on the type of buildings along the roads. Thus billboards began to take on greater importance. A billboard for Clorox, for example, took on the tenor of the McCarthy era by advertising that it made linens not just be white, but "sanitary" as well, going along with the McCarthy era cleansing of the day.

Billboards supported prevailing cultural attitudes, stressing the need for women to serve men and be dependent on them. They emphasized dominant gender roles. Women were to clean while men were to solve problems and handle the technology.

Public Service Announcements came into their own on fifties' billboards. They focused on being good citizens. Smokey the Bear warned about the dangers of forest fires. Billboards also alerted people to the benefits of living in the United States. The war was behind us and it was once again time to enjoy America's bounty. The signs matched the growing American optimism. Billboards showed smiling families with pets enjoying life.

Billboards of the 1950s, then, reflected ideal American life. Billboards portrayed issues Americans felt were important in the postwar world. They were brightly colored, signs of the happiness Americans pursued. Advertisers showed the social and gender roles of the times, as well as the material items essential to American ideas of happiness. Americans, however, were not simply fixated on material items. Family was crucial to fifties happiness. The material items went toward making the family comfortable – a home, car, appliances, security and comfort were intertwined in the psyche.

The government controlled the Interstate Highway system very carefully. In fact, its regulation of billboards demonstrated an attempt at roadside censorship. The government only allowed a limited number of musicals, placed 750 feet away on each side of the road. Moreover, it allowed billboards only in certain designated areas. Ironically, then, while fifties drivers sought the freedom of the open road that very freedom appeared to recede just as quickly as they sought it.

The Marlboro Man

Much of the essence of fifties' advertising is found in the Marlboro Man campaign of Philip Morris.

> "Marlboro. You get a lot to like,
> filter, flavor, flip-top box."
> "Where there's a man...there's a
> Marlboro-with a filter that delivers
> a smoke of surprising mildness."
> "Better 'makins'. Marlboro...More
> flavor...More filter...More
> cigarette."

> "If you think flavor went out when
> filters came in-Try Marlboro."
> "Make yourself comfortable-Have
> a Marlboro"
> "Marlboro. Why don't you settle
> back and have a full flavored
> smoke"
> "Settle Back. You get a lot to like
> here in Marlboro Country."
> "Come to where the flavor is.
> Come to Marlboro Country"
> "Come to where the flavor is."
> "Come to Marlboro Country."
> "Marlboro."

Three elements evoked the essence of fifties culture: a Western landscape, a cowboy, and the color red. Fifties men, becoming increasingly domesticated, liked to vision themselves as John Wayne types. The open road, itself becoming domesticated, symbolized the movement West, toward freedom. Red, not for communism, but for brightness, was significant for its brightness and optimism.

By identifying itself with these American icons, Marlboro went from a basically unknown brand in 1955 to a major one within a few years. It became the leading brand in the United States by the 1970s. It did so by identifying with the visceral American response to the Marlboro cowboy. Marlboro Country became a symbol of the American Eden, a place with fresh, healthy, natural virtues. The identification helped obscure the entirely unhealthy product it offered. It is indeed an object lesson in the shrewdness of fifties advertising.

Conclusion

Advertising reflected and promoted the fifties obsession with optimism, family, and happiness. Ads also captured the essential social and cultural messages of the day, promoting social and cultural hierarchies, approved gender relationships, and adherence to the government and opposition to the Red Menace. Television became the dominant media, replacing radio. However, older forms of advertising remained popular, including roadside signs, billboards, direct advertising, and use of print media.

The physical brightness of fifties advertisements marks them as clearly as their innocence. It is difficult to realize that commercials for cigarettes can be innocent or that tobacco interests dominated so much advertising. However, as the Marlboro example shows, even the most dangerous of products had to identify itself with an idyllic setting. Family, home, security was the trinity that people worshipped in the fifties, and the media had to find a way to reflect that belief.

It is also difficult to understand just how blatantly advertisers controlled the media. They directly sponsored programs and sought to put pressure on the networks to keep programs inoffensive. They tolerated no criticism of their products nor any content they deemed might offend potential customers. Thus, the highly rated Nat King Cole program was cancelled by its network because it could not attract advertisers who feared they would lose Southern customers if they sponsored a Black man, even one so popular as Nat Cole.

The fifties proved to be a transitional period in advertising as in so many other things. TV advertising emerged along with the Interstate Highway System. American life changed radically with the Eisenhower Prosperity, the Cold War, and the growth of suburbia. It partook of both the old and emerging new, for one brief moment looking Janus-like at both past and present.

Suggested Readings and Works Cited
Applegate, Howard L. *Coca-Cola: Its Vehicles in Photographs 1930-1969.*
New York: Iconografix, 1996.
Baker, Eric and Tyler Blik (Contributor), Steven Heller (Introduction) *Trademarks of the 40s and 50s.* New York: Chronicle Books, 1988.
Johnson, Lynn and Michael O'Leary, *All Aboard! : Images from the Golden Age of Rail Travel.* New York: Chronicle Books, 2000.
Kanner, Bernice. *100 Best TV Commercials : And Why They Worked.* New York: Times Books, 1999.
Lears, Jackson. *Fables of Abundance : A Cultural History of Advertising in America.* New York: Basic Books, 1995.
Nava, Mica, et al., Eds. . Cambridge, England. Cambridge University Press, 1998.
Schudson, Michael. *Advertising, the Uneasy Persuasion : Its Dubious Impact on American Society.* New York: Basic Books, 1986.

Chapter 6

Fashion

Women's Clothing and New Fabrics

It seems that much of the material used for women's clothing tended to be stiff. Although many of the available materials were stiff, many others were not. There were many natural fabrics (linen, cotton, wool, silk) as well as synthetics (rayon, acetate, nylon, modacrylic, acrylic, polyester, and spandex). For daytime use, women most often wore clothes made of either natural fibers or rayon, nylon, poly-cotton blends and sometimes acrylic and acetate. Sweaters, however, were generally of wool or, for those who could afford it, cashmere. Sometimes acrylic knit was used.

There were new fabrics in the fifties that found their way into fashions. Acrylic (1950), polyester (1953), and spandex (1959) were the most famous of these fabrics. They were used in various ways to add to the images that characterized the 1950s, such as, the "hourglass shape," accentuated with multiple yards of skirt fabric. The strapless gown worn for proms generally featured tulle and taffeta with glittery details.

The growth of synthetic fibers deeply influenced all fashions. They tended to make clothing cheaper and of "permanent press," a boon for parents, especially mothers in the fifties. Of course, as often happens, these fabrics were not an unmixed blessing. There were some tragic accidents, known as the tragedy of "torch sweaters." Brushed rayon sweaters often burst into flame upon the least contact with fire. The Flammable Fabrics Act of 1953 banned highly flammable fabrics. Despite these dangers, people flocked to purchase clothes made of "miracle fibers." The new automatic washers and dryers made it much easier than previously to care for the family's wash. The fifties were also the period of "drip dry" nylon and polyester apparel, allegedly for travel, although many people who traveled little if at all bought the drip-dry clothing for convenience. There were problems, other than the danger of fire, associated with the new materials. Static electricity was always a danger and the clothes "felt" different from those made with natural fiber. Blends of natural and synthetic material eased these problems.

"The New Look"

The 1940s in contrast with the fifties, according to many, marked the height of glamour in the twentieth century. It was the period of Dior's "New Look." Introduced in 1947, Christian Dior's fashion was a relief from wartime restrictions. The "New Look" was a backlash from the rigors of the war but it was also a taste of the future. It was considered the height of elegance and luxury. Only the best fabrics were used, highlighting a wasp-waisted silhouette with the widely flared skirts that came to characterize the fifties. Christian Dior was the most influential designer of the period. His basic style was to have a silhouette marked by soft but wide shoulders. Meanwhile, her waist was pulled in by corsets to accentuate full hips. To vary these silhouettes women employed a slim bodice with that hallmark of the fifties, a full knee-length skirt. The look could be varied with a fitted short, boxy jacket. A further variation was found in wearing a blouse with a pencil-straight skirt

There were variations, of course, but even the variations, such as one- and two-piece dresses with their small-collared, fitted blouses had the usual full, pleated knee-length skirts. Even the daring fitted eveningwear with their heart-shaped opaque strapless bodices had long, flaring skirts. Most were ankle length presenting a contrast with the strapless top, revealing even with the silk or tulle over bodices. This was the age of proms, and there were many occasions for girls to wear formal gowns with all their decorations – yards of tulle, in pastel colors, ruffles, bows and other frills.

Evening clothing was made of brocades, satin, velveteen, taffeta, nylon net, tulle, and chiffon. Clothing tended to light or medium in weight. Daytime colors covered the gamut from neutral solids through floral prints, dazzling peasant and western styles, and incredible futuristic prints. Flowers were also popular as prints. Abstracts popped up, often hand painted, on scarves or other clothing. At night solids and floral, brocades were popular. Women, who wished to be daring, overlaid sheer chiffon or net on under dresses that were flesh colored. Evening colors also tended to be subtle or bold. Hot pinks began to rival subtler colors. Extremes were the rule, not the exception in clothing.

There was a great deal of flair and daring of another sort in trims. Sweaters were beaded and circle skirts were detailed. Many circle skirts as well as novelty wear was extremely ornate, featuring with appliqué, rickrack, screen-printing, sequins, or glitter. At times, flutter hems, hems that curved evenly, were found on evening clothes and the full skirts that marked the era. Sculpted pleats and sculpted necklines marked eveningwear. Rhinestone and corde added some style to evening clothes.

. Of course, the sacque (usually misspelled or Americanized as sack)dress covered everything up, including the silhouette. The sacque resembled a cocoon. There were both sacque dresses and coats. Sacques were cut to fit shoulders tightly and then ballooned at the waist and featured a full long skirt. It was a backlash against the general fifties styles that accentuated thin waists and youthful figures.

That Itsy Bitsy Teenie Weenie Bikini

Like Dior's New Look, the Bikini was born in Paris in the forties. In 1946, the Bikini, called the Atome, Its name was changed to commemorate the island on which the Atom Bomb was originally tested. It became famous when worn by fifties "love goddess" actresses such as Brigitte Bardot, Anita Ekberg and Sophia Loren. Most people, however, considered the bikini more appropriate to strip joints than public beaches. In fact, many European beaches banned the bikini for years.

Surprisingly, the United States did not ban the bikini officially but it really did not catch on until about 1960. The popular song "Itsy Bitsy Teeny Weeny Yellow Polka Dot Bikini" gives a good idea of its risqué reputation. The song states that the wearer of is "afraid to come out of the water" because she would embarrass herself. In fact, archeologists point out that there are mosaics from the fourth-century villa at Piazza Armerina in Sicily, which depict women wearing bikinis.

Indeed, even in the 1940s there were two piece bathing suits before the bikini as part of the cutbacks due to the war, the American Government, in 1943, ordered a ten percent reduction in the fabric used in woman's swimwear. The skirt panel and bare midriff were sacrificed. The original bikini, however, was but 30 inches of fabric, outdoing the wartime two-piece suit. The bikini was but a bra top and two triangles held together by a string - and a prayer. A woman's navel was actually on display.

The Catholic Legion of Decency pressured Hollywood to keep the bikini off the screen. Esther Williams who was an advocate of two-piece swimwear made an exception for the bikini, declaring "A bikini is a thoughtless act." In 1957, magazine stated, "It is hardly necessary to waste words over the so called bikini since it is inconceivable that any girl with tact and decency would ever wear such a thing." Yet, in but a few years the bikini began to appear somewhat modest compared with other styles of the sixties.

The Collegiate Look

One of the looks for older teens was that of the clean-cut collegian, the so-called Joe College or Pat Boone look. It featured short hair, shiny shoes or white bucks as one chose, patterned ties, and the ever-present sweater. Older teen women generally had short wavy hair bright lips, shiny if possible, tight waists, and a full bust line. In general, this was the most typical look. There were other looks, generally the "greaser" or hood styles made widely known in movies such as "Grease," or "The Wild Ones."

Men's Fashions

America was becoming a more relaxed society, and fashion reflected that change. For example, men returned to the natural-shoulder silhouette. That change may appear minor, but at the time, it was major fashion news. in an article entitled '75 Years of Fashion,' "No style was ever so firmly resisted, so acrimoniously debated - or more enthusiastically received in various segments of the industry. Natural shoulder styling eventually became the major style influence. Brooks Bros., once a 'citadel of conservatism,' became a font of fashion as the new 'Ivy Cult' sought style direction. Charcoal and olive were the colors."

Perhaps, an even more radical departure in style was the introduction from France and Italy of the Continental look. The style included short jackets with broad shoulders, in contrast to the more natural shoulders that American jackets were featuring, and a shaped waistline, slanting besom pockets, sleeve cuffs, short side vents, and tapered, cuff less trousers. A man had to be slim to wear this style and that along with the more natural look of the Ivy League style led to a fashion conflict of sorts. This "slick" look, then, made little impact on those who favored a more American "manly" look. Nevertheless, it was one more push away from the more formal style of dressing of earlier American generations.

However, it was the presumed era of the "gray flannel suit" of the business world. An era that supposedly restricted choices. However, the fifties began to allow more changes as the decade progressed. Brighter clothing made its appearance, and teens began wearing bolder clothing. Some men wore colored dress shirts to work in place of the traditional white on white. Men could even opt to wear colorful and even checked sports jackets, dress shirts with button-down collars or large French cuffs. Sports or casual shirts included the then new Izod crocodile insignia stitched on the breast of the polo shirt. Other loud clothes included Madras shirts, Hawaiian shirts, pegged pants, and the new Bermuda shorts. Sneakers, penny loafers, and leather jackets. There was, in sum, a movement toward the casual and comfortable in clothing. Color was in, despite the assumed "gray flannel suit" image. The period was "gray" only in contrast to the sixties, whose roots were truly in the changes of the fifties.

Children's Clothes

Whenever fifties fashions come to mind images of Poodle skirts that flounced out as a girl's "steady" twirled her to the incessant beat of rock 'n roll. The skirts came far below the knees and stiff crinoline petticoats lent further body to the ensemble. Since there was no panty hose, garter belts, if not corsets, held up the nylon stockings often worn in place of bobby sox under all the other underclothes beneath those famous Poodle skirts. There were, of course, styles that were considered "fads." Among these were the Poodle skirt, Peter Pan collared blouse, scarf-tied ponytail, and saddle shoes. Many young men imitated James Dean. Others took to the "hood" look, dressing like members of motorcycle gangs. Cat-eye glasses, the Beatnik look, Hawaiian shirts, Barkcloth in casual wear, and ethnic scene prints in day and leisure wear were other styles of the day.

In the early 1950s, at least, most young kids did not wear jeans unless they were in the western United States. Certainly, jeans were not appropriate school dress. As the decade progressed, however, jeans became more acceptable, and they were low-cost and "wore like iron." Most boys wore crew cuts; short military style hair cuts. In the early years of the fifties, long pants were a sign of growing up. Younger boys wore shorts for most occasions. Again, custom changed as the fifties progressed. Just as jeans were not considered appropriate school wear for boys, jeans were not appropriate for girls to wear to school. Cotton dresses, perhaps skirts and blouses, and the ever-present cardigan sweater was the uniform of the day. Of course, the uniform had to have bobby sox, Saddle shoes, penny loafers. The full "poodle" skirts, not worn daily as many imagine, was part of the repertoire. In fact, poodle skirts did not always have poodles on them. The full skirts made of felt did in fact often have poodle patches on them. But other patches were also worn, flowers, records, cars and other animals for example. The style ended as teens grow up into more sophisticated adults.

Boy's, meanwhile, come to our imaginations dressed in either skin tight pegged pants, pants whose cuffs were 16" or less at the ankle, or Levi's jeans, equally skin tight. Perhaps, they wore a sports coat, with or without a pink carnation or a Cuban jacket in the style of Desi Arnaz. Under that ensemble were the same type of underwear that boys wear today – jockey shorts or boxers and a tee shirt. Fancy briefs came later to men's wear

Boys, teen or younger, of course, also had their own style. The 1950s was in fact the last time that American and European styles differed greatly from each other. The mass media had not yet developed a general cross Atlantic style for kids. Kids clothing reflected the emergence of the country from the Depression and the Second World War. Prosperity had its rewards as a greater percentage of income went towards clothes. Boys had more than just one good Sunday suit and school clothes. They now had a number of different styles of clothing, not so many as their sisters, but still more than kids of an earlier generation.

TV also aided the movement toward casual clothing for boys. Although many believe that older boys in the 1950s wore suits and jackets all the time, they actually wore suits and jackets less often than boys of previous generations. Suits were for more formal dating and church attendance, but increasingly casual wear for dating and certainly school attendance crept in as the decade aged.

School and sports outfits were more exciting than clothing that is more formal. Comfort was the keyword of the day. Clothes were more simply tailored than in the past, just as TV showed them. In addition, the TV western did much to popularize Levi jeans, although many mothers thought them a bit on the wild side. Even girls fought to wear jeans, and it was stylish for girls to wear boys' jeans when they could get away with it. Most schools banned jeans in the fifties, at least for a time.

Boy's hairstyles caused their elders some discomfort. The D.A. (short for Ducks Ass) was the haircut of the 1950s for cool white males. A lot of greasy hair oil was needed to keep the hair combed back on the sides of the head. Hence, the term greasers came about. Philadelphia barber Joe Cirella created the look. It became popular when a number of movie stars and vocalists adopted it. Sideburns could and did often accompany the DA. James Dean and Elvis Presley popularized this rebel look. The sideburns grew about an inch and a half below their ears. It was part of the juvenile delinquent look, along with leather jackets and cigarette packs rolled up in sleeves, switchblades, and taps on shoes. Taps, steel clips shaped like half-moons, were attached with copper rivets to the back of the shoe by the toe. The shoe of choice was either suede or black leather and always sharply pointed. It remained popular until the British invasion. In fact, some stars still wear a modified version today

Private schools, of course, often had uniforms. Generally, boys had to wear jackets and ties, even in pre-air conditioned building in hot weather. Girls in private schools wore actual uniforms, usually with Peter Pan collars and long jumpers. Although public schools did not require uniforms or jackets and ties, they did have dress codes. Jeans and shorts were high on the list of "no-nos." Tight sweaters for girls and "short" dresses, which few wore in the fifties, also were banned. Needless to say, low-cut dresses or any overly tight clothes, for males or females, were banned. Most dress codes at one time or another usually banned Sneakers. Oxfords tended to be the shoe of choice for males and penny loafers for girls or saddle shoes. In more formal dress wear of the period girls wore the tailored suits modeled after Coco Channel model for girls. Boys wore a rough tweed style. Raincoats became more fashionable while becoming more useful at the same time. They became water-repellent, had removable linings that made them warmer or cooler as weather dictated. Winter coats were lined with those synthetic fabrics that appeared to be but were not fur.

The move to the suburbs had a great impact on fashion. The economic demand of suburban life, leading more women to work outside the home to pay for the pleasures of suburban living, meant that women had to purchase clothes for work that differed from the kick around clothing that was fine for backyard barbecues. Casual pants and tops replaced housedresses for daily life. Housedresses came to be considered as dowdy relics and old-fashioned. Suburban Moms found that they had a new job, that of chauffeuring their kids and picking up and dropping off their commuting spouses. The suburbs also helped spread the popularity of Bermuda shorts. However, teens and preteen boys found shorts generally "uncool."

In 1950 there were five million TV sets in the United States. That number grew astronomically as the decade grew older. Television showed Americans what they were wearing. To be more exact, it showed Americans how "average" people and the "elite," including screen and stage stars dressed. People wanted to wear what they saw others wearing. Teens used TV as a means to choose styles that clashed with what their parents may have wanted them to wear. Moreover, TV did join the movement to bring color to male dress shirts because blue shirts on TV actually looked whiter than white ones.

Shirt manufacturers began making and marketing colored dress shirts to fill the demand The pink shirts, a color that was not worn in the thirties or forties by men, generally was worn with the popular gray flannel suits. Navy blue or black were the conservative standards for boys' suits, although under the influence of TV characters, including Desi Arnaz's Ricky Ricardo, "sharper" patterns soon were seen in jackets, including two different contrasting patterns. As expected, some conservative employers banned colored
shirts from their offices.

The GI "t" shirt of the 1940s got a boost from Marlon Brando who wore them in the 1951 film "Streetcar Named Desire." "T" shirts moved rapidly from being underwear to being typical sportswear. With jeans, they became part of the uniform of the new developing youth culture. Much of the teenager's earnings of $12 per week, more than a 1930's family earned went for clothing.

TV also aided the movement of boy's clothing from shorts and knee socks to boys in long pants. In the late 1940s and early fifties, boys often wore shorts as everyday wear. But by 1953, TV sitcoms like "Father Knows Best," " The Life of Riley," "Lassie," " Leave It to Beaver, " and "Ozzie and Harriet," depicted young boys in long pants, even when in their "play clothes." On of the more famous "Leave It to Beaver" episodes, in fact, recounted what happened when one of the Beave's aunts sent him to Sunday school in a suit of short pants and knee socks. The poor Beaver became the butt of the other second graders' jokes. They told him he was wearing girls' socks.

The fifties reflected the growing prosperity of America in fashions as well as in so many other areas of life. As the decade progressed and the Korean War was put behind it, America began to relax under the leadership of Grandfather Eisenhower. Styles became more informal, suburban life more common, and fun more the order of the day. Leisure style began to gain more popularity as Americans had more money and leisure to spend it in.

The dreary days of the Depression and World War II seemed to be far in the past. The sacrifices of those days, while "worth it" and often retold were not things most Americans wanted to relive. More comfortable, colorful clothing helped put those days further into the past. New fabrics provided greater variety of styles and made it easier to care for clothes. The "drip dry" and no ironing "wash and wear" reflected a preferred style of living that, while seemingly "uptight" to the sixties generation, actually helped pave the way for the "swinging sixties."

Demographic changes such as the movement to the suburbs, growing home ownership, the baby boom, and the explosion in commuting helped change fashion as well. Youth culture and the disposable income of teens helped shape the fashion world. Teens could not only demand their own styles, they could afford to buy their own clothes. Often these clothes were those they had seen in the movies and on television. Increasingly the media discovered the youth market, culminating in the genre of rock 'n roll. James Dean and Elvis became fashion leaders and teens followed imitating their heroes as closely as possible.

It was at time that valued leisure while attempting to discover what it really meant. Certainly, part of that leisure was to be found in comfortable clothes that required a relative minimum of care. Just as meals were "instant" or "already" prepared, so, too, clothes seemingly required minimum care to give maximum satisfaction. The glamour of an earlier period seemed somehow "square." The "relaxed" look was "cool" and "in." It did require quite a bit of effort to appear "relaxed" and "cool" but that effort was supposed to be in the backstage area.

Fifties clothing could be quite restrictive, especially for women at the start of the decade. Foundation garments were rather more formidable than today's versions. The ice-cream cone or torpedo bras were "engineered" to shape women's breasts into a male's fantasy images. The ideal figure had a tiny waist and large breasts. Sexy, form-fitting styles were in. In addition to these sexy styles, there were also elegant cocktail and evening clothes by Jacques Fath, Jean Desses, Charles James, and Givenchy. Movie buffs of fifties movies have seen Audrey Hepburn, Grace Kelly and in a more exaggerated version Jane Mansfield wear these styles. Christian Dior, however, continued to dominate fashion in the fifties. His primary competition was Cristobal Balenciaga, the Spanish designer. The 50s did, however, promote the rise in the "All American Look." Claire McCardell was a major figure in that movement.. McCardell created clothes for American women. She recognized that American women were busy and designed clothes for both home and office.

The fifties marked the rise of teens in the marketing strategy of the fashion makers. However, most styles that were designed for teens consisted of adapted versions of adult fashions or the ever-present poodle skirts, jeans, or Peter Pans. Things were changing and teens were at the root of that change.

It needs to be repeated that Americans were in the mood to celebrate. That mood grew as fifties peace and prosperity continued under Ike. Americans wanted lavish colors and designs. They wanted them in as comfortable fashion as possible. Even undergarments loosened up as the decade wore on. For example, those full-skirted evening gowns made of chiffon, stiff satin and taffeta came with whale-bone corsets sown into the dress early in the decade, giving women an that ideal feminine "hourglass" figures. By the end of the decade, the corset was gone as a standard undergarment. The natural look was in.

However, as one anonymous woman avers, 'we were safer in those horrible panty-girdles. I was quite relaxed when a boyfriend put his hand under my skirt. Wrestling with my 'bullet-proof' corset would take him hours! And I had no fears when he put his hand under my sweater either, he could cares my bra for hours without touching flesh. Bras in those days covered the whole breast and more.'

An, understandably, anonymous man responds, "But it was so exciting! I remember distinctly the first time I touched the top of a stocking, got my first glimpse of a suspender! Yes, it was an effort but incredibly thrilling as each layer of clothing revealed more intimate exciting garments!' Sometimes, it must be admitted, that the clothing was more glamorous and stimulating than what it covered. The imagination had more to work with than in the let it all hang out sixties.

It is important to remember that the baby boom meant that most women, career, or "housewives," were mothers. Most women who lived in the suburbs wore practical styles, called "separates," tops (usually tight, sleeveless and collar less), and skirts (either full or pleated). These were mix and match products, giving women a variety of outfits. Variety at a minimum of fuss is what fifties fashion eventually came to mean. Looking good with seemingly little effort was important. It was, granted an ideal but as with most ideals it helps to define the period.

Suggested Readings and Works Cited

Baker, Patricia, Elane Feldman and Valerie Cumming, Editor. *Fashions of a Decade the 1950s.* New York: Facts on File, Inc,1991.

Ettinger, Roseann. *Fifties Forever! : Popular Fashions for Men, Women, Boys & Girls.* (Schiffer Book for Collectors and Designers.) London: Schiffer Publishing, Ltd., 1993.

Fiell, Charlotte and Peter Fiell, Editors. *Decorative Art 50s* New York: TASCHEN, 2000.

Finlayson, Iain. *Denim : An American Legend.* New York, NY: Fireside Simon & Shuster, 1990.

Ikuta, Yasutoshi, Editor. *50'S American Magazine Ads. 2 : Fashion Apparel.* New York: Books Nippan, 1997)

White, Shane and Graham J. White. *Stylin': African American Expressive Culture.* Ithaca:Cornell Univ Press, 2000.

Wilcox, Claire , Valerie Mendes, Richard David (Photographer), Leonie Davis, Oscar Wilde, and Clarie Wilcox. *Modern Fashion in Detail.* New York: Overlook Press; 1998.

Chapter 7

Fads, Games, Toys, and Sports

There was lost ground to make up for after World War II. The war demanded a number of sacrifices from all; kids had to play with old toys. After the war, however, there was an outburst of new toys, many in the new miracle material, plastic. Plastic joined lithographed tin and precision die-cast metal in the new dolls, games, and toys. The introduction of new playthings began in the late forties with items such as Lionel's new train models, including the colorful Santa Fe diesel set in 1948 and the introduction in 1949 of Silly Putty and Lego building blocks, extremely popular toy in the fifties.

The fifties proper witnessed toys such as 1952's Revell's plastic kits of model aircraft. Model cars soon followed and Matchbox cars arrive in 1954 via England. The matchbox cars came to the United States from England. Lesney Products & Co. first manufactured them. Rodney and Leslie Smith founded the company, producing die-cast toys. The company made its first cars in 1953, adding new cars every year. Eventually there were75 cars. The original distributors were the Moko Company. In 1956 Lesney began the "Models of Yesteryear" series. These detailed cars of the past came in the yellow Matchbox boxes. The company sold out to Universal Toys and in turn Universal sold the matchbox rights to Tyco. Tyco still produces matchbox cars.

The fifties also saw the introduction of the wiffle ball. This lightweight toy made its appearance in 1955. This ball came with many perforated holes, so that it was safe to use in the house as well as outdoors. Play-Doh came along in the same year.

Mr. Potato Head first appeared in 1954. The first versions came without a plastic potato. The kid or parents had to supply the potato. Eventually, the plastic potato became a staple in the set. Gumby, the posable toy, first stretched out on the Howdy Doody Show in 1956. In 1959, Barbie, the fashion doll, made her initial appearance. Ken came along two years later, and, therefore, he is not technically a fifties kind of guy.

Lego first made its appearance in Denmark in 1954. These plastic building toys interlock. Kids can build many different structures with these toys and some of the more fantastic creations are seen in shopping malls today. Virtual Lego lands have blossomed in places such as The Mall of the Americas in Minnesota. Ole Kirk Christiansen, a carpenter, invented these interlocking bricks, a favorite to this day. There are now full scale Legolands in marts and in Disney World. The fifties also gave us Paint-by-Number. It came in with the decade. Detroit's Craft Master Company marketed kits that included paints and a drawing on a canvas with areas numbered for the proper color. Instant artists followed the craze, producing their own prepackaged masterpieces.

Fads

Frisbee, still with us, actually began in the forties. College students tossed pie plates around. The Wham-O company began to sell them in 1957 as Flyin' Saucers on the West Coast. However, their more familiar name, Frisbee, came in 1959. With the name change came the craze. A visiting Australian mentioned to two Californians, Richard Knerr and Arthur "Spud" Melin, about the use of a toy in Australian schools. One toy mentioned was the forerunner of the hula-hoop. These two young Californians were the founders of the Wham-O Manufacturing Company of San Gabriel. They already had slingshots, boomerangs, and similar toys on the market. But this new toy struck them as an opportunity not to be missed. They began perfecting it. They tested it on the local playground and found that kids stuck with it longer than any of their other toys. At its height, the Hula Hoop craze used over one million pounds of plastic per week.

Frisbee has been one of the longest running fads in United States history. Frisbees are thrown by a flip of the wrist. They continue to be a staple of college campuses, beaches, and parks. There is some dispute about who invented the Frisbee. It is clear that some Yale college

students began to toss Frisbee pie plates back and forth. The Frisbee Company was found in Bridgeport, Connecticut. As fads do, this one spread quickly to other college campuses. First it spread down the East Coast. Walter Frederick Morrison perfected the Frisbee and patented it. The Wham-O Manufacturing Company purchased rights to the toy in 1957. In 1959 the Wham-O trademarked the term "Frisbee."
The Frisbee has been part of organized and official sporting events on national and international associations since the 1960s.

Hula-Hoops

The Wham–O company also marketed the Hula Hoop. The plastic hoop composed of a round cylinder tube was modeled upon a wooden toy used in Australian gym classes. The hoop is placed over your head and around your waist. To keep the hoop spinning and from falling off your hips, you have to keep your hips moving like a hula dancer, hence the name. Wham-O first marketed the toys in California. Word of mouth spread interest in them throughout the country. Hula Hoops emerged in 1957 but became a craze during the summer of 1958. At the height of the craze over one million pounds of plastic per week went into the production of the toy.
Within four months, Wham-O had sold 25 million units. Since there were many different versions on the market, Wham-O could not get a patent. "Spin-a-hoop," "Hoop-d-doo" and others flooded the market. Eventually, over 100 million hoops were sold by Wham-O and its knock off competitors. By winter of 1958, the craze was over in the United States. Wham-O then marketed the product in Europe and the Middle East. The fad spread to Japan. There was a hula-hoop in virtually every house in the United States with preteen kids. The fad is over but the hoop lives on.

Slinky

Richard T. James created the Slinky after Word War II, and it became a major fad in the 1950s. James was a shipbuilder who noticed that a coil spring that fell on the deck continued to gyrate and move across the deck. He decided to make a toy and tried it out on a bedridden boy. The boy was thrilled and James began to produce and market the toy. After many rejections, he found a small store that took four dozen unites on consignment. The toys were an immediate hit. The storeowner quickly requested more. James and his wife had a new full time business.
The Slinky was originally made of a long piece of wire, 87 feet. It was three inches and diameter and two inches high when flattened. It amazed people by its ability to walk down stairs. Overcoming many

obstacles, patent disputes, steel shortages, warehouse fires and even difficulties with inspection officials in Philadelphia , he sold 14 million units in a ten year period. Kids continue to find joy in simple Slinky's antics.

Davy Crockett

The song came before the series. It premiered on "Disneyland" on October 27, 1954 as an ad for the Crockett trilogy. It sold ten million records. That's not too bad for an afterthought. It was a filler to make the program run to its full allotment. Tom ("I never wrote a song in my life") Blackburn, the Crockett script writer, and George Bruns, Disney's head staff songwriter/ composer put the tune together in around twenty minutes. The old master Walt Disney came up with the idea of having the song move the story along. The Crockett song was the fastest selling record up to that time. It sold about seven million copies in the first six months of 1955. It was on the Hit Parade for about six months. In fact there were a number of different version, 41 in fact. Three reached the top ten, Bill Hayes's version was the most popular. But Fess Parker himself sold over 3 million copies, and Tennessee Ernie Ford sold over one million. Reruns of Davy surface from time to time, and Disney's Frontierland is a constant reminder of the program.

His Davy Crockett character wore a coonskin cap, which became a big seller. The Davy Crockett coonskin cap reappears from time to time. Davy first appeared on the Disneyland TV show of December 15, 1954. Davy Crockett frenzy did not stop at the cap. That and other toys and merchandise led to over $100 million in sales in 1955. Disney also marketed guitars, underwear, toy guns, and complete outfits, comics, and other paraphernalia Fess Parker and Buddy Ebsen brought the old frontier to life for fifties kids. "Be sure you're right and then go ahead," became a motto for many fifties kids.

Panty Raids

The infamous Panty Raid tradition began on the night of March 21, 1952 at the University of Michigan. About 600 male students decided to flock the female dormitory and steal their underwear. The fad spread. After stealing the underwear, raiders paraded around the entrance of the dormitory boastfully holding up the "stolen goods." No obstacles seemed to thwart the raiders. Men at the University of Miami tore down a wire fence to get into the dormitory.

Women did not take these raids lying down. They retaliated. Women raided male dorms. Five hundred University of Michigan women raided the men's dormitory, stealing boxer shorts and "tighty whities" of their enemy. At Catholic Jesuit run Georgetown University women stormed the male dorms.

Some of the more serious students resented this disruption of their studying. Some felt that their privacy was invaded. Needless to say, police entered the scene on many occasions. Nothing, however, seemed able to stop the raids throughout the fifties. The sexual revolution of the sixties made these raids seem quite innocent and brought them to an end.

Sports

The fifties were as sports mad as any other decade, perhaps a bit more so since the end of the Korean War and the burst of prosperity. A family could still attend a ball game without mortgaging their home. Tickets to the bleachers were under a dollar apiece and typically $.50. Hot dogs were a quarter. Basketball and football, still not really all that important on the professional level sported even lower prices.

Olympics

Boxing

Rocky Marciano dominated the boxing world. Marciano (1923-1969) was the only boxer ever to retire as the only undefeated heavyweight champion in boxing history. His real name was Rocco Francis Marchegiano. Marciano was from Brockton, Massachusetts. Marciano began his career in the army in 1943, and he became a professional in 1947. Marciano defeated his hero, the Brown Bomber, the incomparable Joe Louis 195. Proving that real men do cry, the Rock openly wept after knocking out Louis, who had come out of retirement shortly before. Perhaps, that scene played a major role in his own retirement. In September 1952, Marciano won the heavyweight championship, knocking out Jersey Joe Walcott. Marciano defended his title six times between 1953 and 1955. He retired in April 1956 with an overall record of 49-0. 43 wins were by knockout. In 1969 Marciano died in a plane crash.

The fifties, in many ways, was a great period in boxing history. Jake La Motta, Sugar Ray Robinson, Rocky Graziano, Willie Pep, Sandy Sadler, Tony Zale, Beau Jack, and so many other great boxers were on the scene. TV brought the fights into peoples homes on Mondays and Wednesdays, but ins its desire for huge ratings and with its insatiable appetite, its promoters rushed along too many young fighters and mismatches occurred. The devastating beating that the inept but popular TV fighter Chuck Davey suffered at the hands of the expert Kid Gavilan was but one case in point.

Boxing reached a high point in the 1950s. Television helped bring it into people's living rooms two and even three times per week, live, free, and after the middle of the decade in color. Although overexposure eventually diluted the quality of the sport, it did enable the public to see some truly great fighters in their prime. Perhaps, "pound for pound,' Sugar Ray Robinson was truly the best. Robinson was welterweight (135 – 147 pounds) champion from 1946-1951. Then was the middleweight (147-160) champion from 1951-1960 on five different occasions. At his peak, Robinson compiled a 128-1-2 record with 84 ko's. His one loss was to Jake La Motta, the "Raging Bull," and a middleweight champ in his own right. Robinson, however, won 5 of the six fights the had.

Robinson's became a model for Mohammad Ali. He was not only an outstanding boxer. He also owned a night club, drove a pink Cadillac convertible, mingled with stars like Frank Sinatra, danced professionally, and had an entourage of beautiful women, barber, masseur, voice coach, dwarf mascot, and his manager. That lifestyle caught up to Robinson, and he lost all the money he had made in the ring. He was forced to fight long beyond his capacities to earn money in the 1960s. However, his entertainment career eventually mode him solvent once again, and he remained a popular figure. Robinson died of Alzheimer's Disease in 1989 at 67 years old.

While Robinson was probably the greatest fighter, pound for pound, the greatest heavyweight of the decade, if not all time, was Rocky Marciano. He was far from the idealized version of a movie champion. The "Brockton Rock" was small for a heavyweight champion, 5 feet 11 inches and 185 pounds. He also had a short reach of 68 inches. He had to take many punches to deliver one in return. Fortunately, he had a granite constitution and was able to survive terrific punishment.

On October 26, 1951, he defeated his idol, the great champion of the thirties and forties, Joe Louis. For the Rock it proved his toughest fight. Marciano was the first to rush to Louis's corner to console him after his defeat. On September 23, 1952, Marciano knocked out the champion, Jersey Joe Walcott, in the 13th round to become world champion. Marciano defended his title six times, winning five on knockouts. He had to go 15 rounds only once. That was against the great Ezzard Charles. Marciano won that bout on a decisions and then ko'd Charles in a rematch. His last fight was in 1955 against Archie Moore, a great light heavyweight (160-175 pounds) champion. In 1956 Marciano, then 33 years old, retired at his peak. In 1969, he died in a plane crash.

There were many other great boxers in the fifties. However, the first man ever to win back a heavyweight championship, Floyd Patterson was an interesting figure. Patterson, born in North Carolina but raised in Brooklyn , won a gold medal at the 1952 Olympic Games. In 1956, Patterson won the heavyweight title, knocking out Archie Moore. Patterson lost to Ingemar Johannsson of Sweden in 1959. In 1960, Patterson won his title back, knocking out Johannson. He beat him again in 1961 but lost his title to Charles Sonny Liston in 1962. Patterson is an intelligent and deeply reflective individual who felt he never was appreciated as a champion.

Tennis

Tennis provided its thrills. Maureen Connolly (1934-1969) was the first woman to win the grand slam, the Australian championships, the French championships, Wimbledon, and the United States championships in one calendar year. At 16 she won the United States title. In 1952, she won Wimbledon and defended her U.S. championship. In 1953 she won the Grand Slam. In 1954, a horseback riding accident ended her career. Maureen Connelly, "Little Mo," dominated the game of tennis until her forced retirement from a leg injury when she was but 19. In the short time she competed she never lost a Grand Slam tournament. Little Mo, at 18, became the first woman to win the Grand Slam. She won it on September 7, 1953, at Forest Hills, NY. She remains the youngest ever to win it.

Jack Kramer, a tennis champion, "discovered" Little Mo when he was playing her in a match at the La Jolla Beach Club. She was 14 years old and playing with a local pro. Her play intrigued Kramer and he helped promote her career. Shortly after Connolly began winning tournaments. Between the edges of 16 and 19, she never lost a match. A horseback accident in 1954 ended her playing career. Connolly remained in the game as a coach and commentator, dying of cancer in 1969.

Tennis has long had a reputation of being an elitist sport. That reputation continued into the fifties. As soon as amateurs began making money, they were barred from much competition. Bobby Riggs and Jack Kramer, great 1940s players, kept from many competitions because of their professional status. Both men began to move for an opening of the game. In the 1950s there was some movement in that direction under Jack Kramer's leadership.

Pancho Gonzales, for example, became the U.S. Champion, but had to relinquish his title on become professional at 21. The great Australian players of the '50s, Frank Sedgman, Lew Hoad, Ken Rosewall, and Rod Laver retained their amateur status by being quietly put on the payrolls of sporting goods companies. Eventually, they also turned professional and could no longer compete in the major tournaments, all of which were for amateurs only. Kramer tried a number of ploys to open up the game. He often raided the amateur ranks but gave up the effort in 1962 because of box office failures. Eventually, television came to the rescue of a more open game.

However, there were other successes for the sport. The great Althea Gibson, born in South Carolina in 1927 and raised in Harlem, is a major case in point. Gibson was the first African American woman to play international tennis. In 1957 and 1958 she was the top-ranked woman tennis player in America. In 1966, Gibson became the first black woman to win at Wimbledon.

Hockey

The National Hockey League was a remarkably stable organization, maintaining fan loyalty from the early 1940s throughout the fifties with its original six teams. The Detroit Redwings dominated early 1950s play while the Montreal Canadiens finished the decade on the way to five straight Stanley Cup Championships. Although the New York Rangers gave the league a team in America's largest city, hockey was considered a relatively minor big league sport in the United States. Americans perceived it as a sport for toothless Canadians that was beyond the understanding of most Americans.

Sports fans – Maurice "The Rocket" Richard and Gordie Howe, knew a few greats but it took television to promote it into a major box office attraction. That and great American players of later years, like Wayne Gretzky. In time, hockey would expand and recruit "foreign" stars from America.

Baseball

Baseball remained "America's Pastime" in the fifties, for many people its Golden Age. However, although the great Jackie Robinson had broken the color barrier in 1947, only five teams had integrated by the early fifties, the Dodgers, Cleveland Indians, St. Louis Browns, New York Giants, and Boston Braves. Once the process began it gained a momentum of its own and soon great African American athletes became an accepted and treasured part of the game. The owners most treasured the fans they brought into the seats. By 1953, blacks played on eight of the sixteen teams. The last team to integrate was the Boston Red Sox. The player was Pumpsie Green.

During the 1950s, New York city witnessed the World Series virtually every year as one or more of its teams, the Yankees, Giants, or Dodgers, made it to the Fall Classic. In spite of their success, most New York players had salaries in four figures. Only superstars like Mickey Mantle or Joe DiMaggio made $50,000 or more. Some star players made around $7000, Jerry Coleman's (second base) for a time.

The Yankees were the team everyone else loved to hate. They believed that they were the aristocrats of the game. Therefore, they swaggered, dressed with style and played expecting to win most of their games. DiMaggio, Lawrence (Yogi) Berra, Phil Rizzuto, and Whitey Ford became household names in an era when most of the country saw baseball on television only at World Series time. From 1949 to 1964, the Yankees appeared in 14 World Series, winning nine. It was a way to supplement small salaries, according to Jerry Coleman, who made almost as much in his World Series shares as in his regular paycheck.

Perhaps, however, the most dramatic moment in New York baseball did not belong to the Yankees. It belonged to the shot heard round the world in the third game of the best of three playoffs on October 3, 1951 between the New York Giants and the Brooklyn Dodgers. The Giants had come from 131/2 behind to force a playoff for the pennant. The Dodgers, the visiting team at the Polo Grounds, led 4-1 in the bottom of the ninth. The Giants scored a run off starter Don Newcomb. Two runners were on base, second and third, and Ralph Branca came in to face Bobby Thompson. Thompson a line drive home run to right field to win the pennant. It was the first time a homer had won a pennant clinching game, and the radio announcer, Russ Hodges, went crazy, yelling "The Giants win the pennant!"

Baseball had many heroes in the fifties. Mickey Mantle, Duke Snider, and Willy Mays each played center field for a New York Team at the same time. There were three major league teams in the City – the Yanks, the Brooklyn Dodgers, and the New York Giants. By the early fifties each team saw its home games televised. The Yankees dominated the sport, but there were other great teams and each team had at least one outstanding player in the decade. Ted Williams, whom many knowledgeable baseball fans consider the greatest natural hitter in the game, was, if not at his peak, at least near his peak in the fifties.

The prosperity of the United States after World War II had an impact on major league baseball.. Population shifted ever westward, and five clubs shifted westward by 1958. The Boston Braves of the National League were the first to move. They went to Milwaukee. The St. Louis Brown left for Baltimore and in 1955 the Philadelphia Athletics left to go to Kansas City. These moves caused mere ripples of protest in comparison with the move of the Brooklyn Dodgers and the New York Giants, both of the National League, to Los Angeles and San Francisco respectively.

So great was the furor in New York and the possibility of the new Continental League capitalizing on it that the major leagues expanded from their long-term16 team format. The leagues put two teams in New York and a number of teams into new cities. Additionally, the major league teams found themselves in a bidding war with the new league, driving salaries up. As salaries went up, the pool of talent began to diminish.

Television helped kill the minor leagues through keeping people at home for their free entertainment on the tube and through allowing people to get their ration of sports at home. However, television also subsidized sports that had been considered minor to baseball, attracting great athletes from the overall pool of talent. The broadcasting of major league games did not help the situation at all. Thus, as the leagues began to expand, the talent pool contracted, watering down talent in the league. The drying up of the minor leagues, a drop from 59 in 1949 to 19 in the early 1960s meant that the number of players shrank from over 79,000 to less than 2, 500.

As the talent pool dwindled and labor costs rose, baseball became increasingly dependent on television. Revenues went from $2.3 million in 1950 to over $12 million in 1960, in a period of relative price stability. Television revenues helped determine the location of new franchises. Interestingly, baseball attendance peaked in the 1940s at 21.3 million in 1948 and dropped below 20 million in the 1950s. In attempts to counteract the trend and capitalize on television coverage, baseball turned to night games.Television also made celebrities of players, increasing their salaries and bringing about other changes in the game.

Jackie Robinson opened the door for African American players to come into the major leagues. Robinson was one of the games all-time greats. His playing and deportment made it easier for about 100 black Americans and 80 black Hispanics in the major leagues by 1958. Most of these players were in the National League and included Willie Mays, Roy Campanella, and Roberto Clemente. While a good thing overall, the integration of the major leagues spelled doom for the Black major leagues.

The fifties also saw the growth of unionization in baseball. In 1946 players formed the American Baseball Guild. The union, however, soon faltered. In 1953, however, owners tried to end the players' pension system. Players hired J. Norman Lewis to represent them in the ensuing dispute. The dispute led to the formation of the

Major League Players Association. The Association did little else, however, and languished until 1966 when Marvin Miller assumed leadership. The precedent, however, had been set in the 1950s.

Baseball was probed for possible antitrust violations but managed to get through the 1950s with no legislation hindering the owners' control through the reserve clause, which prohibited free agency among players. Nevertheless, the ground for the eventual end of the reserve clause and the victory of free agency was prepared in the forties and fifties. Danny Gardella won a lawsuit in the Circuit Court of Appeals against major league baseball's black listing of players who had jumped to the Mexican League in 1946. His victory frightened baseball into settling with Gardella out of courts.

The case prompted Congressman Emmanuel Celler to start a congressional investigation of baseball. Celler believed that baseball exerted monopolistic power over the sport and that the reserve clause should be ended. Nevertheless, no legislation came to fruition in the 1950s. However, it would not be long until players gained great power and the salaries of the fifties would appear a joke, averaging between $10,000 and $25,000 per year. Only three players made $100,000 per year in the fifties, Joe DiMaggio, Stan Musial, and Ted Williams.

The fifties were a time of great home run production and pitchers suffered. Teams turned to relief pitching specialists came into their own to try to put out late inning "fires." Joe Page of the Yankees and Jim Konstanty of the Philadelphia Phillies were among the best. The longest-lived in service was Hoyt Wilhelm of many different teams. Wilhelm appeared in 1,073 when he finally retired in 1972. There were many great starting pitchers. Among them were Warren Spahn of the Braves, Don Newcombe, Vic Raschi and Ali Reynolds of the Yankees, and Ewell Blackwell, a sidearm pitcher, who played with the Cincinnati Reds and the Yankees.

There were a number of changes in the game, including better gloves, a smaller strike zone, the reintroduction of the sacrifice fly as not counting as a time at bat and thus adding players' batting averages, lighter bats, protective headgear, the frequent replacement of balls, and shorter distances to the fences, allowing for more home runs. Other changes would soon follow, making the game both more productive in terms of runs and faster in base running.

Basketball

The National Basketball Association was formed in 1949 when the Basketball Association of America, formed in 1946, merged with National Basketball League. Almost immediately, the league integrated racially when Chuck Cooper joined the Boston Celtics. Others African

Americans joined the league, such as, the all-time scoring champion Wilt Chamberlain, Bill Russell, the Big "O" Oscar Robertson, and Elgin Baylor, broadening the league's appeal. In 1954, the league speeded its playing action by installing the shot clock, eliminating serious stalling that slowed down the game. In 1960, it saw the Minneapolis Lakers become the first team to move to the West Coast, becoming the Los Angeles Lakers.

Many of the decade's championship teams came from cities unfamiliar to many of today's fans – Syracuse, Rochester, and Fort Wayne, for example. Nevertheless, the fifties saw the game develop into the run and shoot that became so popular in later decades. It was the last decade in which "small" players of six feet or so, like Bob Cousy of the Celtics, could still shine alongside their seven feet or more team mates, like Wilt "the Stilt" Chamberlain of the Philadelphia Warriors.

Football

Professional football came into its own during the fifties. The decade began with the merger of the American Association Football Conference (AAFC) and the National Football League (NFL). The new league took the name of part of the two partners, the National Football League. The league formed two conferences, the American Football Conference (AFC) and the National Football Conference (NFC). Within a year, the league had twelve teams.

The original teams were the New York Yanks, Chicago Cardinals, Cleveland Brown, New York Giants, Philadelphia Eagles, Pittsburgh Steelers, Washington Redskins, Chicago Bears, Detroit Lions, Green Bay Packers, Los Angeles Rams, and San Francisco 49ers. Of course, there was movement of teams, the Yanks, for example, moved to Dallas in 1951 and then to Baltimore in 1953. The Cardinals moved to St. Louis in 1960. But many of the original teams have kept their locations and names.

The first decade saw the Cleveland Browns with Jimmy Brown, the great running back and sometimes movie star, and with Otto Graham at quarterback, win three championships, matched by Detroit's three. The Baltimore Colts won two championships, and the Rams and Giants won one each. No single team monopolized the league for any great length of time, adding to the NFL's rise in popularity.

Television also added to the game's visibility. From its beginning, the NFl had its games televised. Local games, however, faced "blackouts' to encourage fans to attend games. Attendance, rose to 3, 000, 000 by 1958, up from 1952's 2, 000, 000. The NFL was well on its way toward replacing baseball as America's pastime.

Wrestling

Television aided the growth of professional wrestling. In addition to the "freaks," such as "The Sheik" and Gorgeous George, there were the serious wrestlers. The most impressive wrestler of the fifties, a man who could truly wrestle in the classic styles, was Lou Thesz. Thesz won the National Wrestling Association title in 1948 and remained undefeated until is loss to "Whipper" Billy Watson at Toronto on March 15, 1956. Thesz fought everybody in his day, and his day lasted into his 70s when he was still wrestling. He fought "Nature Boy" Buddy Rogers, Leo Numa Anderson, and others.

In his prime years, During the fifties, Thesz was a celebrity. His photo appeared with Joe Louis, Alan Ladd, Yvonne DeCarlo and other famous people of the period. During a period when the "freaks" were taking over the game, Thesz still managed to give an exhibition of solid wrestling without the gimmicks.

Bowling

TV's insatiable appetite helped make bowling a popular spectator sport. Bowling in various forms had long been a popular participant sport in the United States. TV helped make it one more sport to watch at home as well. It certainly helped professionalize the game. Of course, there were professionals before the fifties. However, TV brought some money into what had been considered a great way to spend a night out of the home with the boys. Most women went bowling with their dates or husbands at that time.

There were three professionals that were well known in the fifties. Andy Varipapa, a fine championship bowler was better known for his trick shots. Floretta McCucheon, a women's champion, gave many clinics and was a good-will ambassador in bowling's "early" pre-TV days. Ned Day was famous for his movie shorts on bowling, which also played in reruns on TV during the fifties.

In 1958, however, spurred by the popularity of bowling due to TV, the Professional Bowlers Association (PBA) came into existence. The PBA set up tournaments patterned after those of the Professional Golf Association. Television, moreover, added to the popularity of the few tours the PBA organized, leading to more tours for television to broadcast. Additionally, each tournament has a series of qualifying steps, each leading to higher stakes. These steps, of course, increase the television time of the tournaments as well as adding to the excitement. At decade's end, the Professional Women's Bowling Association was founded, creating a similar tour, and TV time, for women. There were splits and reunions over time. These led to the creation of the Ladies Professional Bowlers Tour in 1981

Conclusion

As any other decade, the fifties had their fads. Some have lasted, many have faded. Some slang words remain. Things are still "cool," but few are "nervous" or "crazy." However, it is still cool to be "hip" but who is from "Nowhere'sville" or "Lovesville?" Much less "strictly from hunger?" The hula-hoop and Frisbee are in no immediate danger of passing soon. Matchbox cars, trampolines, and other fads of the fifties are safe from immediate extinction. The coonskin cap even makes an appearance now and then and Disney stores still sell them from time to time. Davy lives on in Frontierland on both coasts. But Drive-ins are all but gone. While cars are still important, the old car culture has gone with the Cadillac fins. Real rock 'n roll has given way to various derivatives as is the natural course of things.

In retrospect, the fads of the fifties appear innocent. Little tubes of plastic or coils of metal, three basic chords repeated with more or less artistic skill but those who were about the same age as the audience. Dances that sometimes appeared risqué but often were but juvenile attempts to be sophisticated. The sexuality of the age, which could be deadly serious, appears faintly humorous in retrospect. The clothing defines the age almost as clearly as the styles of the Edwardian era define its age. The girls seem bundled up and hidden in layers of cloth and stiff fabric. The boys seem to be playing at being hoods or college students. Neither pose rings true but both were, often at the same time.

The age of transition was eager for adulthood while reluctant to leave the shelter of adolescence. That blissful period of magical thinking when teenage America was finally defined was the precursor of a new era and the end of an old one. Neither process was fully completed in the fifties but both were present. The innocent panty raids were fun without the responsibility of sexual commitment. They were adolescent pranks with deeper dreams and fears. Davy Crockett's motto could come back to haunt the United States later, and it did. We were sure we were right in 'Nam and went ahead, right into the Big Muddy. The ambiguity of the fifties was gone by the next decade, perhaps, never to be regained.

Suggested Readings and Works Cited

Asakawa, Gil and Leland Rucker.. *The Toy Book : A Celebration of Slinky and G.I. Joe, Tinker Toys, Hula Hoops, Barbie Dolls, Snoot Flutes, Coon-Skin Caps, Slot Cars, Frisbees, Yo-Yos.*

Alexander, Charles C. *Our Game: An American Baseball History.* New York, Holt, 1992.

Angell, Roger. *Season Ticket: A Baseball Companion.* New York, Houghton, 1988.

The Baseball Encyclopedia. New York.Macmillan, 1993.

Burke, Larry. *The Baseball Chronicles: A Decade-by-Decade History of the All-American Pastime.* Smithmark, 1995.

Dworkin, James B. *Owners Versus Players.* Westport: Greenwood, 1981. Baseball unionism, rebel and rival leagues; the reserve clause of 1879 to today's free agents.

Gardiner, Martin. *Fads and Fallacies in the Name of Science*
New York: Dover, 1955.

*Kaye, Marvin.*Story of Monopoly, Silly Putty, Bingo Twister, Frisbee, Scrabble, Etcetera Stein & Day Publishers, 1973.

Schwarcz, Joe. *62 Digestible Commentaries on the Fascinating Chemistry of Everyday Life.* E C W Press;

Strasser, Susan, Charles McGovern, Mattias Judt, *Getting and Spending: European and American Consumer Societies in the Twentieth Century.* New York: Facts on File, 1991.

Chapter 8

Literature

The "Silent Generation" of the 1950s was anything but silent when it came to literature. There was an overlapping of the old and new. In a sense, the past, present, and future of American writing were found in the fifties. The National Book Awards for the period 1950 -- 1960 reflect this process of transition that was so typical of the fifties. The decade began with Nelson Algren's *The Man with the Golden Arm* receiving the National Book Award for best fiction. Algren was in the tradition of hard-boiled realism and drugs were beginning to become a concern to American society. The poetry award went to an old favorite, William Carlos Williams. William Faulkner maintained his popularity, winning an award in 1951 for his collected stories. James Jones, a new figure, won the 1952 award for the war novel *From Here to Eternity*.

The fiction awards were marked with such works of distinction as Ralph Ellison *Invisible Man*, a gentle foreshadowing of the coming Civil Rights movement, Saul Bellow's *The Adventures of Augie March*, Faulkner's *A Fable*, John O'Hara's *Ten North Frederick, John* Cheever's *The Wapshot Chronicle*, Bernard Malamud's *The Magic Barrel*, and Philip Roth's *Goodbye Columbus*. Of the fiction works only Wright Morris's *The Field of Vision* is little remembered today.

Interestingly, each of these honored books was also on the bestseller list.

The list's poetry and non-fiction awards also demonstrate a mix of the old and new. There are biographies of Emerson, Melville, James Joyce, books on environmental issues (Rachel Carson's *The Sea Around Us*), books on the Civil War, empire, and other aspects of history. The poets tended to be more traditional or familiar than the novelists: Robert Lowell, Theodore Roethke, Robert Penn Warren, W. H. Auden, Wallace Stevens twice, Conrad Aiken, Archibald MacLeish, Marianne Moore, and William Carlos Williams.

The fact that the National Book Awards choose books that tended to do well on the best seller lists in contrast to many of their future awards as well as books that tended to last as significant works does not mean that every type of popular work was represented on its list. There is, for example, no work by a member of "The Beat Generation" that came to prominence during the fifties. There is also nothing given to any member of the any school of detective fiction, still, perhaps, the most enduring and popular of all the genres. Moreover, not one of the great science fiction novels of the period received a nod from the award committee. Therefore, although there was a close correspondence between the committee and the public in that prestigious books tended to be popular, there was a divergence in the fact that many popular books were not deemed prestigious.

The Beats

Beats fascinated the public during the 1950s. They brought a fresh air of literate rebellion to what was often viewed as an age of conformity. Their rejection of the gray flannel suit image caught the attention of the so-called "Silent Generation." They tended to be literary people in love with Eastern (Asian) lore and the possibility of mystical experiences, often drug-induced.

Caricatures of them were easily found in the media. Perhaps, the worst insult of all was the character Maynard G. Krebs on the *Dobie Gillis Show*, a TV program based on Budd Schulberg's short stories. Krebs was a bongo playing beatnik with long hair but few brains. Although censors at the time would not allow a marijuana smoking character on TV, it was generally understood that Maynard was under the influence of something that kept him out of touch with reality.

Jack Kerouac

For many, however, the man most associated with the beat movement was Jack Kerouac who always claimed that there was no beat movement. Jack Kerouac's *On the Road*, published in 1957, captured a different aspect of the Beat Movement, a love for movement, and a seeking after the unattainable.

Kerouac was born Mar. 12, 1922, and died Oct. 21, 1969. His *On the Road (1957)*, well received by the establishment critics contrary to myths that have grown up after the fact, became the embodiment of the ethos of that generation. Kerouac became the leading chronicler of the movement. "Beat," he noted for "beatitude," not fatigue.

Kerouac's succeeding books were thematically and structurally similar. These novels included *The Dharma Bums, The Subterraneans* (both 1958), *Doctor Sax* (1959), *Lonesome Traveler* (1960), and *Big Sur* (1962).

His writings are generally thinly disguised autobiography, reflecting his own wandering life. Kerouac chronicles his close but explosive relationships, especially with Neal Cassady. His drug addiction is carefully described. Kerouac's humor does much to relieve the intensity of his works and his obsession with mysticism, drug-induced or not. In many ways, he paved the way for the 60s counterculture, a culture he openly rejected.

Allen Ginsberg

Allen Ginsberg was one of Jack Kerouac's more famous followers, the author of the significant protest poem, "Howl." Ginsberg was born June 3, 1926, in Newark, New Jersey, and continued writing poetry up until his death April 5, 1997. Ginsberg grew up in a rather bizarre home. His mother was a communist and nudist who suffered from a mental collapse. Additionally, he had to face the fact of his homosexuality in a period that did not take kindly to such an orientation. Following his interest in Walt Whitman, he determined on a career as a poet. Nevertheless, his schoolteacher father advised him to become a labor lawyer, a career he began to prepare for at Columbia University.

However, at Columbia he met Lucien Carr and Jack Kerouac and non-student friends William S. Burroughs and Neal Cassady. This early core of the Beat Generation was interested in literature, sex, jazz, and drugs. They helped Ginsberg become worldlier while he gave them grounding in literature.

His new crowd was based at Columbia, but they did not encourage him in his studies, and Columbia suspended him, a fact that did not trouble him at the time. Ginsberg immersed himself in the world of Times Square street people, mostly friends of Burroughs. This encounter with the "real world" had a great influence on him, especially in his trademark poem "Howl."

Ginsberg began a passionate pursuit of Neal Cassady, the model for Kerouac's Dean Morriarity. This cross-country pursuit became a forerunner of the "on the road" romance of the Beat Generation. This period was also one in which he and Kerouac sought an indefinable type of writing they called the New Vision.

This mad pursuit of the New Vision and all that it entailed became a symbolic counterpart to his mother's real insanity. By acting crazy, Ginsberg sought to establish his sanity. This bizarreness as a style of life somehow proved him sane. At this time, the early 1950s, Ginsberg believed that William Blake came to him in a vision. It might, however, simply have been the Benzedrine or marijuana that spoke to him. Nevertheless, he proclaimed that he had seen God.

For a time, Ginsberg went "straight," even proclaiming himself a heterosexual. The triggering event for this transformation was his arrest, resulting from the illegal activities of his friends Burroughs and Herbert Huncke. Ginsberg became a marketing researcher complete with an office in the Empire State Building. The famous 'Brush-a brush-a brush-a!' Ipana Toothpaste campaign was partly of his design.

However, in his psychoanalyst's office, he encountered Carl Solomon, a poet. This meeting led to Ginsberg's return to poetry. He sought out the poet William Carlos Williams, who gave him a letter of introduction. Ginsberg traveled to San Francisco, met Kenneth Rexroth, and joined his new poetry movement.

This move led to Ginsberg's fame. His startling performance of his new poem "Howl" at the now-legendary Six Gallery poetry reading in October 1955 led to his fame, the first Beat writer to achieve popular acclaim. An obscenity charge aided Ginsberg in achieving notoriety. His open homosexuality became a symbol of the depravity of the Beat Generation. In the mid-1950s homosexuality was not accepted and Ginsberg's lack of concern personified rebelliousness and freedom.

Science Fiction

Science fiction became enormously popular in the 1950s, its classic age. In part, it was escape; in part, it was solution, or search for a solution. Space explorations, threat of atomic holocaust, and the anomie that follows a major war – all these factors led people to Science Fiction.

Robert Heinlein

Robert Anson Heinlein (1907-1988) was a major part of the science fiction scene in the 1950s along with Asimov and Clarke. His first Hugo, the "Oscar" of the Science Fiction world was for *Double Star* in 1956. He followed that with a Hugo for *Starship Troopers* in 1960.

There were two more Hugos in the 1960s for *Stranger in a Strange Land* and *The Moon Is a Harsh Mistress*. He became the first Hugo Grand Master in 1975.

Heinlein's work demonstrated the three qualities essential for good Science Fiction. They had excellent plots, strong characters and logical scientific arguments. Moreover, he carried these qualities into related areas of what he termed "speculative fiction," such as fantasy and a combination of Science Fiction with other genres. Heinlein considered social and administrative sciences to be part of Science Fiction and introduced their insights into his fiction. In later years the members of the so-called New Wave Science Fiction regarded him as a precursor.

Heinlein's influence on 1950s popular culture extended into television and films. His juvenile stories had a great impact and the juvenile, intended for adolescents; *Space Cadet* became a television series, adding a term to our language. Another juvenile, Rocketship Galileo was the basis for the movie Destination Moon. It was the first movie to deal realistically with space travel and earned him a posthumous NASA award.

Heinlein's greatest novel came out in the 1960s but was a product of the fifties. *Strangers in a Strange Land* is very much a 1950s work that anticipated coming trends. In fact, Heinlein's editors forced him to cut 30% of the novel because of its graphic sexual imagery. After his death, these cuts were restored. Fans could read the original version and made this version a best seller.

Ray Bradbury

Perhaps, the most personally popular of the science fiction writers of the fifties is Ray Bradbury. His fifties work is recalled with sweet nostalgia. Perhaps, that is because his most famous stories, *The Martian Chronicles* are based more on the fantasy world of Edgar Rice Burroughs novels (*A Princess of Mars* and its sequels) than on science. Bradbury liked this theme of a benevolent Mars so much that he returned to it frequently in his writings. In these stories, it is Earth, not Mars that provides the great threat to peace. There was a contemporary message there for people to ponder in the Cold War.

Bradbury used the Chronicles to put forward progressive political values. He criticizes imperialism, racism, environmental pollution, censorship, and the nuclear arms race. This criticism of American righteousness was a common theme in fifties science fiction. It is a tribute to the good humor of Bradbury and the high affection in which he is held that this sharp criticism of American smugness became the single most widely read science fiction book of the fifties. Bradbury's charm allowed him to get away with lecturing his audience while delighting them with his style, a mix of nostalgia and idealism, and his use of sensory images such as color. Bradbury literally brings a sense to life through appealing to the reader's senses.

Bradbury's charm and the sincere affection his readers have for him hide his deep-seated pessimism. He shared with other science fiction writers of the Golden Age certain fifties traits common to many mainstream writers. These included a deep cynicism about family life viewing it as a trap. Bradbury was pessimistic about progress; He had distrust for the mass of people. There was also an adolescent feeling about sex and its description, typical of much of the attitude of the fifties, a factor that helps explain the success, for example, of Playboy and its girl next door.

Mysteries - Noir, Hard Boiled, and Otherwise

The 1950s proved a transitional time for American popular mysteries. Raymond Chandler continued to write until his death in. Ross Macdonald continued to keep the hard-boiled detective style alive and added a few twists of his own. Hard-boiled detective stories, however, were beginning to go in a number of directions.

In the noir movies, called noir because their black and white film and low budgets gave them a gritty, realistic appearance, hard-boiled detectives like Chandler's Marlowe had a clear cu t sense of morality in a shadowy world. Many of the noir movies of the time had their origin in pulp fiction: *The Big Sleep*, *The Postman Always Rings Twice*, *Mildred Pierce, Double Indemnity*, and others.

Mickey Spillane, however, took hard-boiled writing back to one of its creators, Carol Daley. Whereas most hard-boiled writers had followed the lead of Dashiell Hammett and Raymond Chandler, Spillane went to Daley with his two-fisted larger than life heroes. In so doing, he became the largest selling detective writer in history. His *I, the Jury* and its sequels, featuring Mike Hammer, became the stuff of adolescent fantasies. Mike, too, had a code, aptly expressed in the book's title. It was a code that struck a chord in post-war America.

Film noir took the dark images from the hard boiled school of detective fiction, a school that had few illusions about the way things worked or the trust one could put in political institutions, and gave it life on the screen. The genre really began in the 1940s and reached its peak in the 1950s. The literacy of these films resulted from the great writers who wrote for the screen in those days, including William Faulkner who worked on the script of *The Big Sleep*.

The hard-boiled school sought to entertain while presenting a moral code, one related to Hemingway's but also to the early transcendentalists like Thoreau and Emerson. A man was ultimately naked before his God and had to answer for his own actions. When his moral code differed from what was easy, from what everybody else die, then he had to continue on his lonely path. Therefore, the hard-boiled dick was a modern descendant of the old knight-errant, and the image of the chess set looms large in both Macdonald and Chandler's writings.

However, Chandler and other detective writers had to sell books and entertain. As Chandler wrote, "When in doubt, have a man come through the door with a gun in his hand." (Raymond Chandler "Introduction," *Trouble Is My Business*, 1950). There were times Philip Marlowe, his hero, had to shoot people, beat them up in self-defense, or otherwise show some action. But violence, unlike Mike Hammer's, was never gratuitous nor his first choice.

Some of the dialogue of the hard-boiled schools has become legendary, and there are many attempts to parody or imitate it. The wise cracking private eye is still with us in many forms. A small sample of the style brings it back quite clearly.

Mickey Spillane came along in the 1950s and pleased no one but mystery fans. He has never had the adulation that Hammett and Chandler have. Only the fans have taken to his books. Critics and even fellow writers have looked on him with disdain. However, as time went by and Spillane's books continued to sell, especially his early ones, there came to be a reevaluation of Mike Hammer's impact. After all, in watered down form, Mike had been featured in a number of movies and at least two major TV series; there were a number of, mostly terrible, minor ones from time to time. Anyone that popular was worth studying to find out what meaning his work had for the general public.

Spillane had bothered even hard-boiled fans with his lurid sex and violence and right wing opinions. However, Spillane has won attention through his general good humor and self-parody in TV ads. When asked to explain Mike Hammer he has said that Mike is a righteous man living in violent times. Good people are asked to sacrifice so that evil may prosper. Instead of turning a beautiful woman over to the authorities as Sam Spade does in *The Maltese Falcon, Mike* shoots her, as she stands naked before him in the conclusion of *I, the Jury*. In response to the femme fatale's question of "Mike, how could you?" Hammer answers, "It was easy."

This display of "cool" was the very epitome of 50's style, or at least what the 50s admired as style and a version of what President Kennedy later described as "Grace under pressure." While Hammer may have been too crude for the truly cool in Spillane's original conception, he mellowed on television, which still had strict moral standards watched over by careful censors and program sponsors. Thus, the ultra cool television private eye, Peter Gunn became the symbol of private eye cool with his sexy girl next-door sweetheart and jazz club headquarters. But Mike Hammer remained a secret guilty pleasure for many.

Early private eye writings, culminating in the 1950s, have received The Library of America seal of approval. The Library is by its own mission statement dedicated to preserving the American canon by publishing definitive editions of classic American writings. It has given the stamp of "classic" to Raymond Chandler and other 1950s noir writers, an honor Chandler, for one, would have relished.

The Library, however, is simply recognizing what serious noir fans have long realized; namely, that noir is a thoroughly American genre that employs the conventions of the crime novel and turned them to their use as morality tales, in styles that emulated Hemingway, Hawthorne and Nathaniel West, among others.

These writers often wrote for the pulps like *Black Mask* or *Dime Detective*, learning their craft in the American way, by doing. The 1950s Library of America volume contains a number of classics. For example, it includes Jim Thompson's *The Killer Inside Me*, Patricia Highsmith's *The Talented Mr. Ripley*, the first of her novels with this intriguingly complicated character, Charles Willeford's *Pick-up*, David Goodis's *Down There*, and, the African-American mystery genius Chester Himes's, *The Real Cool Killers*.

Although the 1950s marked the culmination of the noir and hard-boiled genres, their fascination with the dark side of the American drive has persisted. The use of genre literature to explore deeper psychological implications and hidden motives has continued to fascinate Americans. Hitchcock revivals flourish, for example and Hitch drew heavily on noir writers. Patricia Highsmith's The Talented Mr. Ripley has received a glossy 90s treatment that loses some of her bite and complexity but still thrills many and has led to a revival of the book itself. Her earlier noir works, like *Strangers on a Train,* are still read today.

Enter the Ladies
Grace Metalious

When *Peyton Place* (1956) burst onto the market, it became an instant bestseller and *cause celebre*. The book takes place in a small New England town. It concerns incest, rape, and murder. A teenage girl kills her stepfather who has been abusing her. The story concerns the unfolding of the circumstances that led to the murder and its consequences.

Its author, Grace Metalious, had written a book that became many people's guilty secret. The book spawned a new genre of the modern-day soap opera. Metalious was born on September 8, 1924, to Alfred and Laurette de Repentingny. She lived and died in small town New England, Manchester, New Hampshire to be precise. Therefore, her novel depicted rather embarrassingly what she knew at first hand.

In common with many full-time 5os housewives, Metalious looked for some sort of creative outlet beyond motherhood. She began writing and at the age of 32 produced a bestseller. No large publisher would touch _Peyton Place_ because of its "sexual content." Therefore, she turned to a small publisher Julian Messner Publishing Company.

Metalious's book became the basis of a movie and television series. None of her subsequent books achieved the fame of her original. Its shock value could not really be duplicated in subsequent novels although _Return to Peyton Place_ did achieve notoriety in its own right. After all, this was a period in which both Norman Mailer and Hemingway found themselves censored by their publishers. If these chest-beating he-men had to bow to the sensibilities of the times, it seemed all the more shocking that a woman would speak so openly about sex. _The Catholic World_ summed up respectable opinion in its comme

> This novel is one of the cheapest, most blatant
> attempts in years to present the most noxiously
> commonplace in ideas and behavior in the loose
> and ill-worn guise of realistic art

Although not so emotional, "serious" critics found reason to condemn _Peyton Place_, missing the despair many fifties women felt with their lives, a despair later captured in the women's rights movement. _The Saturday Review's_ critic missed the point and his comment is typical. "There is no story, and at the end one cannot say what the book is about" Fans, mainly women, did get the point and took the book and its subsequent incarnations to heart.

Some claimed that publicity alone, brilliantly engineered by the publisher was responsible for this "cheap' book's success. If so, it set the pattern for what has come about since. The publisher's publicity stressed the novel's "two rapes, four seductions, two pregnancies of unmarried girls, two abortions and the murder of a rapist by his victim."

Some critics did grasp that *Peyton Place* had some redeeming social value. Metalious did grasp the realities of small town life and present them with sophisticated irony. Her story did indeed move along at a gripping pace. Moreover, Metalious described female sexual feelings as few American authors had done. These descriptions were, in fact, erotic but in a disturbingly and thrillingly different way from their usual depiction. In sum, Metalious described women in ways that have become somewhat commonplace in succeeding decades but were virtually non-existent at the time.

Interestingly, the recent republication of *Peyton Place* has led to a revaluation of the work. It has become an overlooked modern classic. One reviewer has stated "*Peyton Place* is an under-appreciated classic...that paved the way for many women writers and practically invented the entire genre." *Kirkus* continues the praise: "Metalious was a competent writer with some flair whose punchy workmanlike prose efficiently captured her little inland New England hamlet's earthy (if somewhat unbelievably sexually functional) populace."

Much of the current bestseller list is comprised of sex, violence and murder, much like Metalious's work. However, 1950's readers were not quite ready for *Peyton Place* and its revelations of every secret and rumor of the average household. Metalious's unconventional, sexy story appealed to housewives and rebellious teens. The novel topped the 1956 best-seller list and in 1975, it sold over ten million copies in hardcover and paperback combined it sold, for example, over seven million books in under a year of its release.

Francois Sagan

Interestingly, 1956 was also the year that witnessed another sexy novel from a woman. This novel, however, received excellent critical reviews. Perhaps, the fact that French women, really a teenager, wrote the book had something to do with *A Certain Smile*'s reception. Francois Sagan's coming of age story captured readers and critics alike. *A Certain Smile was* actually Sagan's second novel.

Françoise Sagan was born Françoise Quoirez in the village of Cajarc in France. Her pseudonym came from one of Marcel Proust's characters. Sagan's rebellious youth and admitted intelligence helped her legend. Her failure to gain admittance to the Sorbonne because of her active nightlife further added to the legend. In 1954 she published *Bonjour Tristesse*. It became an international best seller, winning the Prix des Critiques along the way. In 1955 it hit the American bestseller lists. The novel was a cause de scandale, describing a 17-year-old who relishes the loss of her virginity and has a problematic relationship with her father, a playboy. Sagan was writing for a postwar generation that felt marginalized and empty, feeling what t the sociologist would call "anomie." Sagan wrote about the French bourgeoisie and its obsession with sex, leisure, and what she deemed hypocrisy. *Un certain sourire* (1956; *A Certain Smile* in English 1956) and *Aimez-vous Brahms* (1959; translated into English 1960), became popular based on the sweet detachment of her style, her innocence in the midst of "perversion" and on the wit of her theatrical dialogue, as in her best-known play, Château en Suède, 1960).

As with so many other 1950s works, hers borders that nebulous zone between popular and serious literature and between fiction and autobiography. Certainly, her works provided escape to a war weary generation. It continues to capture new fans that find in Sagan's coming of age echoes of their own. The style of her first two novels, moreover, even in translation, is crystal clear and flowing, drawing the reader into the reader into a carefully crafted and perfectly described world, a mark of Sagan's literary integrity.

Lolita

A male author with long established literary credentials also entered the explicit world of depicting female sexuality, further blurring the distinction between high art and popular writing. Vladimer Nabokov (1899-1977) had long been known as a Russian émigré with vast literary skills. However, the general public remained rather blissfully ignorant of his skills.

In a calculated move, Nabokov decided that he would become rich and popular through writing a novel capitalizing on America's strange obsession with sex. As the *Atlantic Monthly* put it, "There is perhaps no better symbol of American society's contradictory obsession with sex -- at once voyeuristic and puritanical -- than the history of Vladimir Nabokov's Lolita (1955) and its delayed publication in the United States, in 1958, when it became a controversial bestseller."

Just as Peyton Place has become a common expression for rampant sexual misconduct behind the veneer of respectability, so, too, has "Lolita" become a term for blatant teenybopper sexuality, for what Nabokov termed "nymphets," coining another term. In fact, the controversy surrounding the release of the remake of the film in 1997 reminded many of the original controversy regarding the book. Like the book, the remake could not find a distributor for some time. It still deals with topics that Nabokov knew fascinated the American public, sex between a middle-aged man and a young girl.

To state that *Lolita* raised a few eyebrows is to understate the matter. Because of Nabokov's great literary skills, the book is more than a voyeuristic pleasure. It raises genuine issues regarding America's puritanical obsession with sexuality and its glorification of the innocence of young girls. The distance from Nabokov's shocking 1950s novel, which did make him rich enough to quit his job at Cornell University and popular enough to write more "serious" and less readable books, to the spectacle of a President's philandering with a young intern is interesting to note. It certainly marks a turning point in American attitude toward sexuality.

Lolita (1955) was published in Paris after being rejected by many American publishers. The French government banned it to protect immature English-speaking readers. The French High Court overturned the ban. The United States Customs office deemed it unobjectionable. It received great critical acclaim in Europe and the United States For a presumed pornographic book there is not on e obscene term. The book is about an older man's affair with a 12-year-old whose mother he has first married and then plans to murder to be with Lolita. An accident saves him the trouble of murdering his wife. It was not an erotic book in the fifties underground sense.

However, Nabokov disturbs readers with a different kind of perversity, a farce of sexual obsession. It is a comic book, and like all books of true comic genius it is about a serious topic. Lolita, after all is more depraved than Humbert Humbert is. It is she who ultimately seduces him and then abandons him for another man. That she becomes a rather drab housewife surely was the émigré snide comment on suburban American life.

Lolita, Peyton Place, and Bonjour Tristesse, marked an interesting turning point in depicting sexuality, especially female sexuality, for the general public. Along with the Kinsey Report findings on male and female sexuality, they began to pave the way toward the swing in sexual depiction that marked the sixties. Whether sixties openness was ultimately more erotic than the more tabooed treatment of sex in the 1950s is an interesting question.

The More "Serious" Writers

Truman Capote

Truman Capote was educated in New York but born in New Orleans. He made an interesting combination of the two experiences. He had come into literary prominence with his short stories in the 1940s but the 1950s were really the decade in which he came into his own. In the 1950s Capote wrote *The House of Flowers*, a musical set in West Indies bordello. He accompanied a tour of George Grecian's

"Porgy and Bess," resulting in *The Muses Are Heard*, an early experiment in a non-fiction novel.

In 1951 Capote's *The Grass Harp* displayed his best qualities, his lyricism, melancholy and whimsical sense of humor. In the novel, a defiant young boy and his cousin learn that sometimes compromise is necessary to live in a community. Strangely, the novel did not become the basis for a movie until 1996. The book's neglect by Hollywood is all the more strange because Capote was a successful screenwriter whose first major film writing was done with John Huston on "Beat the Devil (1954)."

For many people, Capote's best work was *Breakfast at Tiffany's (1958)*. For those people who came of age in the fifties, Holly Golightly, the book's heroine, will always resemble Audrey Hepburn, who brought the character to life on the screen. Holly is a young women who like so many others came to New York to be happy. However, in common with many others, she finds that she must leave the big bad city to find her true happiness with a young writer. Along the way, she gets mixed up with an odd assortment of New Yorkers from the unsavory side of the law.

Capote went on to become more fascinated with journalism, and in 1966 his "non-fiction novel" *In Cold Blood* became a best seller. Capote started with a *New York Times* article on the murder of a wealthy Kansas family. The project took Capote who worked with his mentor Harper Lee six years to complete. They interviewed the killers, their families and the families of the victims. When the killers were convicted, Capote capitalized on the event and recorded their last days for his book. In many ways this book stemmed from Capote's 1950s interest and led to much of the fictionalized journalism of the 1990s.

"I decline to accept the end of man": William Faulkner

William Faulkner (1897-1962) was arguably the greatest American writer of the Twentieth Century. Faulkner's works presented a cohesive examination of American mores and changes in those mores and values in the 20th century through focusing on one small area of Mississippi, the fictional Yoknapatawpha County. The 1950s brought great fame to Faulkner. Faulkner's Collected Stories (1950) opened the decade, impressing people with their quantity as well as quality. Adding to his fame was the awarding of the Nobel Prize for Literature. In his famous acceptance speech, he affirmed his belief in the survival of the human race, even in an atomic age, and in the importance of the artist to
that survival.

Faulkner's prominence led him to be a cultural ambassador, going overseas for the State Department, giving speeches, and becoming active in addressing the South's racial problems. Faulkner spent some time teaching at the University of Virginia. His 1950s fame led him to take more time with his writing than had previously been the case.

In the 1950s he produced such classics as *Requiem for a Nun* (1951), *A Fable* (1954), *The Town* (1957), and *The Mansion*(1959). His final book was 1962's *The Reivers*. Faulkner considered *A Fable* (1955) to be his masterpiece. It won the Pulitzer Prize and National Book Award in 1955. Faulkner spent ten years writing the novel, which is an allegorical story of World War I. It is the most poetical of his novels, and therefore elicits strong reactions from readers, who either love it or hate it. It is set in the trenches of France and supposedly deals with a mutiny in a French regiment. The mutiny is a symbol of despair at the condition to which modern life has reduced us.

The Town and *The Mansion* complete the Snopes Trilogy, which consists of The *Hamlet*, *The Town*, and *The Mansion*. The Snopes were one of the nastiest families in all of literature. Their patriarch was Ab Snopes, a barn-burning sharecropper and former horse thief. Faulkner loved these characters and paraded them throughout his fiction. There seemed to be no end to them. They present an interesting rebuttal to the "lost cause" aristocratic ideals espoused by Yoknapatawpha County's foremost families, who mourn the loss of the Southern glory. The upwardly mobile Snopes replaced the declining planter families of the old Southern aristocracy.

Ab's son Flem Snopes best exemplifies the Snopes and the upwardly mobile class they represent. Flem progresses from sharecropper's cabin to town to mansion. Faulkner charts this social rise in the Snopes trilogy. Of course, Faulkner was not simply writing about one small Mississippi County. He strove to discuss more general truths through careful depiction of the particular.

The Paperback Revolution

In the fifties the paperback became respectable. The "revolution" had begun with prewar Penguins and then spread to numerous other companies. These books were still cheap in price but of reasonable quality. Their price and quality increased with the decade. But they still remained around 25 cents to a half-dollar for most of the decade. A few "quality" or "scholarly" books might reach $3.00 or so, but these high quality "scholarly" books were nevertheless relatively rare in the fifties.

Pocket books came to include a wide variety of material, including a wide range of first-class literature. Their low cost and convenience led to the creation of book readers and buyers on a previously unknown level. Readers collected them, imitating the wealthy collectors of leather bound volumes. These cheap books also helped spread literacy in the developing world, becoming especially popular in Africa. Americans were becoming increasingly aware of the Third World and "the winds of change" as the decade progressed and former colonies became independent. It would be some time, however, before Americans became aware of the dark side of American policy although there had been hints in Guatemala and the Congo of the duplicity of the CIA and of that grandfatherly figure in the White House.

In the fifties, however, Americans were optimistic and certain, by and large, of their benevolence. Therefore, paperbacks were simply another sign of progress. Their seeming omnipresence was a fact of life, a good fact. Paperbacks were found in drugstores, along with lunch and soda counters, bookshops, street kiosks, and newsstands in railway stations, airports, and hotel lobbies. Paperbacks were so cheap that they moved books into the impulse buying category. Many of these books had huge print runs, 30,000 or more at the time.

Most paperbacks were reprints, with a certain market already mapped out. Some originals were produced in paperbacks; experimental publishers often released their books directly in paper. Generally, however, paperback publishers negotiated for rights from hardback publishers. Moreover, as the college population grew enormously in numbers in the fifties, the academic paperback came into fashion for classroom use. Reissues of scholarly books and even originals found their way into the curriculum, cutting book costs. A number of these works were out of print, and paperbacks gave them new life. This great market extension began in America. The original price for these scholarly tomes was between 65 cents to $1.95, terribly expensive in the day of cheap mass-market pocket books. Soon new academic works were issued simultaneously in both cloth (hardcover) editions and paperbacks. Classes usually bought the paper copy and libraries the cloth, selling for $3.50 to $4.00 or even $5.00.

Magazines and Comic Books

The idea of putting comic strips in books was one that blossomed in the late 1930s. By the 1950s, comic books were a staple of life for most kids. Superheroes like the Human Torch, the Sub-Mariner, Captain America, Wonder Woman and Superman were part of everyday life. There were also funny animals, such as those Disney created, and a good deal of teen humor provided by characters like Archie and his friends. By the 1950s adventure, crime, horror/fantasy, humor, romance, science fiction, war, and western comics had arrived on the scene. Stan Lee, Jack Kirby, and Steve Ditko were the superstars of those who created comic strips.

Comics were so popular that a Senate committee, worried about their influence, began to look into their possible corrupting influence. There were psychiatrists as well as senators who argued that the lurid material found in comics caused the increase of juvenile delinquency. The predictable media circus followed, and magazine publishers began to get nervous as many parents tried to keep their kids from reading comics.

Only one major comic book publisher, E. C. Comics failed to band with other publishers to form the Comics Code Authority to regulate their comic books. Presumably, the code made comics wholesome again. In any case, it took heat off the publishers who were joining the fight for decency. The code contained statements such as 'Policemen, judges, government officials, and respected institutions shall not be presented in such a way as to create disrespect for established authority.' and 'No comics magazine shall use the word horror or terror in it's title.' It also stated that drugs would not be glorified and needles not be shown in administering drugs. Those magazines that passed inspection carried a stamp of inspection attesting that they were fit to read.

Magazines kept pace with the popularity of comic books. In fact, they were the most popular media of the period. Women's magazines kept women up to date with culture, fiction, fashion, and homemaking. They were also a powerful influence in shaping American opinion on the meaning of women in American society. Magazines such as *Life*, *McCalls*, *Look*, *American Magazine*, and *Women's Day* presented an image of ideal family life that have remained in popular imagination as "typical" of the fifties.

There were, of course, magazines for each member of the family. *Popular Mechanix* and similar magazines, for example, was aimed at young men along with *Playboy* and its imitators. Young women had *Mademoiselle, Seventeen, True Romance*, and a host of other reading material. Men still had some pulp magazines with detective and western themes as well as *True Adventure, Field and Stream* and many other magazines that portrayed a rugged, vigorous outdoor life. There were a large number of magazines on music, art, literature (*The Saturday Review of Literature*). *TV Guide* became the largest selling magazine of the fifties, even surpassing *The Readers'*

Digest. Newsmagazines like *Time* and *Newsweek* had large audiences. And *The Saturday Evening Post* still featured Norman Rockwell covers. While *Mad Magazine* poked good-natured fun at the entire process, it was, in spire of television, still an age of print media although one that was rapidly moving into the television age.

Conclusion

The novels of the 1950s tended to reflect a mixture of high art and popular culture. Many esteemed writers were quite popular and many popular writers have come to be regarded by critics as American classics It is interesting to note the rise and decline of reputations since the 1950s.

It appears that much of the writing of the 1950s, even the potboilers, was well written and is still readable. As with so much else from the fifties, much of the period's writing is viewed as a "Golden Age." Although much of that attribution is the result, undoubtedly, of nostalgia, there is a certain truth to the assertion in fiction.

Science Fiction writers view the decade as a time when certain aspects reached their culmination while others were engendered. The same is true of hard-boiled detective writing. This transitional feeling is also present in general fiction where high and popular styles met and intermingled. A comparison of the best seller lists of the fifties and nineties would prove quite instructive.

The freer attitude toward sexuality of the sixties was foreshadowed in the popularity of the works of Nabokov, Metalious, and Sagan. It is interesting that only Metalious was born in the USA. The trio certainly helped open up literary treatment of sexual topics, and their works still have power today. *Lolita*, particularly, still holds surprises, even on rereading. The fact that Nabokov's biting satire still stings suggests that the ambivalence and hypocrisy he noted toward sexuality in America still remains in spite of our "freer" attitudes.

Suggested Readings and Works Cited

Benton, Mike. *The Comic Book in America: An Illustrated History*. Dallas, TX:
Taylor Publishing, 1989.
Benton, Mike. *Horror Comics: The Illustrated History* (Tatler History of Comics No.). Dallas, TX: Taylor Publishing Company.
Benton, Mike. *The Illustrated History of Crime Comics* (Tatler History of Comics N.5). Dallas, TX: Taylor Publishing Company, 1993.

Benton. Mike. *Science Fiction Comics*: The Illustrated History (Tatler History of
Comics No. 3). Dallas, TX: Taylor Publishing Company, 1992.

Benton, Mike. *Superhero Comics of the Golden Age: The Illustrated History* (Tatler history of Comics No. 4). Dallas, TX: Taylor Publishing Company, 1992.

Daniels, Les. *Comix: A History of Comic Books in America*. New York: Bonanza Books, 1971.

Goulart, Ron. The Comic Book Reader's Companion: An A-Z Guide to Everyone's Favorite Art Form. New York: Harper Perennial, 1993.

Lardas, John. *The Bop Apocalypse The Religious Visions of Kerouac, Ginsberg, and Burroughs*. Champaign: University of Illinois Press, 200.

Luey, Beth. " 'Leading the Public Gently': Popular Science Books in the 1950s "*Book-History* 2(1999): 218-53.

Polito, Robert, Ed. *Crime Novels: American Noir of the 1950's*. New York: Library of America, 1997.

Chapter 9

Visual Arts

In visual art as in so many other things, the fifties were an exciting transitional period. There were many giants of older forms still practicing their craft while new lions emerged on the scene. Thus, Picasso, Dali, and others overlapped with Pollock, Liechtenstein, and Warhol, Grandma Moses and Norman Rockwell were also practicing their trade to appreciative audiences.

It is important to remember that Pop Art came out of the fifties as a reaction to what they considered the conformity, subjectivity, and overseriousness of Abstract Impressionism. To counter the overpretentiosness and intensity of Abstract Expressionist artists, they moved to the popular material culture that surrounded them, and every other American. Ordinary people watched television, went to movies, browsed magazines, and checked the comics each day in the papers. These simple pleasures gave the group of artists who came to be known as Pop Artists a hook into getting to the general public.

The movement actually began in England in the middle of the 1950s. It quickly caught on in New York City. Pop Artists used images from the media and advertising, fields that exploded in the fifties along with the economic boom of the Eisenhower years. Consumer mass society hit its stride in that period and the Pop Artists began to exploit this fact in the fifties. In fact, the term ``Pop Art'' was first used by the English critic Lawrence Alloway in a 1958 issue of Architectural Digest to describe those paintings that first expressed what came to be the themes of the Pop Art movement; namely, celebration of post-war consumerism, defiance of the subjective psychology of Abstract Expressionism, and worship of materialism.

Picasso and Dali

During the 1950s the painter generally considered the premier artist of the century was alive and still producing works of art. Pablo Ruiz y Picasso (1881-1973) was a Spanish painter and sculptor whose figure dominated the century. He produced over 20,000 works of art, in itself an amazing feat. The influence of his art on other artists, however, is even more amazing.

Picasso himself came under the influence of Paul Gaugin, the Postimpressionist genius, the Symbolist painters of the Nabis Movement, and Edgar Degas and Henri de Toulouse-Lautrec. These influences led to his famous Blue Period. Picasso continued to master various styles of painting. His cubist works, for example, influenced many artists and encouraged a fascination with African art. Perhaps, his greatest work was Guernica, painted in response to Francisco Franco bombing of that Basque town. It goes beyond that disaster to address the general topic of the horrors of war. World War II increased his anti-war feeling, expressed so eloquently in his paintings.

During the 1950s, Picasso continued to attack war, painting pictures that expressed his opposition to US involvement in the Korean War. Unfortunately, he hurt his cause by depicting the US as engaging in germ warfare, something America did not do in that horrible conflict. The works he produced, moreover, were far from the peak of his Les Demoiselles d'Avignon. Although he was from his peak periods in the fifties and sixties, he continued to be a presence in the art world and a major influence on artistic production.

Like Picasso, Salvador Dali's greatest works, perhaps, were in his past as the fifties unfolded. However, like Picasso, his works could not be ignored and he remained a force throughout the period. Dali was born in 1904 in Figueras, Spain. He spent his college years with Luis Buneul, the great filmmaker. His political conservatism seems ill at odds with his artistic radicalism, but as with so much dealing with Dali, it is hard to know what was fantasy and what reality.

It seems destined that he came under Freud's theory of the unconscious. It also appears inevitable in retrospect, that he came to work with the surrealists, and writers led by the French poet Andre Breton. Under the sponsorship of Joan Miro, Dali went to Paris in 1928 where he met France's foremost surrealists. In 1929, he moved to Paris and became one of the greatest of the surrealists. His blend of realism and fantasy, akin to dreams, captured the public's imagination. Dali became noted for pitting bizarre objects against desolate landscapes. He juxtaposed incongruous, unrelated, and often bizarre objects. Dali described her surrealist works as "hand-painted dream photographs," are inspired by dreams, hallucinations, and other unconscious forces that the artist is unable to explain; they are produced by a creative method he calls "paranoiac-critical activity." Dali's most characteristic works show the influence not only of the surrealists but also of the Italian Renaissance masters, mannerists, and the Italian metaphysical painters Carlo Carra and Giorgio de Chirico.

Dali and Gala, his wife, left Spain for the US during the Second World War. Dali always knew how to promote himself and America gave him the opportunity to exploit his talent for public relations. He continued his tremendous output and produced not only paintings but also graphic works, book illustrations; and designs for jewelry, textiles, clothing, costumes, shop interiors, and stage sets. Additionally, he wrote poetry, fiction, and a controversial autobiography, `The Secret Life of Salvador Dali'. Earlier in his career Dali was involved in two films with Luis Bunuel: `An Andalusian Dog' (1928) and `The Golden Age' (1930). His most famous painting is `The Persistence of Memory', painted in 1931. Dali's images stick in the imagination. His melting watches, startling crutches, and the overpowering image of a cubist cross with Christ once seen are never forgotten.

In America, Dali's touch can be seen in a number of movies. Alfred Hitchcock's 1945 classic "Spellbound," for example, has a dream sequence complete with melting objects in a Freudian nightmare. Directly or indirectly, Dali's touch is evident in a number of other films, including Hitchcock's late-fifties "Vertigo." Dali's sets graced many movies and plays of the period, reflecting his earlier work with Luis Buneul in Spain.

There are other connections between Picasso and Dali. Picasso came under the influence of Surrealism and his "Les Demoiselles" and cubist works owe a debt of gratitude to the movement. After World War II Picasso became an almost mythological figure, and his personality, like Dali's, overshadowed his work. Both artists had an enormous output, and critics accused them of simply exploiting the economic demand for their work. Both stood accused by some of simply repeating themselves and putting out commercially viable, and popular, items. Both artists found their later works to be quite popular with the general public while the high art critics were not so pleased.

Abstract Expressionism

Abstract Expressionism was more about sharing a feeling of revolt and freedom of expression, akin to that shared by jazz musicians of the period. Although Robert Coates first used the term in the March 1936 issue of the <u>New Yorker</u>, it was basically associated with the fifties. Much of the fifties abstract expressionism was dominant. It is also known as "action painting" and the New York School. A number of major figures are associated with the movement. These figures include Arshile Gorky, Jackson Pollock, Willem de Kooning, Hans Hoffman, Robert Motherwell, Franz Kline, and Mark Rothko. It was certainly easy for comedians and others to poke fun at the movement with its enormous canvases and splashes of color, often resembling the work of pre-school children's art. However, the movement is important for its conscious rejection of European styles. As so much else in America after World War II it declared conscious independence from Europe while influencing European art itself. Whether art for art's sake made sense to the tired worker or "average Joe or Joanne" did not influence the New York School. Indeed, its very unpopularity in the hinterland served to validate its value to its practitioners.

Jackson Pollock

To most of the public the name Jackson Pollock is virtually synonymous with Abstract Impressionism, since Pollock may be the most parodied painter in American history. Pollock had a rather prototypical American background. He was born in Cody, Wyoming in 1912, raised in California, and moved to New York City. He studied with that very American artist Thomas Hart Benton and came under the influence of Mexican muralists, Native American art, Jungian archetypes, Picasso, and various other modernists. All of these influences stamped with his individual mark. He first applied these lessons to working for the Depression era Works Progress Administration. Eventually, his works went from the more naturalist style of Benton to a surreal one influenced by Dali.

By 1947 Pollock was firmly within the abstract expressionist school. He developed his action-painting style, producing works such as Full Fathom Five and Lucifer (both 1947, Museum of Modern Art). He changed his style around 1950 using brown and black lines to crisscross on pure white canvass. Ocean Grayness (1953, Guggenheim Museum, New York City) is an example of this style.

The change in Pollock's style illustrates an important fact about Abstract Expressionism; namely, that not only is it not an accurate description of the work of all the accepted members of the school but that the movement encompassed many different styles under its umbrella. However, there are certain characteristics that do unite the members of the school. Obviously, the paintings are abstract. They do not draw from the visible world. The paintings are also free and emotional. The techniques are also free and not restricted to the "normal" methods of painting. The members of the school place great stress on the character of paint and use it to suggest sensuousness, dynamism, violence, mystery, and lyricism. Intuition is also given an honored place. Improvisation in which the artist follows the creative unconscious is honored. There is a unity of feeling to their huge wall-size paintings.

Pollock died young, in a car accident at 44, and had not done much painting in the last two or three years of his life. Of course, "not much" is a relative term; he had painted four significant pictures in that period, a small output for him but more than most artists produce in a long lifetime.

Ironically, Pollock's death in August 1956 added greater mystique to the planned survey of his work that opened at New York's Museum of Modern Art in December 1956. The Museum's retrospective was the first to honor a member of the Abstract Expressionist school and helped establish Pollock's reputation as abstractionist in American art history. The retrospective became a memorial, one that associated the movement firmly in the public's mind with Pollock

It was Jackson Pollock and Willem de Kooning who brought these trends together, building on the work of Arshile Gorky and Hans Hofmann as well as the Surrealists who came to the United States fleeing Nazi oppression. In the fifties Abstract Expressionism was at its height, making New York City the center of the art world and replacing Paris in that position. By 1960, however, action painting was out of style and other movements had replaced it.

Pop Art

Many of the artists who left Abstract Impressionism as well as new artists went into Pop Art. Although Pop Art is associated with the 1960s it emerged in the late fifties as protest against the over serious attitude of Abstract Expressionism. Painting become fun again as the pop artists used comic strips, advertisement, and objects from popular culture familiar to the general public. What they did with these objects often had a serious intent, forcing people to look at the familiar in unfamiliar ways. Leaders of the movement included Roy Liechtenstein and Andy Warhol. Pop artists saw no boundary between popular and high culture and sought to erase what they considered arbitrary distinctions

Andy Warhol, in fact, presents an interesting study in the manner in which an artist can use popular culture to promote himself while still making a significant statement about the world beyond him. Of course, his major work belongs to the sixties but his emergence in the fifties is one more sign of that decade's own creativity and essential position as a meeting of old and new styles.

Andy Warhol and Roy Liechtenstein

Warhol (1930-1987) was born in Philadelphia. Warhol's silk-screen paintings made him famous. Their use of soup cans, dollar bills, and other ordinary objects immediately marked him off from the abstract expressionists. Warhol refused to discuss his art, hinting that unlike that of the Abstract Expressionists, it was all surface and was what it was. There was, he seemed to insist by his refusal to comment, nothing beneath the surface.

Roy Liechtenstein drew his own first Pop Art inspiration from the work of Walt Disney, specifically Mickey Mouse and Donald Duck. True, "Look Mickey," was painted in 1961. But its spirit is late fifties return to the popular and a lifting of a spirit of fun. Like Warhol's fifties erotic cherubs, Liechtenstein takes familiar items from popular culture and gives them a twist. They are familiar but somehow different. They appear to be nothing more than a big, bold, colorful work, like Disney's general artwork. However, Liechtenstein takes it beyond the commonplace while still keeping his sense of humor. It takes the commonplace and brings it to a level that reminds the viewer of more "serious" works of art. In so doing, a critique of popular culture and forces the thoughtful viewer to reconsider the world around him or her.

Liechtenstein's ideas matured in the fifties. He concluded that the artists of the fifties had lost touch with the real world and were too engrossed in looking inward for reality. Others artists agreed. By the end of the 1950s a group of artists had formed a movement that rejected some of the major tenets of the Abstract Expressionists; namely, the belief that constructs of personal experience were primary, emotional intensity and the inward search for images. Out of this mix of talent, including Ed Rushca. Larry Rivers, Richard Hamilton, Claes Oldenburg, James Rosenquist, Jim Dine, Warhol and Liechtenstein emerged the Pop Art movement that ushered in the '60s with a new attitude toward popular culture, one that co-opted and celebrated as the "reality" of what American truly was, at least for them.

A branch of Pop Art that began in the fifties was Kinetic Art. Essentially, it was "art in motion." Kinetic artists wanted to show the connection between art and technology. Their focus was on movement itself. The "subject" of Kinetic Art, then. Was movement itself. Movement was a basic theme of the fifties and the general public took to the new style, which had its origins in the middle 1950s. Kinetic Artists began simply enough with moving strings attached to weights, using air power or currents to form shapes. Soon light sources, motors, and other devices provided further effects. Art took on a "becoming" aspect.

Grandma Moses and Norman Rockwell: Red, White, and Blue, and More Complex Than We Thought

Anna Mary Robertson was better known as   "Grandma" Moses. Her simple, primitive paintings warmed many people's hearts. Her famous scenes of farm crafts, winter views, and rural seasonal celebrations found their way into many reproductions and calendars that people hung on their walls. Often Abstract Expressionist works were put down and those of Grandma Moses held up as "real art." "And," someone was certain to remark, " She only started painting at 78!" She kept at it until she was 100.

Grandma Moses became a legend for her so-called primitive paintings. The legend grew up that she was a simple woman, a legend she nurtured carefully. In fact, she was a competent woman who was not just a Connecticut farm wife with five children, but a woman with remarkable gifts who managed to stay focused. Moses also had a great sense of light and color. As soon as her kids had grown, she decided to move off and "try something different."

Norman Rockwell began his career at a much younger age, in his twenties. Rockwell is best remembered for presenting the public with images of everyday life that everyone could recognize but were better than people remembered them. In sum, they were truly idealistic. In many ways, his work resembled that of Frank Capra, the Hollywood director of films such as "It's a Wonderful Life," and "Mr. Smith Goes to Washington." Both their works present a view of what life in American should be, and, in their opinion could be.

It is interesting that this enormously popular artist who was painting images from popular culture long before the Pop Art phase came into being has had his high art reputation polished recently. Representatives of high art no longer mock the longtime Saturday Evening Post illustrator's work. Most of his work was meant for immediate popular consumption. They were meant for mass production and had to use the colors of the processes that prepared them for such production.

Rockwell created a democratic world in which history came from the bottom up. He showed how great events affected the average person. His world was filled with tolerance, love, hard work, and respect. It was a rural world that recalled a day gone by but one that many Americans remembered with fondness.

Rockwell was born and raised in New York City and finally moved to a rural setting, Stockbridge, Massachusetts, in 1953 and lived here until his death in 1978. His 1950s paintings featured many of the town inhabitants as models. Many of his more famous Saturday Evening Post covers were made during this period.

Rockwell captured many of the basic ideals of American life and his reputation among the common people remained high. Even when the "more sophisticated" mocked him, they generally would mention one or two exceptions to their putdowns. His covers, however, show a true grasp of what was happening at any given period in which he worked. Rockwell was both a part of popular culture and a shaper of it.

Interestingly, the blurring of distinctions between popular and high culture that began in the fifties have aided his reputation. Norman Rockwell (1894-1978) represented everything the serious art world hated. From the age of 18 he worked as a commercial illustrator. He went on to make a handsome living producing advertisements for Ford and covers for the enormously popular Saturday Evening Post, providing an idealized set of story pictures of some town USA.

Rockwell's style was deceptively photographic. High critics, those who appointed themselves representatives of what was best in art, mocked him for his simplistic works that would leave no visible mark on art history. The general public ignored the critics who were filled with praise for Abstract Expressionism and other art experiments. Compared with these works, his paintings appeared as a traditional holdout against "progress." His works appeared to be too sweet and sentimental for the modern age of anxiety.

Although Rockwell's work is undergoing a revival in the early 21st Century, it is fair to ask whether only the general public appreciated his work in the fifties. As a matter of fact, there were a number of artists who favored and collected his art. Among them were Willem de Kooning and the man most associated with Pop Art, Andy Warhol. Warhol admired Rockwell's understanding of the commercial value of his art.

Rockwell understood the span of art history and found ways to put in classic references in his work, using a figure from the Sistine Chapel, for example, in his Rosie the Riveter cover. He tried to escape commercialism by escaping to Paris, but he always came back to his magazine covers and commercial art. The art he called Santa Down the Chimney and most Americans felt that nobody did it better. Today art critics tend to agree. Dave Hickey, for example, an art historian, compares Rockwell to Hogarth, Vermeer and Franz Halls, terming Rockwell as ``the last best practitioner of a tradition of social painting that began in the 17th century.' '

Rockwell's close friend, Maxfield Parrish worked in a similar vein, and it is appropriate the Rockwell Museum in Stockbridge, Massachusetts, has room set aside for his work. Maxfield Parrish (1870-1966) was one of the finer illustrators in American history, as well as a painter of note. Parrish illustrated Washington Irving's Knickerbocker's History of New York, among other works. He also did a number of magazine covers and posters. The St. Regis Hotel still has his Old King Cole murals on its walls. His romantic landscapes are marked by vivid color and flat, decorative treatment. Granted that some of his work is dreamy and differs from Rockwell's. But some of Rockwell's best work differs from what some consider "typical Rockwell" as well.

Although Parrish's greatest period of public acceptance was over by 1935, he remained popular throughout the 1950s. He did many magazine covers, books, and even illustrated seed packages, did advertisements, prints, calendars, posters, and elaborately decorated candy boxes. His posters decorated many fifties homes. Parrish managed to capture a feeling of childhood in his works, and he often explicitly used themes from children's literature, like the Pied Piper or Old King Kole. His use of color and light drew the viewer into a land of magic, reminiscent of childhood. Parrish completed his illusion by adding real things to his imaginative paintings. For example, he used his pet cat, friends, and his children in his works. He even made himself into the Pied Piper for his famous illustration, and it was his own son, Maxfield Junior, who followed him in the painting.

Photography

Interestingly, photography as an art was quite neglected in general. Many people considered it more a hobby than an art. Things began to change in the fifties, as more people became interested in the art of photography. Really beginning in the fifties there have been two aesthetic approaches to photographic art. The first makes use of photography's basic characteristics in a functional manner. The second seeks to relate photography to other mediums of art. The fifties combined yet another approaches to these two; namely, an expressive, emotional use of photography pioneered by the photographer Alfred Stieglitz.

Minor White served to popularize Stieglitz's approach in a number of ways: writing, teaching, and his founding and editing of the influential magazine Aperture. White believed that each photograph should have an inner message, a deeper one, not perceived in a surface manner. The photographer must place that message in the photograph through art. Aaron Siskind, a photographer who worked with what he termed "the detritus of our world," agreed with this sentiment. Siskind worked with wall scrawls, weathered wood and plaster, torn billboards.

Andreas Feininger learned his craft through working for Life magazine. After World War II he launched out on his own, using his early training as an architect to produce dramatic close-ups of architecture and nature. Design, composition, and structure are clearly evident in his best work.

In the 1950s artists like Aaron Siskind, he became fascinated with wall scrawls and graffiti. There were other developments demonstrating a point of view. Robert Doisneau, for example, used humor and satire to capture the absurdity in everyday life. Lucien Clergue, on the other hand, used the natural world and the nude in surf to present his point of view. Experimentation was not lacking. The Belgian Pierre Cordier furthered the tradition of camera less abstraction. In 1958 his "chimigrammes"--color images made, not by light, but chemical action on photographic paper opened new possibilities for photographic art.

Unfortunately, in spite of these innovators many people did not really consider photography to be an art. Because cameras are so cheap and relatively easy to use, many people see little of art in their use. His or her belief tends to be that anyone can take a good picture. Indeed, from time to time, anyone can. The genius of the great photographer, however, often lies in seeing art where others see the commonplace – or nothing at all.

Ansel Adams

Ansel Adams (1902-84) was just such an artist. He was born in San Francisco and rebelled against the proletarian, realistic art of the Depression. He preferred to capture gorgeous landscapes, most significantly those of the Southwest. Adams seemed to understand that the days of the beautiful landscape were running out. It seemed that he knew that shopping malls and developments would encroach on the landscape space.

Adams spent a good deal of energy lobbying for environmental causes, fearing that strip mines, malls, and other signs of progress would destroy the virgin forests and the farmland he loved. His work conveys his passion for nature and a simpler America that was on its way out in the fifties.

Adams was always aware of time in his work. There is a sense of the great geological periods that have passed as one looks at canyons or rain forests or mountain ranges. There is an awareness of what is to come to spoil those scenes as well as what has been over endless ages of the past. Adams was capturing the potent wilderness before it disappeared. He described the experience in this way after climbing the Sierra Nevadas.

> The silver light turned every blade of grass and every particle of sand into a luminous metallic splendor; there was nothing, however small, that did not clash in the bright wind that did not send arrows of light through the glassy air. I was suddenly arrested in the long crunching path up the ridge by an exceedingly pointed awareness of the light . . . There are no words to convey the moods of those moments.

There were no words but Adams's photographs did convey their moods and beauty. His romantic nature and great skill enabled Adams to capture a vanishing wilderness and preserve it on film so that we could note what was lost and strive to save what was left. Interestingly, his mood that seems so at odds with the consumer culture of the fifties actually captured the imagination and loyalty of many people and made him a popular artist as well.

Edward Steichen

There was also Edward Steichen (1879-1973, who had been born in Luxembourg. Steichen was known in Paris for his photographs that looked like painting. Steichen sought an emotional, impressionistic of material in his photography. Steichen came to the United States at a young age, and he began his career as a teen. At 21 he went to Paris to perfect his art through studying painting. In 1905 he joined Alfred Stieglitz in New York City in founding the 291 Gallery. Steichen worked as the main photographer during the 1920s from Vanity Fair and Vogue. He was a key figure in developing an appreciation for photography as an art form. In wartime, Steichen found military uses for photography, helping to develop aerial photography aiding U.S. naval combat photography in World War II. After the war he headed the Museum of Modern Art's photography department (1947-62), where he organized the Family of Man

Fifties Furniture

As new homes were built and renters became owners, there was a call for new furniture. American furniture designers not only answered the call, they came to prominence. Among the best known were the architects Charles Eames and Eero Saarinen. These architects turned furniture designers adapted technology that had emerged during the war. They used wood, metals, and plastics, collaborating on the design of the so-called Eames chair and ottoman, which they constructed, of subtly curved molded plywood with deeply padded leather upholstery, set on a metal pedestal base. In 1956 Saarinen designed an entire range of pedestal furniture in molded plastic and metal. His famous white chairs resembled in silhouette wineglasses. These chairs have loose cushion seats in bright fabrics. His tables, which range in size from small side tables to long conference tables, have tops of either marble or wood. Although few Americans in the fifties owned the originals, many people purchased mass-produced copies.

The sculptor Harry Bertoia produced the lightweight wire mesh chair in 1952. Knoll Associates; Florence S. Knoll was a graduate of the Cranbrook Academy of Art in Bloomfield Hills, Michigan, as were Eero Saarinen and Bertoia. Paul McCobb, another graduate of the same Academy of Arts, based his popular Planner group on 18th and 19th century Shaker furniture. This simple and functional furniture captured the public's fancy.

Conclusion

Visual art in the fifties exhibited the same transitional nature as music, dramatic art, architecture, and so many other fields. It was a period in which older forms coexisted with new ones, and in which the future was present in nascent form. In spite of the seeming dominance of Abstract Expressionism, Surrealism, representational art, the various contributions of Picasso, and newer forms coexisted in some sort of harmony and mutually influenced each other. Photography began to come into its own, in turn influencing and being influenced by other visual art forms and even architecture.

The general public often paid little attention to the pronouncements of the high art critics. The popularity of Rockwell, Grandma Moses, Parrish, and Ansel Adams, for example, made their feelings clear, as did the general delight in Pop Art and kinetic art. As the fifties moved toward the sixties, indeed, a greater sense of play clearly emerged and the arts reflected that emotion. In retrospect, it is clear that the general public was often correct in choosing where to place its allegiance. Rockwell, for example, has weathered the years well while the reputations of many of the Abstract Expressionists have not. Parrish and Moses continue to have the power to delight.

Current trends in art stem from many of the changes of the fifties, finding their roots in that transitional decade. Abstract Expressionism, early Pop Art, the later works of Picasso and Dali – each and all of these still stir young artists, challenging them to find their own mode of expression to carry on the tradition.

Suggested Reading and Works Cited

Greenberg, Cara and Tim Street-Porter (Photographer). *Mid-Century Modern: Furniture of the 1950s.* New York: Harmony Books, 1995.

Hennessey, Maureen Hart and Anne Knutson , Editor. *Norman Rockwell: Pictures for the American People.* Norman Rockwell, High Museum, 1999.

Fryer, Jonathan. *Character Sketches: Soho in the 1950s and 1960s.*Washingon: National Portrait Gallery Publications, 1998

Von Hase-Schmundt, Ulrike, Christianne Weber, and Ingeborg Becker. Theodor Fahrner Jewelry...Between Avant-Garde and Tradition: Art Nouveau Art Deco in the 1950s. London: Schiffer Publishing, Ltd.: 1991.

Chapter 10

Architecture

Architecture is more than merely the construction of buildings. People have used architecture to convey political and ideological messages, as long as there have been political entities. The tensions between these very diverse, but interrelated goals, produce much of the dynamism of architecture.

Architecture is deeply related to a people's culture, expressing its deepest characteristics and ideals in a visible form. No matter the style architecture in general has three main characteristics. First, the work is designed to be suitable for humans engaged in specific human activities. Next, the architect designs the work to last. It is meant to be a permanent and stable work. Finally, the work expresses experience and ideas through its form.

The "new architecture" of the fifties was designed to be functional and striped down. It was what the architect David Handlin in retrospect termed as "less is a bore" architecture. At the same time, old masters such as Frank Lloyd Wright and Le Corbusier were still practicing their art while new architects appeared to challenge them. Moreover, the new Googie architecture, the architecture of space age car culture, combined many of the elements of "serious architecture" with popular culture and captured the mood of mass America. That mood was one of exuberant optimism that embraced the new.

During much of the 20th Century the Midwest was the motive force for American creative architecture. There were, of course, prominent architects in other parts of the country, such as the California brothers Charles Sumner Greene and Henry Mather Greene. However, by and large, the Midwest dominated the scene. Among the second generation of architects of the Chicago school, such as William G. Purcell, G.G. Elmslie, and William Drummond, and Frank Lloyd Wright's "prairie architecture."

Frank Lloyd Wright

Frank Lloyd Wright (1867 – 1959) is generally considered America's greatest architect. He was born in Richland Center, Wisconsin, and entered the University of Wisconsin at 15. Because the university had no course in architecture, Wright studied engineering.

About 500 of his designs were built. Wright was a prolific architect, more so, when one realizes that he died leaving plans for several hundred more projects. He began his career working for J. Lyman Silsbee and Louis Sullivan. In turn, he trained numerous architects at his own school, the Taliesin School in Arizona where he championed "organic architecture." During his career he developed the Prairie and Usonian residential styles as examples of organic architecture. Organic architecture challenged the dominance of European styles, presenting an American style for the way Americans lived. So influential was Wright's idea that most Americans have at least some elements of his style of architecture in their homes. Wright designed all sorts of buildings from single-family homes for middle class and wealthy Americans, to skyscrapers, places of worship, resorts, public building, bridges, and even gas stations. The diversity of his work demonstrated clearly just what he meant by organic architecture and how it could be applied to a wide range of work.

Frank Lloyd Wright began his career in Chicago working for Louis Sullivan, the father of the American skyscraper. Before World War I, Wright took architecture in new directions with the development of his early works, such as the "prairie houses." These prairie houses were, in fact, houses in the suburbs outside Chicago. Wright experimented to get simplified spaces that were, however, unified and articulated. Moreover, Wright designed his prairie houses so that space flows between interior and exterior, adding to the unified nature of his buildings. He called his homes prairie houses because he sought to suggest the wide midwestern prairie in their design. In addition to using flowing space toward that end, Wright also used long horizontal lines of eaves to further unify the design.

Frank Lloyd Wright's architecture met the three criteria for architecture quite well. It fit into and expressed its site clearly. It adapted to its region through its structure, using materials that belonged to the area. By the 1950s Wright had mastered the form. In spite of his genius, it is fascinating to realize that Wright spent a long period of his career trying to gain acceptance for his ideas. As late as 1943, the date of his autobiography, he feared his work would remain the property of a few clients.

The major characteristics of his architecture consist of reducing his works to a minimum number of rooms and emphasizing the building's association with its site through extended and emphasized planes parallel to the ground. Wright believed that there should be a free flow of space. As part of planning an organic whole, he incorporated mechanical equipment and furniture as integral parts of the building's structure. Wright's ideas concerning a more universal geometry of design had matured by this era. The sculptural Solomon R. Guggenheim Museum at New York City (1956-59) stands as evidence of his grand design. It is an apt symbol of his architectural genius, marking the climax of his lengthy career.

From Formalism to Functionalism

Wright brought to the Guggenheim his version of a movement that had been present in the works of many who followed the Functional or International style. Hidden beneath the rectilinear style of Functionalism was an emphasis on ornate sculptured design. Eero Saarinen's Trans World Airlines terminal at John F. Kennedy International Airport, New York City (1956-62) meanwhile followed the "form follows form" dictum of the Formalists. These single form buildings allowed interior space to be divided for many functions and were not limited to a single use. The McGregor Building for Wayne State University in Detroit (1958) is one of the more famous buildings in the Formalist style. Minoru Yamasaki, a Japanese-American architect, solved some of the structural problems of the style through making structure decorative.

In the fifties, moreover, the Modernist style shifted from Functionalism to an emphasis on grand or monumental Formalism. Interest focused on a sculptured look for massive areas of the work. Additionally, decorative aspects of building materials as well as exposed structural systems came increasingly into favor. Frank Lloyd Wright put these interests into full focus in his design for the Guggenheim Museum.

International Style

The New Brutalism is related to earlier styles of architecture, especially to the Formalist style that emerged from the International Style of architecture, which Le Corbusier, Ludwig Mies van der Rohe and Frank Lloyd Wright created. This style with its functional demands encouraged certain starkness in approach. For the Smithsons, Le Corbusier use of the International style and its contrast with Mies's glass and steel aesthetic was stark. Le Corbusier's employment of monumental structural shapes and raw unfinished molded concrete evoked images of a raw confrontation, a New Brutalism. For many, it was a reform movement, advocating a return to Functionalist principles. Hence, there was a deliberate avoidance of polish and elegance. Structural elements are deliberately exposed to the elements, and the relationship of form and function laid bare.

The International Style of architecture that became an important part of Modernism that reached its peak in the fifties owes a great deal to the emigration of many German and Austrian architects from their homelands to the United States in an effort to escape Nazi oppression. Nazi hatred of avant-garde architecture aided the development of American architecture. Among the more prominent of these architects were Rudolph Schindler and Richard Neutra, in Los Angeles, Walter Gropius and Marcel Breuer, in Cambridge, Massachusetts, and Ludwig Mies van der Rohe, in Chicago. These architects brought to the U.S. the aesthetic principles of the Bauhaus school of art, a school of abstract impressionism that developed in Germany. It clearly set out principles of the relationship of function and structure and a sense of abstract composition. This style came to be known as the International Style.

Mies developed the steel structure; around which was stretched the nonbearing curtain wall, often mostly of glass. To him we owe the glass-box style of skyscraper so common in the fifties. Gropius's student Philip C. Johnson worked with Mies to design the greatest example of the style, New York's Seagram Building (1958).

The New Brutalism

The fifties saw the emergence of a style called the New Brutalism. The architects Alison Margaret Smithson, née Gill, and Peter Denham Smithson were British architects whose design for the Hunstanton Secondary Modern School, Norfolk (1954) is usually taken as the first example of New Brutalism. This approach to architecture often stressed bare staging of materials and structure. The Hunstanton School was the prototype for the New Brutalism. It followed the Formalist aesthetic, stressing a formal severity and clarity. The building exposed steel- and brickwork as well as its electrical conduits.

In keeping with the transitional nature of the fifties, a reaction against the less creative aspects of the International Style began. Concrete slabs were becoming more of a cliché and less of a creative statement. In reaction to this lack of creativity, architects moved toward a more fluid expression in their designs. They made their engineering more conspicuous. Eero Saarinen, for example, sought bolder composition and more forceful appearance of the materials he employed, especially concrete.

The New Brutalism had its American counterpart, especially in the works of Paul Rudolph. In the 1950s and '60s Louis I. Kahn used the ideas of the movement to design a number of works. His Salk Institute (1959-1965) in La Jolla, California, for example, combines the ideas of monumental elegance of form with utility of function. I. M. Pei, a Chinese-American had American buildings to match his great work in Montreal, the Mile High Center complex (1955) in Denver, the East Building wing (1978) of the National Gallery of Art in Washington, D.C., and the Fragrant Hill Hotel (1982) in Beijing, China. Although the latter buildings were built after the fifties, they are expressions of developments that began in that period.

Le Corbusier

These fifties developments owe a great debt of gratitude to the pioneering work of Le Corbusier, Le Corbusier, born Charles-Edouard Jeanneret in Switzerland in 1887, was certain that the new industrial age required a daring style of architecture to match its audacity. For that reason, his love of newness and energy, it is no surprise that he took quickly to New York. New York's skyscrapers fascinated him but he deemed them not large enough. However, he was intrigued with the geometric regularity of the city and its embrace of the new.

Le Corbusier assumed that name, his maternal grandfather's, when he moved to Paris at the age of 29. In Paris, he began to apply his visionary ideas, seeking to form a style to replace Art Nouveau. Le Corbusier felt that Art Nouveau had become bogged down in over ornamentation. Art Deco was on its way to extinction in his opinion and the Arts and Crafts movement was no match for the industrial age.

Le Corbusier called for a new beginning for architecture. "We must start again from zero." This new architectural beginning was called the International Style. Le Corbusier promoted his new style in manifestos, pamphlets, exhibitions and his own magazine. In addition, Le Corbusier wrote numerous books. It is worth looking at his "recipe" for an International Style building: "raise the building on stilts, mix in a free-flowing floor plan, make the walls independent of the structure, add horizontal strip windows and top it off with a roof garden."

The International Style was more an attitude toward design than a coherent style. There was a belief that clarity and precision of design matched the modern clarity of action of those who used the buildings. The International Style buildings had nonsymmetrical forms, the interior spaces were flowing, there were flat roofs, and large areas of glass and undecorated walls. There was a machine-like simplicity to these buildings that matched the industrial age. Indeed, Le Corbusier termed his works "machines for living in."

Mies van der Rohe

Mies van der Rohe presented a different, but related, path for architects. Ludwig Mies van der Rohe designed buildings that were mainly steel-and-glass structures. Mies employed simple geometric forms. Some art critics have noted that his works have such a detailed aesthetic vocabulary regarding steel detailing that they approach a kind of religious pitch.

Although Mies developed his ideas around the time of World War I, it was not until his moved to the United States that he had an opportunity to build large structure. The Lake Shore Drive apartments of 1948-51 in Chicago were his first. It was in the United States that Mies came hit his stride. He came to the United States in 1938 and taught architecture at the Illinois Institute of Technology in Chicago. There he designed high-rise office and apartment buildings, which influenced 1950s commercial and institutional architecture in America. Most of the high rise office buildings in America since the fifties have been influenced by Mies's ideas, especially the steel-and-glass curtain wall. The 1958 Seagram Office Building is still the model of what steel and glass office

Googie

Googie architecture was the major form of popular architecture in the fifties. It was architecture for the masses. When the fifties are depicted, it is generally Googie architecture that TV and movies use to recapture the era. Bright neon, swooping roofs and endless glass walls of diners, motels, and bowling alleys mark its style. American Graffiti and Grease, for example, both really staged and filmed after the fifties, used huge gobs of Googie to capture the feel of the period.

The name "Googie" came from the roadside world of the fifties, indeed, from the Los Angeles region that epitomized it. Googie's was the name of a chain of Los Angeles roadside coffee shops. The original Googie's chain had everything the style represents: oversize signs to curved, padded booths in turquoise and salmon shades. It used flagcrete, terrazzo and plenty of dingbats. Of course, there were spaceships, martini glasses, tiki torches, complete in A-frame buildings.

The Googie style of architecture had a great influence on popular culture. Disneyland is probably its most famous example. The entire Anaheim resort area, in fact, was a great centers of Googie architecture and the entire fifties style.

When Disneyland opened its gates in 1955, the area around it boomed. Disney did not have the control he did later in Florida with his Reedy Creek Development to control growth around his park. Thus, the surrounding area of Disneyland quickly mirrored the popular culture of its day. There was the galloping camel of the Caravan Inn. A genie popped out of the Magic Lamp's tiki totem pole of the Samoa Motel. The Satellite Shopland sign spun and the Anaheim Convention Center had a domed arena. Of course, there were the famous Eden Roc and Kona Kai signs. The architecture was "Space Age" in its day and reflected the optimism of the fifties when it seemed that everyone would soon be able to go to the moon.

Although the Googie style is named after the original Googie's Coffee Shop, which was next door to Schwab's Drugstore, the legendary site of the discovery of movie starlets, Las Vegas and Miami Beach heavily influenced the style. As it developed, the style combined the car culture of southern California with the space age. It was a style that expressed the optimism of the day. Googie can be spotted rather quickly by its use of a boomerang and outer space shades of blue, green and orange. Many fifties diners and bowling alleys bore these trademarks. These garish features captured the attention of drivers who otherwise might have zipped by roadside attractions.

It is important to understand that Googie developed in response to a car culture, defining a modernistic roadside architecture. It was cheap but also hip. It spread from its original architectural use for popular cheap highway drive-ins to Tupperware parties, tailfins, car washes, and other fifties cultural markers. However, it was indeed primarily a gravity-defying architectural style marked by giant, look-at-me neon signs, diagonal lines, boomerang curves, starburst sparkles, bubbling circles, out of whack squares, undulating canopies, zig zag roofs, amoeba shaped cutouts and sloping glass walls. It was an optimistic style and the coffee shops and diners that popularized the look support its spontaneous and optimistic nature - Biffs, Ships, Pann's, Chip's and Googie's itself.

The use of Googie as a term to mark this architectural style came from Douglas Haskell who used it in a 1952 <u>House and Home</u>

Magazine issue. Soon architectural schools used the term to describe the style. Technically, a true Googie building should have characteristics; its design themes should be a mixture of styles combined abstractly, it should defy gravity, its various structural systems should not only be a mixture and combined but also be visible, finally, the newest building material, such as glass and plastic should be used.

Fans of Googie nostalgically remember the days when the line between Disneyland and its surrounding area were blurred. In many ways it seemed that there was no barrier between the two, echoing Wright's principles of architecture in a strange way that there should be no distinction between interior and exterior. The jet-like tailfins on cars that zoomed past giant tiki gods, rockets and flying saucers on their way to Disneyland appeared to be part of Tomorrowland itself. The Magic Kingdom really seemed to be part of a real world that was just as interesting outside its walls as within. One wit has encapsulated the Googie philosophy in this fashion, summarizing the story that is inherent in every Googie building.

> Man left his caves and grass huts and through hard work and ingenuity has built an amazing modern world. Tomorrow he will conquer any remaining problems and colonize the rest of the galaxy. However, for all his achievements and modern science man will never lose touch with the natural world and his noble roots.

Thus, in the midst of space age architecture, historical themes emerged. There were decors of the Old West, the South Seas and even caves. New materials enabled architects to express the man-nature link. Rock and permacrete walls, extravagant landscaping, gardens brought inside buildings, plate-glass windows, and plastic. New technology allowed for giant windows and, reflecting the dictates of Modernist architecture and Frank Lloyd Wright, the inside and outside merged. "Alien" buildings might have a palm tree growing out of an overhanging roof. They might also have a rock wall and three glass ones.

Googie was an integral part of popular culture, reinforcing an integral vision of an ideal future. That future was one, which humans could shape through hard work and ingenuity. The Vietnam War and the loss of innocence and the birth of pessimism that war engendered, however, killed Googie. Ray Bradbury sums up the pessimism that killed American innocence in "The Toynbee Convector." He has its hero say:

I was raised in a time, in the sixties, seventies, and eighties, when people had stopped believing in themselves. I saw that disbelief, the reason that no longer gave itself reasons to survive, and was moved, depressed and angered by it . . . . . Everywhere was professional despair, intellectual ennui, and political cynicism . . .. The impossibility of change was the vogue. . . . Bombarded by dark chaff and no bright seed, what sort of harvest was there for man in the latter part of the incredible twentieth century? Forgotten was the moon, forgotten the red landscapes of Mars, the great eye of Jupiter, the stunning rings of Saturn...Life has always been lying to ourselves . . .. to gently lie and prove the lie true to weave dreams and put brains and ideas and flesh and the truly real beneath the dreams. Everything, finally, is a promise. What seems a lie is a ramshackle need, wishing to be born.

The fifties, despite some pessimism, tended to be optimistic than the following decades. If there were problems, they could be solved. Googie expresses this optimism. Googie architecture, much of it designed by Armet & Davis, designed many of the Googie coffee shops, including Bob's Big Boy. Denny's, Tiny Naylor's, Ship's, McDonald's, Norm's, Cliff's, Biff's, Coffee Dan's, Taco Paco, Clock's and Carolina Pines Jr. also adopted Googie style.

The "Typical American House "

There were many different style American houses in the fifties – ranch, split-level, colonial, Cape Cod, and others. The size of the houses varied according to the size of families, location in suburb or city, and income. However, as families grew larger at the height of the Baby Boom and public transportation declines, middle class families typically had three or four bedroom houses with two or three car garages. Homes typically had family rooms, patios, large yards, and functional fireplaces. There were formal dining rooms and a living room. The kitchen, at the rear of the house, was state of the art, often with a work island in the middle from which the "ideal" mother supervised the family work and watched young kids in the play area in the back yard.

The Levittown house that had inspired the suburban developments had been more modest than later houses. They didn't have garages, and most homes had two bedrooms and one bath. However, there was room for expansion and Bill Levitt expected people to raise their roofs, literally, and add rooms on a second floor. People, in fact, did expand their Cape Cods and other homes. They personalized the homogeneous community, adding touches here and there to make them their own. As the American family changed, so did Levittown and other developments it inspired.

Developments became more elaborate as the fifties rose to new heights of prosperity. The building boom continued throughout the decade and a greater variety of affordable housing for many Americans became available. Young married couples bought "starter" homes, fully intending to move up as their families and incomes increased. The "dream house" seemed to be an attainable goal for many fifties families.

Conclusion

The popular architecture of the fifties brought the innovations of Le Corbusier, Wright, Mies and others to the public. It expressed an all-embracing optimism that recognized that there were indeed humans but that believed that any problem humans created could solve problems. The prosperity of the Eisenhower era propelled that optimism, creating a youth culture that came into its own in the next decade.

The Eisenhower era also continued the expansion of American highways that aided the development of Googie architecture. A nation on the move needed a space age motif to express its enthusiasm. It also needed bright colors, mammoth architecture, and eye-catching designs to slow it down enough to stop at drive-ins of all types. The blurring of interior and exterior that dominated Wright's architecture was adapted to the things of everyday life. That southern California became the center of Googie architecture is itself an apt metaphor for the era.

Disney, moreover, grasped its power in his design for Disneyland in Anaheim, near Los Angeles. Although he grumbled about the desecration of the area surrounding his park, it was in fact an appropriate complement to it. It continued its themes outside the confined space of the park in a manner that the more controlled Disney World does not. In time, especially in Tomorrowland, Disney incorporated Googie motifs into the park from the motels, drive-ins, coffee shops, and other attractions outside his park.

Both "serious architecture" and its popular culture version Googie captured the spirit of the age rather well. The fifties saw no barriers to the expansion of the American spirit. History was itself an affirmation of the American drive to expansion and amalgamation. That great architects from Europe and Asia contributed to the American style of architecture surprised no one. If Le Corbusier said that American skyscrapers weren't high enough, well, maybe he was right! Monumental architecture is not foreign to the American spirit. That Pei built the mile high stadium is only appropriate.

In the fifties, American architecture shouted with the enthusiasm of a naïve people who believed that raw energy could overcome any problem. Blurring boundaries was further evidence that reason could solve difficulties and that somehow amalgamation of both opinions might be possible. Whitman, the quintessential American poet, after all had proclaimed, "Do I contradict myself? Very well, then, I contradict myself. I am large, I contain multitudes." Action, not theoretical consistency, was America's strong point.

It was, alas, the pride that went before the disasters of the sixties.

Suggested Readings and Works Cited
Curtis, William J. R. *Le Corbusier at Work.* Cambridge: Harvard University Press, 1978.
Glancey, Jonathan. *20th Century Architecture: The Structures That Shaped the Century.* New York: Overlook Press, 1999.
Handlin, David P. *American Architecture. London:* Thames and Hudson, 1997.
Hess, Alan. *Googie: Fifties Coffee Shop Architecture.* New York: Chronicle Books, 1986.
Jackson, Lesley (Editor). *Contemporary: Architecture and Interiors of the 1950s.* Phaedon Press, 1996.
Larkin, David and Bruce Brooks Pfeiffer, Editors. *Frank Lloyd Wright: The Masterworks.* New York: Rizzoli, 1993.
Pawley, Martin. 20th Century Architecture - A Reader's Guide. New York: Architectural Press, 1999.
Solomon R. Guggenheim Foundation, *The Solomon R. Guggenheim Museum, Architect: Frank Lloyd Wright.* New York, 1960.

Chapter 11

Music

Although most people today associate the music of the 1950s with rock and roll, 1950s music was incredibly diverse. Rock and roll did not simply storm in and overwhelm jazz, classic crooners, show tunes or American classic pop. These older musical forms existed side by side with the newer ones throughout the fifties.

Big Bands and Vocalists

The decade began with a mixture of post big band music, dominated by vocalists and vocal groups who had sung with the big bands. Pre-rock and roll teens continued to support this music, claiming that modern jazz "was too difficult to dance to." "The Singing Rage, Miss Patti Page," for example, not only had the top song for the year, "All My Love," but also songs more closely associated with her, "The Tennessee Waltz, " "I Went to Your Wedding," and "How Much Is That Doggie in the Window." These songs were quite popular at record hops, dances that featured records rather than live bands, not only early in the decade but also later on when rock became king. Although she had none of her other tunes placed in the top ten for the years after 1953, she did have her own variety television program, continued to sell records and filled auditoriums for her concerts. Patti Page was a symbol of the decade's "innocence" and its continued ties to the big band past. She was barely out of her teens in 1950 when she had her first hit "Confess."

Even more impressive for the decade was the success of Perry Como. Como had recordings in the top ten throughout the decade. In 1950, for instance, he had the number six record for the year, "Hoop-de-Doo." In 1958, against such rock and roll competition as the Everly Brothers, Danny & the Juniors, Elvis Presley, and others, Como had the number four record in the U.S., "Catch a Falling Star." The secret of Como's enduring popularity during the rock and roll era has long been something of a mystery. Perhaps, his easy acceptance of the new music and his featuring it on his popular television program helped contribute to it. Certainly, his very relaxed manner and "cool" personality made him a natural for television and his weekly exposure enabled him to promote his music to his large weekly audience.

While Como's popularity was unique, there were always more "sedate" or jazz-like recordings on the charts. In 1959, for example, Bobby Darin's "Mack the Knife "was number eight for the year. In 1960, Ray Charles's hit "Georgia on My Mind" was number six for the year. Percy Faith and His Orchestra had an instrumental hit with "The Theme for a Summer Place." Interestingly, a number of later rockers were moving into "the mainstream" with songs like "Are You Lonesome Tonight" and "It's Now or Never" (Presley), "El Paso" (Marty Robbins), "I'm Sorry and I Want To Be Wanted" (Brenda Lee). In addition, there were hits by ballad singers who used a slight rock beat such as Connie Francis ("Everybody's Somebody's Fool," "My Heart Has a Mind of Its Own"). The Platters, always a sweet group more in the rhythm and blues tradition, had a number of hits in the period such as "Smoke Gets in Your Eyes," "The Great Pretender, "and "My Prayer." Additionally, Johnny Mathis became very popular during this period with songs like "Chances Are," and "The Twelfth of Never."

In contrast, Frank Sinatra, "The Chairman of the Board," had only one top ten hit in the period, 1955's "Learning the Blues." Sinatra, however, had not only diversified his talents, having various TV shows, winning an Oscar for *From Here to Eternity*, and a successful night club act, but he also turned to the potentials of the LP (long-playing record). Sinatra overcame his throat troubles of the early 1950s and moved to Capitol Records. His vocal problems, caused by polyps on his vocal chords, left him with a deeper and huskier voice. A world-wearier one that along with his publicized personal problems appealed to an older audience and more sophisticated college students replaced the young romantic sound.

That audience tended to be more affluent and willing to plunk down the cost of an LP, from $2.99 to $3.99 compared with the $.75 of a single. Sinatra found that he could stretch out in the LP format and develop a common theme, or concept, in these albums. He had Capitol hire Nelson Riddle and the best studio musicians available, especially the distinctive trumpet sound of Harry "Sweets" Edison from the Count Basie Band. These Capitol albums "Close to You, " " Songs for Swinging Lovers," "Only the Lonely, " and others are classics of their types.

Bing Crosby, whose successful career stretched back to the 1920s, continued to be popular in various media. His movie career continued. Its 1950 high point for many was his role in *High Society*, a musical remake of *The Philadelphia Story*, co-starring Grace Kelly, and Frank Sinatra. His duet with Sinatra on "Well, Did You Ever" is not only a highlight of the film but shows where some of Sinatra's talent came from. Similarly, his duet with Louis Armstrong demonstrated that Armstrong was the ultimate father of jazz and popular singing.

Crosby was, perhaps, Armstrong's earliest most famous disciple. Crosby, himself, acknowledged his debt on many occasions. That heritage was passed on to a number of "crooner," the term used for male vocalists who mastered the use of microphone and "crooned" into it, rather than belting out a song. He continued that style through the fifties and sixties. Only Crosby's death in 1977 stopped his various media activities.

Rhythm and Blues

There were early signs that a new music was slowly gaining popularity among a young audience. In 1952, for example, "Her Nibs, Miss Georgia Gibbs" covered a rhythm and blues tune, "Kiss of Fire," and it was the number eleven hit song of the year. Kay Starr covered "The Wheel of Fortune" and it finished as 1952's number 13 song. In 1954, the Crew Cuts hit it big with "Sh-Boom," and Georgia Gibbs had a hit with "Dance with Me Henry," a cleaned up version of "Dance with Me, Annie" and "Annie Had a Baby (Can't Dance No Mo')." Interestingly, none of the top ten or even twenty hits featured one black rocker. There is no Chuck Berry, Little Richard, Big Jay McNealy, Little Anthony, or any of the others whom those who were teens remember from the fifties. Not even the white rocker Bill Haley and his Comets is on the list.   The reason for that is that rhythm and blues and its child rock and roll were found on separate lists. Race music was generally segregated from the mainstream, and early rock and roll was definitely considered race music. 1955 saw the popularization of rock and roll with such hits as Pat Boone's number one song "Ain't That a Shame," a watered down version of Little Richard's song.

The reason that rhythm and blues had a separate listing of its hits is the same one that made it appeal to primarily a black audience; namely, segregation in American society. Black artists were generally separated from white ones and the "race" music that was R&B was free to develop black themes for a predominantly black audience, using black idioms in its presentation. As the fifties saw the first serious cracks in segregation, that music began to reach a white audience, often in diluted form. That ending of segregation, slow as it was, meant that black artists who had been confined to a R&B ghetto were freer to cross-over into the big money of the top ten, helping to end one of their major complaints Chuck Berry was the first black artist to become truly popular with white audiences. He broke through the barrier with the aid of Alan Freed in the mid-1950s with his own composition "Maybelline." In the 1960s rhythm and blues would break from rock and emerge as soul music.

Rock and Roll

Rock 'n' Roll, of course, is perhaps the most enduring of the fifties fads. It burst on the scene in 1954-55 with hits by singers including Chuck Berry, Little Richard, Jerry Lee Lewis, and Elvis Presley. Rock also generated its share of novelty songs, including David Seville's "Witch Doctor" and "The Chipmunk Song," Those loveable chipmunks still plague us every Christmas with Alvin still interrupting his other chipmunk friends, Simon and Theodore. Two other novelty tunes of note are "The Purple People Eater" by Sheb Wooley, and "Willie and the Hand Jive" with its own dance craze of 1958.

Rock & roll was certainly related to R & B and the blues. It was also related to other forms of African-American music, a fact that often appears to surprise its supporters as well as its detractors. All forms of African American derived music, including the popular doo-wop street music are related. Whatever else it was to become, the music categorized as rock & roll was African American derived music, or in the terms of the day "race music."

There is some argument about the "origins" of rock and roll. Nelson George (1988: 67) describes its beginnings in his book _The Death of Rhythm & Blues_. After discussing the role of the white rhythm and blues deejay Alan Freed, he notes

> Rock & roll – the words alone evoke notions of hedonism, romantic wandering (taken from the blues),

and pseudo rebellion akin to the blues but without the mature battle of the sexes essential to that black expression. Nevertheless, as Freed knew, rock & roll wasn't a music but a marketing concept that evolved into a life-style. Years later critics and fans would search for the first rock & roll record, a quest Freed would probably have laughed at, since he never seemed to know what rock & roll was. The many recording made under his name in the 1950s reflected a taste for big-band swing with bluesy sax breaks and covers of standard tunes. . .

One of the primary influences on both rhythm and blues and rock & roll was Joseph Vernon Turner (Big Joe Turner). Big Joe's music was widely imitated by the early rockers and he, himself, often appeared on early rock & roll bills. Turner was famed for his recordings with his partner, the pianist Pete Johnson. The duo became famous in Kansas City saloons.

As was the case with many other musicians, John Hammond "discovered" them and took them to New York City. Turner was a star of the 1938 Carnegie Hall "Spirituals to Swing" concert. Turner remained in New York and became quite popular, helping to popularize boogie- with Pete Johnson. Turner became a frequent singer with jazz bands, including the enormously popular Count Basie.

In 1951 Turner hit the R&B charts with "Chains of Love," and followed it with a series of top R&B hits "Sweet 16," "Honey, Hush," "Shake, Rattle and Roll," and "Flip, Flop and Fly," all of which were covered by young white musicians, notably Bill Haley, The white musicians generally cleaned up the lyrics for the white teenage crowd.

Alan Freed, in a similar vein, used the term rock & roll to "disguise the blackness of the music," according to Nelson George. The attempt did not work, as we have come to be told through numberless movies and oral histories. Perhaps, its failure to mask its blackness was its best selling feature. However, if it failed to mask it what came to be identified as rock & roll did water it down a bit. One its earliest divas, Laverne Baker, is reputed to have said, "The blues is for bourbon. Rock & roll is for Coca Cola."

That evaluation was generally true in the early days and became even more valid as black artists, like Little Richard and Fats Domino began to be crowded out by white adolescents like Fabian and Frankie Avalon. That development is not surprising because the purpose of rock & roll was to exploit the white teenage market. Rock & roll, unlike rhythm and blues, did not specifically address a black audience of all ages. Instead, it addressed the coming of age concerns of white adolescents. Again, George (1988: 68) describes the situation well.

The generational schism and teen-eye view that has always been the crux of the rock & roll ethos was mostly foreign to black consumers, young as well as old. That is not to say that all blacks rejected rock & roll, both as a business term or social attitude, but R & B made a connection to black listeners that was both musical and extra musical. Music made by the white bands was inevitably (and often deliberately) adolescent, addressed to adolescent ears about adolescent fears. Black teens might listen, but their heads were in different places, and R&B articulated that difference not just in vocal or aural effect but also in attitude.

Alan Freed (1926-1965), as George notes, is generally given credit for putting the marketing term rock & roll on a collection of related black music. Freed was an R&B deejay at WJW in Cleveland in 1952 when he applied the black euphemism for sexual intercourse to a conglomeration of music. His sponsor, Leo Mintz, encouraged Freed to play R&B originals, and Freed generally stayed away from white covers of black music throughout his career (Larkin 1998: 151). Freed moved to New York's WINS in 1953 and began to host rock & roll concerts, first in New York and then elsewhere. He appeared in a series of rock & roll films, making enemies in the music world for his championing of rock & roll. Eventually, a riot at a Boston concert in 1958 and a conviction of payola in 1962 ended his career.

Freed's career was greatly aided through his collaboration with Chuck Berry, the duck walking master guitarist and composer. More than anyone else, Berry brought the electric guitar to its preeminent position in rock & roll. Berry had a great deal of sexual energy and an ability to focus it on the problems of adolescents. He was able to give content to what Freed had only hinted. Berry was a classic blues storyteller who had soaked up the lessons of the great Louis Jordan.

According to Larkin (1998:52), Berry was born in 1926 in San Jose, California, not in St. Louis as he claims. Like Ray Charles, Berry cites Nat Cole as a great influence on his singing. Berry's first hit was "Maybelline" in 1955. He quickly followed that up with "Thirty Days," "No Money Down," "Roll Over Beethoven," " Brown-Eyed Handsome Man," School Days," "Sweet Little Sixteen," and many others that topped the R&B charts. Larkin (1998: 32) sums up his success in this way.

> Between 1955 and 1960, Berry seemed unassailable.
> He enjoyed a run of 17 R&B Top 20 entries, appeared

in the films *Go Johnny Go, Rock, Rock, Rock* and *Jazz on a Summer's Day* . . .

Larkin also indicates that it was Berry who clarified rock & roll's message through bringing a needed discipline to its vocals and performance. He also set a template, which the next generation followed.

The mix of black music tailored to white adolescent audience becomes even more curious when the case of Leiber and Stoller is considered. Jerry Leiber and Mike Stoller were two Jewish boys who managed to write from a Black perspective without condescension and with total authenticity. Leiber and Stoller managed to catch the Black idiom and attach it to stories of urban life that blacks could sing with comfort.

Both Leiber and Stoller had grown up around African Americans and had embraced black culture, especially its music. They felt that writing music was a sign of respect for the culture. Interestingly, they did not feel that whites should perform the music. Both Leiber and Stoller were well grounded in that music, Leiber in blues and Stoller in jazz.

Their first R&B hit the Robins', later renamed the Coasters, "That's What the Good Book Says," came out in 1951. The next five years were a period of intense R&B activity in which Leiber and Stoller wrote songs for the black R&B audience. These songs attracted such artists as Ray Charles, the Isley Brothers, Jimmy Witherspoon, Big Momma Thornton, and Joe Turner. They included "Hound Dog" and "Kansas City," among others.

Leiber and Stoller turned to the new Rock & Roll along with the Coasters and others of their clients. They, too, began to address the white teenage audience that favored the more commercial music that addressed their needs. They managed to keep their sounds soulful even if they began to address mainly white teens rather than a broader black audience.

Larkin (1998: 224) states that songs such as "Smokey Joe's Café," "Searchin'," "Yakety Yak," and "Charley "Brown," each a hit for the Coasters, marked a transition from straight R&B to Rock & Roll. Each hit the wit, urban black language, and story-telling genius associated with Leiber and Stoller at their best.

Inevitably, the duo expanded their repertoire and wrote hits for Elvis Presley ("Jailhouse Rock"), Ben E. King ("Stand By Me"), and such stalwarts of non-rock music as Peggy Lee ("I'm a Woman"). They even wrote for Dion. According to Larkin (1998:225), they seemed unable to cope with the later changes in the music and went into and out of retirement. Their work is still on Broadway in Smokey Joe's Café.

Doo-wop Music

The success of the Broadway musical *Smokey Joe's Café* also illustrates the continuing popularity of what has come to be called doo-wop music. This type of music was exemplified by a number of groups in the 1950s. Doo-wop music featured a simple four-part harmony that young male teens could, and often did, sing on street corners. Groups such as the Ink Spots anticipated doo-wop music. The Ink Spots popularized simple four-part harmony with a falsetto tenor and deep booming bass voice. They also put in human sounds to replace musical instruments, a major feature of later doo-wop tunes. These characteristics became dominant among fifties doo-wop groups.

The Drifters, for example, were a black doo-wop group. The height of their popularity was from the mid to late 50s to the mid 60s. The group had very gifted members, including at one time or another: Clyde McPhatter, Gerhart Thrasher, Andrew Thrasher, Bill Pinkney, Ben E. King, Rudy Lewis, and Johnny Moore. (Collins, 3/17/99). The drifters had a string of hits that transcended many of the changes in music that occurred during this volatile time. They included "There Goes My Baby," "On Broadway," "Save the Last Dance for Me," and " Under the Boardwalk," among others.

The Spaniels were another popular doo-wop group. Their biggest hit was "Goodnight Sweetheart Goodnight" which continues in popularity to the present. The popular movie, *Three Men and a Baby*, for example, used it throughout the film. The rock revival group, Sha-Na- Na used the tune as its closing theme. "Pookie" Hudson, the Spaniel's lead singer, wrote the song. As an example of the complex mix that was 50s music, several musicians during the 1950s, including The McGwire Sisters and Pat Boone covered the hit and had successful hits of their own with the song.

Elvis, Orbison, Perkins

On the other side of the divide, as Morris puts it, was Elvis Presley. In many ways, The King came to transcend the divide and become an icon by himself. Nevertheless, in 1956 there was no real way to know that he would become his own category. Elvis Presley was born in Tupelo, Mississippi, on January 8, 1935. By all accounts he was a rather shy misfit and something of a mommy's boy in his adopted hometown of Nashville. However, after some false starts he became a star, a white boy who could sing like a black man, as Sam Phillips put it. 1956 was his breakthrough year. "Heartbreak Hotel" went to number one on the charts. Presley had 18 top hits and 20 others that made the top ten list. His fame carried him through generally forgettable movies, although he did begin his career with an obvious talent that could have been developed as were Crosby's and Sinatra's.

Some of Presley's hits were "I Want You, I Need You, I Love You," "Jailhouse Rock," and, of course, his first major hit, "Heartbreak Hotel." Although most of his hits are in the general rock & roll vein of the times, others demonstrate Elvis's rather wide range – from soft ballads to gospel-tinged renditions. There are successful efforts to crossover to the "establishment" with "The Wonder of You," and "Can't Help Falling in Love (With You)," not to mention "Are You Lonesome Tonight."

Presley influenced a number of imitators and followers. Prime among them was Roy Orbison. Orbison tended to accent the Rockabilly joined with rhythm and blues side of Presley. Over the years he developed his own personality and made his own contributions to the evolution of the music but his roots were deep in Presley's music. Orbison was a multi-talented performer. He was a fine guitarist and songwriter as well as a vocalist with a three-octave range who knew how to use his soaring falsetto tones to add depth and mystery to his performance.

Orbison began as a country vocalist for the same record company, Sun that signed Elvis. His first hit was also in 1956, "Ooby Dooby" (1956). He left Sam Phillips to join Monument Records, achieving distinction as a melancholy romantic singer. John Belushi, one of his biggest fans, parodied Orbison's trademark dark glasses, dark clothing, and black pompadour hairdo, both as one of the Blues Brothers and as a Roy Orbison imitator.

Carl Perkins, who had the original hit on "Blue Suede Shoes," is another artist who was very much in the Presley vein. Perkins also went on to establish his own style and voice. Perkins pioneered Rockabilly, a fusion of blues, country, rhythm and blues, and gospel that is one of the sources of what became rock and roll. Perkins's hit "Blue Suede Shoes" became the definitive theme of the movement.

In common with many of the early stars of rock & roll, he began playing at a young age and formed a band in his teens. In Perkins's case, he played with his two brothers. After hearing Elvis, the trio noted the similarity of their styles and decided that Nashville was the place to be. Perkins joined the Sun record stable and opened for Presley in the mid-50s. Sun Records gave him the opportunity to compose and produce. An accident, unfortunately, stalled Perkins's career. He continued to write hits like "Honey Don't" (1956) and "Matchbox" (1957), but Presley's popularity far outstripped his own.

Presley's version of "Blue Suede Shoes" reached Number one on the charts; ahead of Perkins's number two. Perkins, however, did become a major influence on the development of the music through his compositions and guitar playing. His hard-rocking guitar playing influenced the Beatles, among others. His songs received wide circulation among rock & rollers and country performers, including the Beatles and Johnny Cash.

America's Oldest Teenager, Dick Clark, and the Teenage Idols

Dick Clark was born in 1929. Thus, he was well out of his teens when he became American Bandstand's second host in 1956. Bandstand was a local Philadelphia show when Clark became its host but so popular was big brother Clark that ABC distributed it nationally in beginning August 5, 1957. For the next six years, it was live every weekday afternoon.

Clark's low-key style helped gain fans for rock and roll since many figured if a nice boy like Clark liked the music it couldn't be too dangerous. Clark broke with the tradition of having black artists' music covered by white performers. On Bandstand, he played the original recordings for his teens to dance to. And his teen regulars danced every popular dance – The Slop, The Hand Jive, and The Bop. Bandstand even introduced new dances of its own – the Stroll, the Circle, and the Calypso among them.

Clark made it a practice to introduce the original talent behind the records on his show. Bill Haley and the Comets, James Brown, Buddy Holly, Connie Francis, Bobby Darin, Fabian, and Ritchie Valens, among others, got their national start on Clark's show. For over forty years, Clark, the man who never grows old, continued to play popular music on the air.

He is often credited in helping to make rock the success that it became. He introduced many new records for teens to judge. Their stock reply, "It's got a good beat and you can dance to it," has become part of the lore of the fifties. But dancing was much of what the music was about at the time. Clark emphasized the fun that the music represented and became a clean-cut spokesman for that music, an older brother reasoning to Mom and Dad about this new music that many feared so much.

Clark's regulars, like Justine Carrelli and Bob Clayton, started many clothing and dance trends. The fact was that there were no other national shows targeted to teens at the time. Clark used this advantage to press quietly for integration. On his show, Blacks and Whites were together, peacefully dancing and performing.

By proving that there was a viable teen audience, Clark had a further impact on popular culture. Other shows came along to tap that audience, Soultrain, Hootenanny, among them. By the 1960s, others had discovered the teen market and the value of targeting that market. Integration was progressing in the entertainment industry and Black performers carved out their niche on center stage.

But Clark had been among the first to push the trend and his quiet demeanor and understanding of his audience served him well as he moved on to other endeavors in show business without ever quite abandoning American Bandstand in the process.

Bachelor Pad Music

A musical form of the fifties that has become popular once again is bachelor pad music. It has become known as Space Age Bachelor Pad Music. Bachelor Pad Music was directed toward an older sophisticated crowd. Exotic Latin and Brazilian rhythms and sounds marked it; parrots and other exotic birds were often on the sound track.

Les Baxter had a series of hits in the 1950s, for himself and others. For example, he arranged Peruvian singer Yma Sumac's 1950, "Voice Of The Xtabay," which became a landmark of exotic music. Baxter went on to produce a number of albums for Capitol, including - - *Tamboo* (a top 10 hit in 1956), and between 1956 and 1959 *The Sacred Idol*, *Rita Of The Savage*, and *Skins*. *Skins* demonstrated a new dimension of the genre, one that exploited its puling exoticism. Perhaps, Baxter's most famous composition is "Quiet Village." This song became an instrumental hit for Martin Denny, reaching number four in 1959. Its exotic birdcalls are still imitated and those who lived through the period often parody the sound at parties. The album, in fact, reached number one during 1959. During the 1960s, there were a number of exotic "Bachelor Pad" instrumentals. Part of the explanation for the music is found in the fact that it exploited the relatively new phenomenon of hi-fi stereo systems, toys for older boys of the time.

The genre lies on one side of a great divide in American popular culture. That rift was visible to millions of viewers on "The Milton Berle Show" of June 5, 1956; there, the King of Rock'n'Roll was pitted against the Godfather of Space Age Bachelor Pad Music. Elvis Presley's swiveling, erotic performance of "Hound Dog" that night set off a storm of national protest, leading Steve Allen to garb Presley in a tuxedo and Ed Sullivan to shoot him from the waist up in later TV appearances. At the benign end of the sonic spectrum was Berle's other musical guest, Les Baxter, who performed "The Poor

People Of Paris," a chirpy hit that had been displaced at No. 1 on the charts by Presley's "Heartbreak Hotel" that April.

Jazz

The LP revolution did a great deal to enhance and preserve jazz's popularity. It allowed not only for longer solos in contrast with the limitation of the old 78s but also for concept albums. In addition, jazz fans tended to be older and a bit more affluent than rock fans, as Playboy had noted. There were many changes in jazz during the 1950s, the Golden Age of Jazz. Thanks to the creation of the jazz festival and its predecessor the Jazz at the Philharmonic road show, it is possible to note the similarity of the different jazz styles as well as their connection. Moreover, it is possible to appreciate in retrospect the fact that most of the important jazz musicians who had lived were alive and working in the 1950s. Jazz' past, present, and future were all there in the 1950s.

Jazz was still a young art form in the 1950s. The Original Dixieland Jazz Band recorded the first jazz record in 1917. Louis Armstrong and Sidney Bechet, the first two outstanding jazz soloists, were still performing. The great swing musicians were well represented. The be-bop revolution had become part of the mainstream and the new revolutionaries who would blossom in the 1960s, like John Coltrane and Ornette Coleman, were launching their careers or consolidating them in the 1950s. In sum, all forms of jazz could be found in vital live performances not by revival bands or repertory aggregations but by the originals, many of whom were not out of their fifties, like Louis Armstrong, even though younger musicians might consider them old men.

The first of the great festivals was the Newport Jazz Festival. George Wein a pianist and nightclub owner in the Boston area decided to promote a jazz festival in Newport, Rhode Island. Jazz still had a slightly unsavory reputation and the wealthy inhabitants of Newport did not have the reputation of being great supporters of the art form, a fact that added to the spice of the movie *High Society*, the successful remake of The *Philadelphia Story*.

The festival began over the July 4th weekend in 1954 and soon grew to a weeklong event with hundreds of performers. Its excitement can be viewed in a documentary of the 1958 festival entitled Jazz on a Summer's Day. The film made by Bert Stern, gains from the work of Aram Avakian. It was the forerunner of other concert documentaries and is still unmatched for its general quality and the matching of music and setting. It combined a sense of 50s high quality fashion with its love of the cool and the hip.

Stern juxtaposes tryouts for America's cup with the best of jazz. Big Maybelle, Chuck Berry, and Mahalia Jackson show jazz's roots and relatives in performances. Jazz musicians and the relationship of Blues, Rock 'n Roll, and Gospel become quite clear through the performances accompany each of these non-jazz performers. The range of jazz in the 50s is also remarkable. Some of the performers whom Stern highlighted are now mere footnotes to jazz history, known only to aficionados. Their 50s reputations appear inflated in retrospect. Others have stood the test of time and their reputations are still strong. Among the performers were Chico Hamilton, Jimmy Giuffre, Anita O'Day, Theolonius Monk, and Louis Armstrong. There were interesting brief interviews with fans, giving the viewer a good glimpse into the way real people looked and talked in the 50s, rather than the way Hollywood later came to portray the 50s look. Additionally, there are some excellent candid shots of fifties fans reacting to the music and dancing in the aisles, giving the lie to the old canard that you can't dance to "modern jazz."

The Newport Jazz Festival has spawned over 2000 other national and international jazz festivals. Its success has made it common for jazz to be performed in venues other than clubs and auditoriums. Nevertheless, the Newport Festival had other predecessors, most notably Norman Granz's Jazz at the Philharmonic series that began in the late 1940s and reached its height in the 1950s. A 1953 Time magazine piece on JATP's second European tour began in this fashion.

> Two thousand Swedish fans turned out in Stockholm last week to hear a rocking sample of the best brand of U.S. jazz, beaten out and bellowed by some of the best U.S. practitioners. First, half a dozen instrumentalists gave them a round of modern combo numbers, including C-Jam Blues and Perdido. Then Songstress Ella Fitzgerald stepped forward, let loose with Why Don't You Do Right? In addition, St. Louis Blues. Finally, the stage was darkened, and Gene Krupa, his face spotlighted from below, flailed away on the drums.

> Between numbers, the packed hall resounded to roars and whistles of approval and the stamping of teen-age feet. Afterward, it took the performers 45 minutes to fight their way through the ecstatic crowd outside. For U.S. Jazz Impresario Norman Granz, it was a comfortably reassuring beginning for his

second annual invasion of Europe with his package
show, "Jazz at the Philharmonic." In the next ten
weeks, he and his musical tourists expect to put on
much the same kind of program -- and get much the
same kind of flattering attention -- in such cities as
Oslo, Brussels, Paris, Geneva, Zurich, Milan and
Turin.

The Jazz at the Philharmonic series grew out of Granz's
promotion in his junior year at UCLA of a concert featuring Nat Cole,
Lester Young, and Billie Holliday on the same bill. It gave jazz fans a
chance to hear a number of stars perform with their own groups on the
same bill. He felt that it filled a niche seriously lacking in jazz. After
being in the Special Forces for a time in WWII, Granz sponsored a
concert at Philharmonic Auditorium in Los Angeles. "The posters were
supposed to read "Jazz Concert at the Philharmonic Auditorium," but
there was too little space. The cards read "Jazz at the Philharmonic,"
and the name stuck. "
          Granz left Los Angeles after the directors of Philharmonic
auditorium told him that they did not appreciate integrated
performances. He never booked his JATP back into the auditorium that
gave his show its name. Beginning in 1946, he took his show on the
road to about 60 cities a year. Granz summed up the reasons for the
success of JATP, and for the festivals that followed in the 1950s. "I
give to people in Des Moines and El Paso the kind of jazz they could
otherwise never see or hear." A glimpse into 1950s prices incidentally
is given by his advice on scaling a house. "He also believes that he has
learned as much as any living man about scaling a house, i.e., deciding
how many seats to price at $4.80, etc. "You can't get piggish," he says.
" On the other hand, you can't be easy. I've got a sixth sense about it."
          The Festival Scene came at an opportune time for jazz, for
dancers had gone to rock 'n roll, either live or in the sock or record
hops that featured records played by disk jockeys. The big ballrooms
had either closed or were deemed not appropriate for most of the
modern jazz musicians. The jazz clubs were hurt by the luxury taxes
left over from World War II, extended through the early Cold War
period and the Korean conflict. The college kids fueled the Festival
culture in great measure, and the king of the college circuit was Dave
Brubeck.
          Brubeck was associated with the "cool" West Coast sounds of
jazz. He also seemed to be part of the more cerebral movement in jazz
that tied into the jazz with classics movement. The Dave Brubeck
Quartet was immensely popular and its sound was one of those that

helped identify an era. In spite of being considered "too white" by some critics, the Dave Brubeck quartet won the first jazz poll conducted by a black newspaper, _The Pittsburgh Courier_. Brubeck further angered some jazz critics when his picture appeared on the cover of Time Magazine. Nevertheless, Brubeck's album" Time Out," and its singles, "Take Five" and "Blue Rondo a la Turk," became the first in modern jazz to "go gold."

Brubeck took part in the jazz ambassador program by going on several world tours sponsored by the State Department in the Middle East and Eastern Europe. These tours gave Brubeck many ideas for multirhythmic performances and further increased his popularity. They also led to an album of a play he wrote, "The Real Ambassadors," setting forth a program for civil rights that carried over into the sixties. The album featured a number of jazz musicians, including his quartet and Louis Armstrong.

Country Music

The fifties witnessed a major change in country music and its spread to mainstream popularity. It spread from an isolated base in the south to nationwide acceptance. It did so through incorporating electronic sounds, such as amplified guitars and a more popular approach to music, one in keeping with popular music in general. Hank Williams, one of the most popular country singers, began his career in the forties and never claimed to be anything else but a country singer, exploring the many diverse forms of that genre. Williams was at home in any kind of country setting but was most noted for his honky-tonk tunes, such as "Hey Good Looking, What You Got Cooking?" Along with Williams, Lefty Frizzel and Ernest Tubbs helped popularize the honky-tonk style, noted for its amplified guitar riffs and hard-driving beat and tales of "outlaw" life. In addition to being a stellar performer, Williams composed a number of famous tunes; many recorded by artists in no way associated with country. Tony Bennett, for example, had a hit with Cold, Cold Heart. Sadly, on New Year's Day 1953, Hank Williams died in the back of his Cadillac, a victim of living the life he sang about. Pills and booze did him in, making him a legend at 29.

A number of people carried on in William's tradition. Others developed a new style. Gentleman Jim Reeves brought crooning to the country world, for example. The most popular of the new styles, however, was the mixture of black music with country. Elvis Presley began as a country singer who mixed rock with country, a "white man who had the Negro feel," in the words of Sam Phillips the owner of Sun Records. "That's Alright Mama," a cover first recorded by rhythm and blues singer Arthur "Big Boy" Crudup, startled the music world, especially country fans, as did the flip side, a souped-up version of Bill Monroe's bluegrass classic, "Blue Moon of Kentucky." This recording was the first of the "rockabilly" genre. Johnny Cash, Carl Perkins, and Jerry Lee Lewis, among others, would develop and profit by the rockabilly sound, changing country music, and the country's perception of it. Country stars no longer had qualms about incorporating popular sounds into their performance, a trend that continues to the present.

Conclusion

As the decade ended, the various musical forms continued to evolve. In the 1950s there was still a type of uneasy alliance brought about by the confusion of the marketing label rock & roll and the promise of great money to be made from fifties teens and their disposable incomes. However, as the 1950s end and the world began to get more complex with the escalation of the Vietnam War in the 1960s and the maturing of the baby boomers, the music began to split into various factions.

White rock would go its own way into "progressive" rock and its many forms. It would become increasingly amplified and often turn its back on the steady beat of old time rock & roll. In the 1960s, much of its momentum would come from protesting the war and the establishment. From time to time it would remember its roots and pay tribute to black blues musicians as the Beatles and Stones did but it became increasingly enamored with experiments and tricks that advancing technology made possible, such as tape splicing and recording. Toward the end of their partnership, for example, the Beatles became mainly a studio band.

Rhythm and blues evolved into Soul Music and later allied itself in the strange partnership between black musicians and gay men that characterized disco. In the sixties, however, the Motown Sound carried on a more polished rhythm and blues tradition with incursions from B.B. King and Muddy Waters and their colleagues, providing an updated blues sound for the black musical mix that inspired so much of the sixties musical sound.

Country music continued its musical evolution into glitzier and more popular acceptance. Dolly Parton, Johnny Cash, and others continued to incorporate and tame wilder rock and rhythm and blues sounds. Glen Campbell and John Denver crossed over into the pop scene as often as they made country records. The genius of Ray Charles united soul music with a country sound that pleased Nashville audiences as well as urban boomers.

The big bands were often pronounced dead but Ellington and Basie continued the tradition and Dizzy Gillespie managed to revive his big band periodically. The State Department helped Benny Goodman and others revive their big bands as part of the cultural exchange program. Moreover, Woody Herman's Herds just kept getting better as the sixties went on. Maynard Ferguson and his high note trumpet and Buddy Rich and his drums kept up the big band tradition. The reports of the death of the big band were greatly exaggerated.

Jazz entered a period of protest as the sixties evolved. Much of sixties jazz was for a very small audience as it often became incoherent. Much of the old Dixieland and bop tradition continued, however. Miles Davis and others tried to become popular with the youth through changing their styles and becoming electrified. The old core audience, however, tended to abandon these new styles, arguing that there wasn't much jazz in fusion or jazz-rock groups. Chicago and Blood Sweat and Tears as well as Chase did manage a popular blend that kept touch with their jazz roots.

Fifties music was regarded as old hat and even "Uncle Tom" by many of the sixties rebels. Only in the 1980s did a fifties revival begin that has lasted into the 1990s. It was a vital period for music and in retrospect, the roots of much of today's music can be readily discerned.

Suggested Readings and Works Cited

Ake, David. Re-Masculating Jazz: Ornette Coleman, 'Lonely Woman,' and the New York Jazz Scene in the Late 1950s. *American Music* 16: 1 (Spring 1998), 25-44.

Cross, Alan. *20th Century Rock and Roll: Alternative (20th Century Rock & Roll Series)* New York: Collector's Guide, 2000.

Goldberg, Joe. *Jazz Masters of the Fifties.* New York: Da Capo Press, 1998.

Larkin, Colin, Editor. *The Virgin Encyclopedia of Fifties Music (Virgin Encyclopedias of Popular Music)* New York: Virgin, 1998.

Marvin, Elizabeth West, Editor. *Concert Music, Rock, and Jazz Since 1945: Essays and Analytical Studies (Eastman Studies in Music).* Boydell & Brewer, 1995.

Hill Trent. The Enemy Within: Censorship in Rock Music in the 1950s. *South Atlantic Quarterly* 90: 4 (Fall 1991), 675-707.

McKeen, William. *Rock and Roll Is Here to Stay: An Anthology.* New York: W. W. Norton & Company, 2000

Morrison, Greg. *Go Cat Go! Rockabilly Music and Its Makers.* Champagne: University of Illinois Press, 2000.

Pruter. *Doowop: The Chicago Scene.* Champagne: University of Illinois Press, 2000.

Romanowski, Patricia, Holly George-Warren, and Jon Pareles, Editors. *The New Rolling Stone Encyclopedia of Rock & Roll.* New York: Fireside, 1995.

Wilmer, Valerie. *As Serious As Your Life: John Coltrane and Beyond (Five Star).* New York: Serpents Tail, 2000.

Chapter 12

The Performing Arts

The 1950s was a transitional period in the area of performing arts. Movies, theater, dance, and, yes radio, had examples of past, present, and what was to come. It exhibited the best and worst of these periods but in a context of change and experimentation that was exciting in itself. Often what was popular was also what has come to be regarded as high art. Perhaps just as often, it was simply schlock, schlock that has achieved a certain classicism of its own.

Each of the performing arts had its "high art" and its schlock, but it interesting to see how much overlapped and how reputations and opinions have altered over the years.

Changes in Hollywood in the 1950s

The 1950s marked major changes in the Hollywood. Perhaps, the most significant change was the end of the studio system. There were two major reasons why the studios lost their dominance over the industry. Certainly, television's popularity eroded movie profits. It was so easy to stay at home after a hard day's commute that many people decided not to leave their homes for entertainment when it was available so cheaply and easily at home. The Federal courts' decision to force studios to give up their monopoly on distribution and exhibition of films also ate away at their control.

Studios had actually been losing business to Independent distributors and theaters since the end of the Second World War. To survive, they sacrificed their huge staff of creative talent and turned to technology as a means of salvation. Thus, the fifties observed numerous wide-screen processes: CinemaScope, Cinerama, VistaVision, 3-D, and stereophonic sound systems. People often went to the movies to see what they couldn't on TV, technological wonders and full color.

The stress on technology did not mean that good movies were no longer made. There were good movies and even some glamour was left in. Think Marilyn Monroe, Grace Kelly, Audrey Hepburn and Jayne Mansfield. Movies, in fact, became more daring in an attempt to go beyond what the censors allowed on TV. The films became more realistic and allowed greater freedom for directors like Elia Kazan, John Frankenheimer and Sidney Lumet. There were also great film stars in a sense that no longer was possible after the fifties when the studio system broke down and competition from television and other media reduced the influence of the screen. There were stars such as Marlon Brando, Marilyn Monroe, Burt Lancaster, Montgomery Clift, Judy Holliday, James Dean, Paul Newman, Elizabeth Taylor, Charlton Heston, Doris Day, George C. Scott, Audrey Hepburn, and Sidney Poitier.

Eventually, however, by the mid-fifties, studios found it necessary for survival to produce material especially for television. Many studios turned to producing commercials, and for some the worst insult of all was the selling of older films to TV. In effect, movies were competing with themselves. Many studios became mere distribution centers, leaving production to independent producers.

The independents did provide a wide variety of films appealing to various tastes. Since their profit margins could be lower, they were more willing to go for smaller audience. Moreover, many of these new producers filmed on very low budgets. Thus, there were the teen exploitation horror, science fiction, and rock 'n' roll stories. The big studios struggled to find a winning formula, turning to big musicals, vast screens, and finally fighting censorship to allow the presenting of a harsher and sexier reality.

More Stars of the 1950s

The fifties were really the climax of super movie stars. Marlon Brando (b. 1924) was among the greatest of them. Brando was the epitome of the "method actor," following the precepts of Lee Strasburg of the Actor's Studio. Strasburg stressed a naturalistic performance style. Brando recreated his portrayal of Stanley Kowalski in Tennessee Williams's *A Streetcar Named Desire* (1950), starred in *Viva Zapata!* (1952), played Marc Antony in Shakespeare's *Julius Caesar* (1953), won the Best Actor Oscar for his performance as a battered dockworker in *On the Waterfront* (1954), and even sang in *Guys and Dolls* (1955).

Marilyn Monroe (1926-1962) was perhaps the most famous American motion-picture actor ever. Certainly, her fame has lasted longer than her brief life, as has that of James Dean and Elvis Presley who were her contemporaries. Like Dean and Presley, Monroe became a sex symbol, the most famous of the fifties and possibly of the entire 20th century.

The transformation of Norma Jean Mortenson born significantly in Los Angeles into Marilyn Monroe is a story that has been often told. Her mother was mentally unstable and Norma Jean spent much of her early life in foster homes.

At 16 she entered into a doomed marriage. In 1944 she began her modeling career, posing for pin up posters for soldiers. The next step was the movies where initially she failed. She worked briefly for 20th Century- Fox and Columbia. However, in 1950 2oth Century-Fox gave her another chance, and her acting in *The Asphalt Jungle* (1950) and *All About Eve* (1950) drew favorable attention. She ignited the screen in *Don't Bother to Knock* (1952) in which she portrayed a psychotic babysitter. In 1953 she starred in *Niagara, How to Marry a Millionaire*, and *Gentlemen Prefer Blondes.*

Although Marilyn could act, the studios choose to accent her obvious physical charms. She became an international sex symbol, and her films, many of them quite good, became famous for showing as much of her body as the censors would allow. She starred in a number of films in this "sex symbol" period, including *River of No Return* (1954), *There's No Business Like Show Business,* (1954), and *The Seven-Year Itch* (1955).

Monroe married the great baseball hero Joe DiMaggio in 1954 but divorced him the next year because of his possessiveness and desire to have her become a good housewife. She then decided to attend the Actors Studio and change her image. But her studio did not want to lose its number one box office attraction to serious art.

20th Century-Fox gave her more money and creative control. Monroe made a critical success playing opposite Laurence Olivier in The *Prince and the Showgirl.* Her next film gave her a chance to satirize her sex symbol role. *Some Like It Hot* (1959) has become a classic, and her performance with Jack Lemon and Tony Curtis is among her best. She finished the decade with Yves Montand in *Let's Make Love* (1960), a mediocre film.

James Dean so captured and symbolized the fifties that he still stirs interest today. His few movies still play frequently on TV and are in demand at video rental stores. Dean projected an androgynous sexuality that came into high favor in the sixties. (Think Mick Jagger and all those longhaired hippies.) Teen aged bobby soxers preferred to think of it as a "boyish vulnerability." Guys generally related to his suffering toughness. After all, Bogie (Humphrey Bogart) projected a good deal of brooding in his own acting. Dean's looks were more delicate than earlier male heroes but in *Giant* Dean proved he could be rugged and malicious in a more orthodox macho fashion. Only Elvis Presley and Marilyn Monroe have proved to be greater Hollywood icons in their deaths than James Dean. Dean, however, was the only one of these fifties icons to do in the fifties and to solidify his "serious" reputation as an actor by the time of his death.

Notable Films of the 1950s

The great movies of the fifties include many that were enormously popular, such as *Rebel Without a Cause, The Wild One, Invasion of the Body Snatchers,* There were a number of films that dealt openly, sometimes trivially, with adolescent rebellion. *Blackboard Jungle* (1955) concerned teenage violence in an inner-city high school. Glenn Ford plays a teacher who has problems with high school punks. It was deemed so violent that the American Ambassador to Italy, Claire Booth Luce, had it excluded from the Venice Film Festival. It was among the first of many films dealing with teen violence in schools.

Rebel Without a Cause, dealing with teenage violence through a feeling of anomie, or loss of a sense of meaning and purpose, was an extraordinarily influential film in a period in which there were supposedly no rebels. James Dean proved that he was an actor who could capture a generation in this film.

The fifties witnessed many fine film noir movies. Among them was the detective classic, *Kiss Me Deadly* (1955). This film found Ralph Meeker portraying Mickey Spillane's pulp detective hero Mike Hammer. Meeker brought a cool toughness that was part of Mike's charm in the series. Perhaps, Meeker was the best of the many screen Mike Hammers. Meeker was able to display Mike's moody, lurking violence and vigilante sense of justice. The movie was a major influence on the French New Wave movement. It also had the distinction of introducing Mary Richards future neighbor, Cloris Leachman.

There were a number of "quiet" movies that told stories about average people in everyday situations. Many of these movies came to the big screen from television. Perhaps, the most famous and best was "Marty." The film won a number of Oscars, including one for Ernest Borgnine in the title role. Borgnine, who was also in 1953's "From Here to Eternity," played a Bronx butcher who is much under his mother's control. Marty is not a glamorous person but a good hardworking stiff. He has basically given up any hope for romance. He does find love with a plain woman who is not Italian, a fact his mother and aunt find reprehensible. Paddy Chayefsky adapted his script from his TV play and won an Oscar as well. The movie won the 1955 Oscar for Best Picture Oscar as well.

The United States began to confront some its racism through movies. One of the better films to do so used American racism toward Japanese American, a subject that few Americans wished to confront in the fifties One of the first Hollywood films to deal openly with white racism toward Japanese Americans during World War II, this drama directed by 1950s action maestro John Sturges ("The Great Escape") stars Spencer Tracy as a one-armed stranger named MacReedy, who arrives in the tiny town of Black Rock on a hot day in 1945. Seeking a hotel room and the whereabouts of an ethnic Japanese farmer named Komoko, MacReedy runs smack into a wall of hostility that escalates into serious threats. In time it becomes apparent that a local racist police chief Reno Smith (Robert Ryan) has murdered Komoko. This local cop also plans on dispensing with MacReedy. Tracy's hero is forced to fight his way past Smith's goons (among them Ernest Borgnine and Lee Marvin) and sundry allies (Anne Francis) to keep these other alive, setting the stage for memorable suspense crisply orchestrated by Sturges. Casting is the film's principal strength, however: Tracy, the indispensable icon of integrity, and Ryan, the indispensable noir image of spiritual blight, are as creatively unlikely a pairing as Sturges's shotgun marriage of Yul Brynner and Steve McQueen in *The Magnificent Seven*.

B Movies and Drive-Ins

On the other hand, there were the movies that American International Films' producer Sam Arkoff made, drive-in classics. These films were the forerunners of Scream, *Nightmare on Elm Street*, *I Know What You Did Last Summer*, and other slasher horror films. They played well at the drive-ins because drive-ins were where 1950s teens went to get to know the opposite sex a little better. The A.I.P. films were rather stale melodramas but the fifties equivalent of a date movie. The films, however, did produce what is now the modern language of rebellion. These movies demonstrate t hat the fifties were a rather complex period, comprised of more than just hula-hoops and Vaseline greasy hair.

The main purpose, however, of drive-movies for a "guy" was to encourage his "date" to move closer to him, on his lap if possible. There was little interest in the possible classic or campy nature of the horror and Sci-Fi films that were the main fare of fifties drive-in movies. The scarier the better was the motto of many teens.

During the fifties the drive-in reached fad status. Drive-ins had been around since at least the early 1930s. But the car culture of the fifties turned these gravel pits into a major date place. Kids could check out their friends' cars and dates. They could show off their own steadies and cars in turn. It didn't really matter what movie was showing, because no one really watched the movie.

Drive-ins resembled gravel and dirt fields. Most were set at the town's edge. They had a large screen across from a concession stand. Small speakers were on poles and were hung on your window. Each car had its own mount and speaker. The sound was bad, but no teen was really listening to the movie. Rain caused some excitement for someone was certain to be stuck in the mud.

In 1958, the number of drive-ins was 4,063, an increase from 1948's 820 Drive-ins. Hollywood cranked out Drive-in movies. There were virtually no plots and the acting ranged from bad to very bad. No one really cared. Teens were in their own space and with a date. Sci-Fi and Horror movies were the most popular, for they were reputed to be great "make out" movies. Drive-in were a focal point of entertainment for many teens. Their huge screens, car speakers that often were pulled free by careless drivers who forgot they were there, refreshment stands that brought in more money than the low admissions – all these added to their charms for fifties teens. A carload of teens could often gain admission for one-dollar. Despite the low cost, many fifties teens claim to have sneaked in via the car's trunk. Each week, or even more frequently, there was a new feature. There was always a double bill and sometimes there were three feature movies. The titles of some of the more popular drive-in movies gives an idea of their content: *Creature From The Black Lagoon*, *Revenge Of The Creature*, *Invaders From Mars*, *It*, *Terror from beyond Space*, and *Forbidden Planet*.

Forbidden Planet (1956) was an inspiration for *Star Trek* and all that followed. Leslie Neilsen, in his more serious acting days, starred in the film as Commander Adams. He leads an expedition of astronauts, equipped with a flying saucer, to Altair 4. The expedition's purpose is to rescue two survivors of a previous expedition. Walter Pidgeon plays

Professor Morbius. Anne Francis depicts his daughter, Altaira. These two survivors, with Robby the Robot's aid, have made a home for themselves. Morbius does not want to be rescued. However, the inevitable monster makes rescue the only alternative to death.

Walt Disney and Animation

Walt Disney continued his reign as the magical Pied Piper whom parents trusted and kids adored. He found various ways to keep his product before the public, using all media available at times. Walt Disney was simply America's purveyor of wholesome entertainment that pleased the family. He moved into the 1950s big screen sweepstakes with 1955's *Lady and the Tramp*, his first CinemaScope feature. Disney based his version on Ward Greene's story *Happy Whistling Dog* about a rakish dog named Tramp who helps pedigreed canine named Lady. The movie is original, with a charm that is not mawkish.

It tells the tale of Tramp, a street-wise but loving dog that falls in love with an aristocratic dog, Lady. Tramp comes to Lady's rescue when she gets into trouble. The film has a combination of innocence, sophistication, romance, and the great tunes that Disney films cultivated. Peggy Lee, a jazz vocalist and songwriter adds a good deal to the film with her vocals and portrayal of one of Peg, one of Tramp's friends, a wise street dog with a heart of gold.

The most famous musical scene is the one with the Siamese cats who get Lady in trouble and help set up the climactic scene in which Tramp saves the Darling's baby. It is true Disney Americana, and very much in the fifties vein of admiring the tough outsider who can be tamed by a loving woman.

Foreign Films

The 1950s witnessed a growing interest in foreign movies. It was an interest related to America's continuing immersion in world affairs as an aftermath of World War II. Americans found that it was not so easy to go back to prewar isolationism. Besides, foreign films explored themes that American movies often did not or could not.

Among the foreign directors, who had achieved *auteur* or author status none was more highly respected than Ingmar Bergman. Bergman achieved his initial fame with his brooding melodramas about sin and guilt. Films such as The *Seventh Seal* (1956), *Wild Strawberries*, (1957) and *The Virgin Spring* (1959) gained him a reputation as a brooding figure with little sense of humor. Certainly, these films established his reputation and influence. However, none of them won so wide a popular following as his classic melancholy comedy about the romantic entanglements of three 19th-century couples during a weekend at a country estate, *Smiles of a Summer Night*.

The film certainly has the Bergman thoughtful cynicism about it but it is at the same time exactly what a classic bedroom farce should be. It is sharp, serious, pensive, austerely sexy, and grave. It forces the viewer to think amid the laughter.

That is not to say that the film does not have a sense of humor. Indeed, much of its punch and further influence comes from finding out that the brooding Swedish director did indeed have a wicked sense of humor, and a romantic streak as well. In orchestrating the moves of his bourgeois cast of character, Bergman elicits not simply laughs, but belly laughs.

Briefly, he has a prosperous lawyer named Björnstrand married to a young shapely woman, Anne. Somehow Ann remains a virgin, in itself an amusing poke at the worldly lawyer. To complicate matters somewhat Bjorn strand's son from an earlier marriage, Henrik, is in love with Ann. To occupy his time, Henrik is having a fling with the maid. Henkrik's affair bothers him because of his deep Christian piety. Bjorn strand's former mistress, Desiree comes to town. While visiting her, Björnstrand discover that she is having an affair with Count Malcolm, an uncouth lout. Surprisingly, he is jealous of the Count. Adding to the already complex complications, the Count is married to Anne's best friend, the depressed and suicidal Charlotte.

Bergman then brings the ensemble to Desiree's mother's estate for a weekend. Confrontations, illicit romances, dinner, dueling, and comedy ensue. Since this film is a comedy, people pair themselves with the right romantic partner. Interestingly, Bergman intriguingly conveys various aspects of both young and mature love.

Stephen Sondheim adapted the film for his play *A Little Night Music*, with its poignant song *Send in the Clowns*. Woody Allen, who has often paid homage to Bergman in movies, used the film as the foundation for *A Midsummer Night's Madness*. The story is a solid one and beguilingly Bergman made the film because his studio was on the verge of bankruptcy and he wanted to raise money to do more "important" films.

Las Vegas

In the 1950s Las Vegas became a major center of entertainment. Interestingly, while Nevada was the first state to legalize casino gambling, it was also the last western state to ban it. On October 1, 1910, Nevada outlawed gambling. The law was so strict that it outlawed flipping a coin for a drink. Illegal gambling quickly returned to Nevada.

In 1931, Nevada legalized gambling, basically to pay for public schools. In fact, over 43% of Nevada's general revenue comes from gambling taxes and 34% of its general revenue goes for education. During the 1930s, gambling remained a small but lucrative business. Las Vegas remained prosperous, for example, during the worst of the Great Depression.

However, Vegas' greatest growth had to await the conclusion of World War II. During the late forties Vegas witnessed a building boom in casinos. These hotels, built along a two-lane highway that led from Los Angeles to Las Vegas, were the start of the famous Strip. One of the key hotels on the strip was the Flamingo, the brainchild of mobster Benjamin "Bugsy" Siegel. Unfortunately, an unknown assailant murdered Siegel in 1946.

The fifties, however, marked the peak of Vegas as it has entered popular imagination. In 1952, the Sands and the Sahara opened. The Sands became the headquarters of Frank Sinatra's Rat Pack, featuring Sammy Davis and Dean Martin. Sinatra aided Davis in integrating Vegas' entertainment and housing. Sands Hotel opened that same year. In 1955, the high-rise hotel in the form of the Riviera came to the Strip. The Royal Nevada, Dunes, Hacienda, Tropicana and Stardust hotels on the Strip and the Downtown Fremont Hotel-Casino also opened in the fifties.

In 1955, outside the Strip, the Moulin Rouge Hotel-Casino opened. The Moulin Rouge was the first club to integrate its show and audience. It attracted great stars and set a pattern for Las Vegas. Joe Louis, the former heavyweight champion of the world, was a Moulin Rouge owner-host. In spite of its popularity and that of Joe Louis, the Moulin Rouge has had not had an easy time. It has closed and reopened many times over the years. Louis became a greeter at Caesars Palace on the Strip. The Moulin Rouge finally gained a long overdue recognition in 1992 when it became a national historic site.

Beginning in 1941when there was only one casino in town; the El Rancho, entertainment and Las Vegas became conjoined. The new fifties hotel casinos followed the El Rancho's lead. In addition to big stars, Vegas showgirls have become part of the Vegas scene. In 1957, the Dunes introduced topless showgirls on the Strip.

In the fifties, the lounges of the casino have provided non-stop 24-hour entertainment for the price of a drink. A number of great entertainers played the lounges: Don Rickles, Buddy Hackett, Shecky Greene, Alan King, Louis Prima and Keely Smith, and the Mary Kaye Trio among them. The theory was that if the casino could get people inside the door, gambling would prove too appealing to resist. Vegas became known as the place where anything goes. There was no cover, no minimum, no state speed limit, no sales tax, no waiting period for marriages, no state income tax and no regulation of gambling. Those days ended with the waning of the fifties.

Theater

1950s drama witnessed a flowering of magnificent talent. Certainly, the rise of Tennessee Williams and Arthur Miller was simply the peak of an enormous wave. The postwar prosperity reached Broadway as well as other entertainment centers, and Broadway profited from the work that New York based television and its thirst for writers brought forth.

Tennessee Williams

Thomas (Tennessee) Williams was born on March 26, 1911, in Columbia, Missouri. Although best known for his plays, Williams wrote film scripts, novels, and short stories as well. He was considered shocking for his time because of his exploration of underlying sexual tensions. However, his overriding talent, ear for dialogue, and use of seemingly quaint Southern idioms. Williams won Pulitzer Prizes for *A Streetcar Named Desire*, and *Cat on a Hot Tin Roof*, both made into powerful movies. For many, however, their favorite Williams's play is the one for which he should have but didn't win an award, *The Glass Menagerie*.

Williams attended two universities, the University of Missouri and Washington University, before being graduated from the University of Iowa in 1938. Williams seemed to mature slowly in his writing as in his college career. However, his 1945 play, *The Glass Menagerie* won the New York Drama Critics' Circle Award. It became a classic American movie in 1950. The play was largely autobiographical and caught the attention of generations of theatergoers.

Williams, however, became more notorious for his treatment of sexual frustration than for his basic sympathy for his characters, a sympathy he always exhibited along with a profound ironic sense of humor. Perhaps, the most famous of his works was *A Streetcar Named Desire*. Although the play was produced in 1947, the film was very much a part of the fifties, being released in 1951. It vaulted the stage actor Marlon Brando into Hollywood prominence as Stanley Kowalski who has an affair with his wife's spinster sister Blanche Dubois. It is virtually the model for portrayals of personal disintegration.

Summer and Smoke, The Rose Tattoo, Cat on a Hot Tin Roof (1955; film, 1958)" deal with frustrated female passion. *Cat on a Hot Tin Roof* is the first of Williams's plays to deal openly with homosexuality, a theme toned down a bit in the movie. Williams began to deal more openly with the theme of male homosexuality in *Cat on a Hot Tin Roof*, and *Suddenly, Last Summer* (1958; film, 1960), *Sweet Bird of Youth* (1959; film, 1961). The later films use classical themes for modern plays. Williams explored the darker aspects of the human mind in dealing with murder, cannibalism, and emasculation. Paul Newman starred in each of the movie adaptations of these latter plays and used them to help secure his screen reputation

Williams proved he hadn't lost his sense of humor with *Period of Adjustment* (1959), a perceptive play and later movie about the problems of the newly married. In the play, Williams depicts two newly married couples and the minor problems that each must face. To the characters, of course, these minor problems appear to present major problems. But after a short "period of adjustment," in which each person must make compromises to achieve a more satisfactory married life, all works out well. The play is an often-overlooked small gem in his career.

The fifties proved to be the high point of Williams's career. He continued to write until his death in 1983 and some of his latter works are indeed good but none is so fine as his uniformly good productions in the fifties. Similar comments can be made about Arthur Miller who also had a long series of critical and popular hits in the 1950s.

Arthur Miller

Miller was born in 1915 and had his first success in 1947 with *All My Sons*, a family drama, which told the story of a factory owner who caused the death of several American pilots during World War I by selling defective parts to the government. The factory owner did so even though one of his own sons was in the military. Miller's work continued to be concerned with responsibility and guilt. *Death of a Salesman* became an instant classic and was performed to great acclaim in 1999 in a brilliant revival featuring Brian Dennehy.

Despite argument about whether Miller's play was really a tragedy, it captured the 1949 Pulitzer Prize for drama. Miller argued in a democratic fashion that any play that dealt with the willingness of an individual to die for his dignity was a tragedy, no matter how "little" that person may be.

Miller has been deeply concerned with the human condition in America and takes great pains to bring social factors into his works.

The Crucible, as so many of his plays, is a criticism of a social evil he feels to be of major concern in American life. As one critic wrote, "The merit in Miller's treatment of his material lies in a certain clean, moralistic rationalism." Miller is concerned with the struggle of the individual to achieve dignity, to develop their talents, and to avoid self-defeat. He believes that to achieve these goals the individual must know his or her limitations and adjust to them.

Miller "put his money where his mouth" was when he refused to cooperate with the House Un-American Activities Committee in its search for Communists in the entertainment world. Miller acknowledged his own earlier Communist ties in the 1930s but refused to name names and thus save his own skin in so doing. He chooses instead to be brought up on contempt of Congress charges. John Steinbeck, a giant in American literature wrote an article defending Miller. In that article he wrote," There is no doubt that Congress has the right, under the law, to ask me any question it wishes and to punish my refusal to answer with a contempt charge. The Congress has the right to do nearly anything conceivable. It has only to define a situation or an action as a "clear and present danger" to public safety, public morals, or public health. The selling or eating of mince pie could be made a crime if Congress determined that mince pie was a danger to public health--which it probably is. Since many parents raise their children badly, mother love could be defined as a danger to the general welfare. Surely, Congress has the right to ask me anything on any subject. The question is: Should Congress take advantage of that right?"

Steinbeck concluded that if law were not moral, it would not survive. The record of the House Un-American Activities Committee was such as to cause any reasonable person to wonder about its judgment and morality. It used liars and perjurers, not to mention betrayers of friendships for its purposes, and did so to no decent end. "I feel profoundly that our country is better served by individual courage and morals than by the safe and public patriotism which Dr. Johnson called "the last refuge of scoundrels."

Miller decided to tackle the great dilemma of loyalty to country and personal dignity allegorically in *The Crucible*, an attack on the witch-hunts of the fifties through depicting the Salem witch trials. Miller's play *The Crucible* (1953), although concerned with the Salem witchcraft trials, was actually aimed at the then widespread congressional investigation of subversive activities in the United States. It won the 1953 Tony Award. The play probably helped lead to his appearance before the House Committee that found him guilty of contempt, a verdict later reversed on appeal.

Miller had great success in the fifties with plays such as *A View from the Bridge* (1955)," about a dysfunctional Italian-American family from Brooklyn. He gained more fame for his marriage to the screen idol, Marilyn Monroe, winning her from baseball legend Joe DiMaggio. His 1964 play *After the Fall* is based on that incident from his life. Miller has continued to write and with some success but has never had the sustained success that he did in the 1950s.

Modern Dance
The fifties saw a continuation in the evolution of "serious" dance. While classical ballet remained popular, popular enough for Ed Sullivan to feature the Bolshoi Ballet whenever they came through New York City, modern dance continued to attract attention, a fact that Sullivan also noted on his TV show.

Generally, modern dance rose to prominence in America in the 1930s under the influence of Martha Graham. The angular movements of modern dance are its most noticeable, and satirized ones. In contrast to the light and graceful movements of ballet, they often appear comical to the average person. Moreover, Graham clad her performers in costumes that emphasized their bodies. The overall effect was to stress simple, stark emotions, those very emotions that classical ballet neglected.

A new style of music aided choreographing these basic emotions. Composers like John Cage and his contemporaries minimized music into its elements. This "minimalism" allowed dancers to dance to a single instrument rather than a symphony, striping emotions to their core.

Grahman inspired a number of dancers: Merce Cunningham, Paul Taylor, Twyla Tharp, and Mark Morris among others. Even those who laugh at her style find that Graham has influenced their work.

The 1940s was her most successful decade, laying the groundwork for fifties dance styles. Aaron Copland and Samuel Barber wrote scores for her works, which were concerned with her symbolic dance dramas.

Graham peaked in the fifties, insisting on dancing well past her prime. However, in the fifties she was still capable of choreographing and dancing, thrilling audiences by her sometimes-horrific ideas, such as having Medea eat her own entrails. Her floor movements and lack of leaps and swoops brought dancing more to the level of depicting everyday feelings.

Her greatest rival was George Balanchine, the master and proponent of neoclassical ballet. Together with Taylor and Cunningham, who had worked with her but repudiated her work, neoclassicism became more popular than her dance works. Balanchine centered his work at the New York City Ballet, which he founded in 1948. Balanchine came to the United States from France in 1933, developing a modern version of classical ballet. Finally, at the New York City Ballet over the fifties, Balanchine's vision came into view. He wrote works for the ballet and choreographed them. ` Jerome Robbins joined Balanchine in 1949, having written two ballets, including the masterpiece "Fancy Free," and choreographing four successful Broadway shows. The partnership worked well. Balanchine was responsible for 113 ballets in the period between 1948 and 1983 while Robbins created 43.

There were many other dance highlights in the fifties. In 1952 Merce Cunningham established a dance company at Black Mountain College, N.C., leading to a lengthy collaboration with composer John Cage. Bob Fosse was gaining popularity on Broadway and in 1953 brought the pelvic thrust from Burlesque to the hit play *The Pajama Game*. "Steam Heat," was the hit song to which the dance was performed. More elegantly, perhaps, 1953 marks the founding of Paul Taylor's dance company. In 1954 George Balanchine created *The Nutcracker* (Tchaikovsky/Balanchine), for the New York City Ballet. It is still a holiday fixture as well as the most performed ballet in the world. Another great and popular dance company emerged in 1956. Robert Joffrey took takes six dancers in his station wagon and began a tour. Ten years later he made it official and founded his company, the Joffrey Ballet. Jerome Robbins introduced his style of ballet to Broadway in 1957's *West Side Story* (Leonard Bernstein/Jerome Robbins). It became a hit. When it went to Hollywood, it won 10 Oscars. America has always had a fascination with black dance. Alvin Ailey took advantage of that interest to found his own dance company in 1958, a company dedicated to African-American choreography, dancers and music. Modern dance had its first complete televised program in 1959, Hanya Holm's *Tragic Exodus*.

Both Ailey and Joffrey exhibit much of fifties culture in their lives and dances. Both came of age in the fifties. Joffrey was born in 1928 and Ailey in 1931. Both loved classic ballet but merged it with modern techniques. Joffrey and Ailey produced dances that were famously accessible to the general public. So much so that staid critics faulted them on their popularity alone.

Katherine Dunham was a major influence on Ailey, especially her *Tropical Revue*. Ailey came to New York from Texas in order to perform in Truman Capote's Broadway adaptation of *House of Flowers*. In 1958 Ailey's troupe performed their first concert. At the end of the decade in 1960, Ailey presented his most famous and successful work, *Revelations*, a stunning dance based on spirituals.

Robert Joffrey, a Seattle native, Joffrey's major influences were the Hollywood dancers, Gene Kelly and Fred Astaire. Instead of the boxing lessons his parents wanted him to have because of his small size, he pleaded for dance lessons. He moved to New York, determined to teach ballet, using his acting ability to compensate for his five feet four inches. Joffrey's first concert with his own company was in 1952's *Persepone*. His greatest successes came during the remainder of the decade, especially 1956's *Pas Des Deesses* and the 1955 *Pierrot Lunaire*.

Merce Cunningham took Graham's ideas and merged them with traditional ballet. Cunningham used the spine as the source of movement, organizing dance on chance and making it independent of movement or setting. He wanted his dancers to experience the here and now rather than history or setting.

The dance innovations of the 1950s continued to influence changes in later decades. Dancers such as Paul Taylor and Twyla Thorpe, for example, have incorporated many of the innovations of fifties dance and continued to apply them in new ways.

Popular Dancing

Latin music really became popular in the 1940s. It never entirely left the popular scene, and the cha-cha and mambo among other dances helped keep America dancing. The limbo came from Trinidad, West Indies. Originally, it was a funeral dance. Basically, mourners walked toward a horizontal bamboo pole and attempted to walk under it while leaning backwards. The point was to move under it without knocking it down. The dance symbolized the passage of the soul between this world and the next. The dance symbolized the difficulty of the journey between the two worlds. Limbo is the place between heaven and hell where the soul would spend this difficult time. As each successful person went under the pole, it was moved closer to the ground.

American tourists brought the dance back to the United States in the 1950s and it caught on as a fad. A Trinidadian dancer, Boscoe Holder, became famous as a limbo dancer, using the step in his routine. Teens were first to popularize the craze and then beats followed. Soon older people followed suit. The dance reached its peak in 1960 with the movie *Where the Boys Are*, in which it was featured. It was revived with Chubby Checker's 1963 hit *Limbo Rock*.

However, rock 'n roll became the dominant form of popular dance. Hip rolls moved onto the popular dance floor, thanks to Elvis the Pelvis Presley. Presley first major record, "Heartbreak Hotel" hit

the charts in 1956. Just before Elvis's hit, Bill Haley and His Comet hit it big with "Rock Around the Clock," featured in the film "The Blackboard Jungle" (1955), one of the better teenage rebellion movies. Dick Clark's "American Bandstand" was almost as famous for its cast members' dancing as far its music. Of course the two went together.
The Bunny Hop, a conga line "dance" from a hit record by bandleader Ray Anthony has also maintained its popularity, at least at wedding dances and other group party gatherings.

Soon the show's teens began inventing dances to supplement the basic Lindy Hop step inherited from an earlier age. The stroll, Monster Mash, and eventually the Swim and other steps seemed to multiply without end. Certainly, rock 'n roll had "a good beat and you can dance to it," as the cliché line on Bandstand went. The decade ended with Chubby Checker's Twist, a dance performed with gyrating hips and body and an attitude that said it all. "Doing your own things" became the norm. The fifties ended having paved the way for the sixties.

Suggested Readings and Works Cited

Byars, Jackie. *All That Hollywood Allows: Re-Reading Gender in 1950s Melodrama (Gender and American Culture.)* Chapel Hill: University of North Carolina Press, 1991.

Kobal, John. *Film-Star Portraits of the Fifties: 163 Glamour Photos.* New York: Dover, 1980.

Mordden, Ethan. *Coming Up Roses: The Broadway Musical in the 1950s.* New York Oxford University Press, 2000.

Russo, William. *Junior Bad Guys: Movie Delinquents of the 1950s.* New York: 22 Publishing, 2000.

Wilmeth, Don. B. and Christopher Bigsby, Editor. *The Cambridge History of American Theatre: Post-World War II to the 1990s (Cambridge History of American Theatre, Vol 3).* New York: Cambridge Univ Press, 2000.

Chapter 13

Television

When the 1950s began, there were four television networks. NBC, CBS, ABC, and the Dumont Network. CBS and NBC had been very successful in radio broadcasting, and they continued to dominate television in the 1950s. ABC was formed in 1943 because of a lawsuit, which the Roosevelt administration won against RCA, the owner of NBC. RCA had two national radio networks. Edward J. Noble, who owned Lifesavers Candy Company, purchased RCA's Blue Network. In spite of its willingness to experiment, ABC never finished better than third in the ratings. At least it survived the fifties, while Allen B. DuMont's network folded in 1955.

The top three networks convinced a compliant Congress to keep TV competition limited. Thus, Paramount Pictures and Zenith, among others, were victims of some strange regulations. For example, in 1948 the Federal Communications Commission (FCC), yielding to the networks' pressure, instituted a freeze on the issuance of new station licenses making only the 12 very high frequency (VHF) channels available for broadcasting. This effective ban on the other 69 stations, the UHF channels, led to an artificial scarcity. With the boost of a compliant Congress, then, the Big Three controlled network TV and the huge revenues that control made possible.

From their inception, the TV networks followed the commercial lead of network radio. Sponsors produced virtually every television program. It was common in the fifties to have a sponsor's name in the show's title like *The Texaco Star Theatre* (1948-1953). The Nielson rating system that is still with us sprang from the desire of sponsors to know how many people their ads reached.

Television in the 1950s was by necessity experimental. Everything that was being done was being done for the first time - and it was live. There was no tape in the early days. There was something called kinescope, a filming of the TV program from a monitor. If it weren't for those fuzzy black and white images, we would only have the memories of those performers and viewers who were lucky enough to be present to rely on. Fortunately, we can view the programs that are preserved and judge their quality for ourselves.

Although that quality is not, alas, consistently high, it is surprising that so much of it is of superior integrity. There is indeed wholeness in much of early television, a unity between intent and achievement. Certainly, that integrity was not accidental. Early television evolved from radio and had the benefit, and drawbacks, of its experience. It also began with relatively young people, those most likely to experiment in a medium in which no one was an expert.

By 1950 radio had achieved an expertise that brought certain sophistication to program production. There were many performers and writers who had developed clear-cut styles but who were also able to improvise on their feet. A variety of formats had been tested, and the general public's taste been measured. Writers learned their crafts on the job, and many had learned them well. Many radio programs simply prepared a version for television and into the 1950s stars such as Jack Benny kept their radio programs while succeeding in television.

However, television soon learned that the demands of a visual medium are different from these of an aural one. The master pantomimist Red Skelton had adapted to radio by developing a stable of characters. Television allowed him to display his great skill at mime. Groucho Marx, similarly, was great as host of *You Bet Your Life* on radio but his facial gestures added a great deal to the television version.

Fortunately, in its early years people would watch test patterns and tended to let television's novelty amuse them while people worked out the kinks. Working out the kinks produced some brilliant experiments with freshness that only live TV can bring. When Jackie Gleason found the door to his television apartment stuck, he climbed in through the window. The audience roared.

In ways similar to the early days of the computer revolution, youngsters in their early 20s dominated the new medium. Steve Allen seemed to be on television all the time. He was young, healthy, and full of charm and ideas. Sid Caesar was also in his twenties and his brilliant writers appear to be little more than kids learning by doing, and do they did.

The Comics, Talk Shows, and Variety

Steve Allen was born Stephen Valentine Patrick William Allen on December 26, 1921 in New York City. He died in Los Angeles in October 2000. He had a remarkable show business career. Among his many achievements are hosting the first *Tonight Show* on NBC, having a successful variety show that competed with Ed Sullivan for three seasons, being a better-than-average pianist, composer, fiction writer, radio host, and political activist, among other accomplishments. In 1986, Steve Allen was inducted into the Television Hall of Fame.

On July 27, 1953, Allen, already a show business veteran though barely in his thirties, began a late night program on a local New York City station. On September 27,1954, it became *The Tonight Show* on NBC. Allen stayed with the program until January 25, 1957, when he left to concentrate on his Sunday evening variety show.

Many of his regulars went on to forge respectable show business careers of their own. His "regulars" included Steve Lawrence, Eydie Gorme, Don Knotts, Bill Dana, Andy Williams, and Skitch Henderson, the show's musical director. The show was a mixture of conversation, sketches, and performance. Allen featured many jazz artists on this and his other programs, often joining them and displaying his own talents in that area.

His wife, Jayne Meadows, joined him on *The Steve Allen Show*, and it survived from June 24,1956 to May 3, 1959 in spite of being opposite the unbeatable *Ed Sullivan Show*. Allen had his regulars, many from the late-night program, and kept a steady pace, filled with jazz guests. The show appealed to the hip but finally had to yield to Sullivan's wider family appeal.

A different type of comedian is Red Skelton.   Red   (Richard) Skelton born on July 18, 1913, in Vincennes, Indiana, is the proverbial star of stage, screen, and radio. He is also the proverbial paradox of one whose talent spans low and high comedy. His skill as a mime is second to none but the bread and butter of his act has been "low comedy" characters; such as, Willy Lump-Lump, Freddie the Freeloader, Junior the Mean Widdle Kid, and Clem Kaddidlehopper.

Skelton's father was a circus clown and for a time Red followed in his footsteps. He began his career at ten years old with a traveling medicine show. Only when an established star did he begin to catch up on his education. Skelton left the medicine show to enter the Clyde

Beatty Circus, following the same circus his dad had worked in. After viewing Beatty being mauled, Skelton left the circus, no longer dreaming of being a lion tamer. He entered vaudeville and a new phase of his career.

He met his future wife, Edna, while playing burlesque in Kansas City in 1928. It was one of those hate at first sight turning into love themes that Hollywood later perfected. Edna became his partner and writer and, in 1931, just before he was 18, wife. In Montreal, Edna noticed a man nervously dunking his doughnut. She wrote the skit up and it became a Red Skelton trademark.

He used it in his first movie 1938's *Having a Wonderful Time*. Although the movie had Ginger Rogers and Lucille Ball, it was a flop. His first appearance in a film included his classic donut-dunking bit, a masterpiece of pantomime. He was a hit.

He appeared in a number of movies and on radio before succeeding in television. Rather forgettable films, such as, *The Fuller Brush Man*, followed his first film. Skeleton hit his stride on radio where he was somewhat of an anomaly, a pantomimist on a sound medium. It was for his radio program, essentially, that he developed his string of characters, which he later successfully adapted to TV.

TV, however, gave him the opportunity to display his ability to do pantomime. Skeleton is also a consummate actor and he could wring tears from his audience in the midst of their belly laughs. That acting ability was nicely displayed on a 1956 Playhouse 90 program, *The Big Slide*. His Civil War veteran sketch in which an ancient veteran watches a Fourth of July parade was a classic mixture of pathos and humor.

Skeleton's show was a CBS Tuesday night staple from September 22, 1953 to June 15, 1970. Before that he was on NBC from September 30, 1951 to June 12, 1953. Although his CBS show was still in the top ten in 1970, CBS canceled it to appeal to a younger audience.

The premier comedy program of the 1950s, however, was *Your Show of Shows*, variety show (1950-1954). The variety was excellent but what distinguished the program was the state of the art satire and parody performed by an ensemble led by Sid Caesar. Caesar was blessed with a stable of young writers that included, at one time or another, Neil Simon, Woody Allen, Mel Brooks, Carl Reiner, and Larry Gelbart.

The program took advantage of television's ability to be topical. It was live TV at its best and Caesar and his partner, Imogene Coca, could parody recent films, including foreign films at will. Because of the dangers of McCarthyism, however, they could not parody politics. The ability of its performers to ad lib was essential in its success, since there were no retakes in live television.

Caesar was born in Yonkers, New York, in 1922.He entered show business as a Juilliard trained saxophonist and enjoyed success in a number of famous big bands. During his army service, Max Leibemann, who became his producer on *Your Show of Shows*, noticed his ability to make his fellow band members laugh. He decided to feature Caesar as a comedian in future productions. In 1949 after appearing in nightclubs and on Broadway, Caesar began his television career in the forerunner of *Your Show of Shows*.

The program took six days to put on, from writing to performing. Caesar notes the difference between *Your Show of Shows* and television today in an interview for *The Saturday Evening Post*.

> I didn't come in and have a script handed to me. Never happened. The show took six long days to write, and I was there on Monday morning, working with the writers, putting in the blank sheet of paper. See the show had to be written by Wednesday. Thursday we put it up on its feet. Friday we went over it with the technicians and Saturday was the show – live."

The program ran for 90 minutes and was number one for four years. NBC decided to have two programs that would be highly rated and *Caesar's Hour* and *The Imogene Coca* show were born. "Caesar's Hour" was highly rated for a time but Caesar's descent into alcoholism and pill taking finally took its toll and its fourth season was its last.

Although Caesar eventually had a number of female partners on his various shows, Imogene Coca is the one best remembered by fans. She began acting at 11 and had a long career before joining Caesar on *Your Show of Shows* She became a comedienne under protest. Leonard Sillman drafted Coca and Henry Fonda into doing comedy bits for scene changes for his *New Faces* Broadway production. Until then, she had been noted for her singing, dancing, and acting. However, she so impressed the critics that she became hailed as the next great comedienne .In 1949 she joined Caesar in the Admiral Revue that was the forerunner of *Your Show of Shows*. She left to do her own television program after the 1954 season. It failed, as did her reunion with Caesar in 1958.

Your Show of Shows paved the way for *Saturday Night Live* and other similar live revues like *Second City*. It has remained popular on PBS and in the sale of videos. The movie *Ten from Your Show of*

Shows, featuring ten of its classic skits did well commercially and is still available on video.

Ed Sullivan's success is a harder to understand because he had virtually no performing talent at all. He was a successful newspaper columnist and had some success as a radio emcee. But from the beginning in 1954 his program, originally the *Toast of the Town* was a solid hit and became a Sunday evening family staple. He introduced over 20,000 acts during the course of the program, his "Re-e-aly Big Shew." His acts covered virtually the entire gamut of show business from the Italian mouse/puppet Topo Gigio, through Bob Hope, who made his first TV appearance on Sullivan's program. Sullivan discovered the great violinist Itzhak Perlman, presented Elvis, cut off at the waist on his last of three appearances, and, continued courting the teens of the family with the Beatles in 1964. He presented Grand Opera, circus acts, comics, mimes, and anything else, including scenes from Broadway plays. There were certainly more talented hosts than the somewhat wooden Sullivan but there were none more successful.

Sit-Coms

TV has bequeathed the sit-com to us. They filled up a good deal of space on the channels of the fifties, just as they do today. In fact, TV sit-coms came from radio, as so much else on television. Many of the early television sitcoms came over completely from radio versions.

The once exceedingly popular *Amos and Andy* (1952)-radio program did not make it on TV even though Alvin Childress and Spencer Williams, two black actors played its lead characters. On radio Freeman Gordon and Charles Correll, two white men, played *Amos and Andy*. The NAACP protested the racial stereotypes and the CBS network cancelled it in 1953. Given today's fare that supposedly appeals to the African American audiences, *Amos and Andy* seems tame. *Abbott and Costello* (1952) brought their radio program to television and did Eve Arden with her *Our Miss Brooks* (1952), *Burns and Allen* (1956), and William Bendix with his *Life of Riley*.

The best of the sit-coms was undoubtedly Lucille Ball and Desi Arnez's *I Love Lucy*. It is still seen somewhere in the world every day of the year. This program also had its roots in radio. It began with a 1948, Lucille Ball program called "My Favorite Husband" on CBS radio. Lucy starred with Denning. Her program character was Liz Cooper, a scatter-brained wife whose imagination got her into trouble most of the time, a theme familiar to *I Love Lucy* fans.

. *My Favorite Husband* was one of many hits CBS series slated for transfer to TV. Lucy's marriage was in serious trouble, so Lucy tried a desperate move, refusing to move to TB without her husband. The network initially refused, arguing that no one would believe she was married to a Cuban, an interesting observation since she was married to a Cuban.

Lucy embarked a vaudeville tour with Desi to prove that the country would accept her marriage to a Cuban. The tour was a huge success, and Lucy followed it up with a hit movie, teamed with Desi. So CBS was convinced and agreed to let Desi play her husband, Phillip Morris sponsored the show, and *I Love Lucy* was born on October 15, 1951.Because of network problems, Lucy and Desi began Desilu Studios. The basic plot is familiar to any TV viewer. A bandleader named Ricky Riccardo is married to a housewife named Lucy. Their neighbors, Fred and Ethel Mertz are also their landlords and best friends.

I Love Lucy won 5 Emmy Awards and had more than twenty nominations. Sadly, Desi never received a nomination. The show was number one in the ratings for each of its seasons. Its regular run ended in 1957 when Desi's executive responsibilities made it too difficult to do a weekly show. Thirteen specials were done each year as *The Lucy and Desi Comedy Hour*. Lucy and Desi's divorce in 1960 also ended the program, except in syndication.

Desi, whose contributions are often overlooked, was a master straight man, a brilliant executive, and a fine director. He introduced the use of three cameras in TV production, a major innovation. His skills at administration helped the show's success, and Lucy never found another professional partner who suited her better.

There were many other sit-coms but only Jackie Gleason's Kramdens could ever come close to matching the Riccardo's for popularity and staying power. *The Honeymooners* was a spin-off from his variety program. The episodes showed a more urban, rather than suburban perspective on American life. Even Lucy and Ricky eventually moved to the suburbs. Gleason's Ralph Kramden viewed Prospect Park as the outer reaches of the suburbs and would have been lost in Scarsdale or Connecticut.

Ralph was, in his words, a working class stiff, and Ed Norton, his buddy, was his perfect pal. Certainly, they were an inspiration for grittier shows to come, including *All in the Family*. There was no doubt that Alice and Ralph loved one another, and their shouting and carrying on was closer to what viewers saw at home than the careful politeness in many sit-com homes.

There were many other sit-coms in the 1950s that still have their share of fans and that have left their mark on others that have succeeded them. Among the more notable are *Topper* (1953) with Leo G. Carroll and Lee Patrick as Cosmo and Henrietta Topper and Robert

Sterling and Anne Jeffreys as the "ghosts" George and Marion Kirby, *Make Room for Daddy* (1954) with Danny Thomas as Danny Williams and Jean Hagen as Margaret Williams, Love *That Bob* (1955) with Bob Cummings as photographer Bob Collins and Ann B. Davis as Charmaine "Schultzy" Schultz, *The Real McCoys* (1957) with Walter Brennan as Grandpappy Amos McCoy, Richard Crenna as Luke McCoy, Kathy Nolan as Kate McCoy, Lydia Reed as Hassie McCoy, and Michael Winkleman as Little Luke McCoy, the comic strip character *Dennis the Menace* (1959)with Jay North as Dennis, and Joseph Kearns as Mr. Wilson (1959-'63), Finally, there was *The Many Loves of Dobie Gillis* (1959) with Dwayne Hickman as Dobie Gillis, Tuesday Weld as Thalia Menninger and Bob Denver as Maynard G. Krebs. And of course, there was the Beav of "Leave It To Beaver."

Action Programs

Perry Mason's two-hundred-forty-five episodes are seen somewhere in the world every day. They have never stopped running in syndication since the demise of the original series on September 4, 1966. The original hour-long series ran from September 21, 1957 to September 4, 1966 and was set in Los Angeles. Very few of the original programs were in color.

There had been ample preparation for the debut of Perry Mason on television. The character had first appeared in *The Case of the Crimson Claws* in 1933. Fifty-three Perry Mason novels had been released before the first Perry Mason television show was aired. Warner Brothers released the first Perry Mason movie, *The Case of the Howling Dog*, in 1934. In 1943, Perry Mason went on the radio in a five-day a week soap opera format. The soap portion of the series became *The Edge of Night* in 1956, complete with the radio cast. Gardener separated the soap and the detective quite consciously and shrewdly and kept script approval of the series until its final episode.

The original cast included Raymond Burr as Erle Stanley Gardner's lawyer-sleuth Perry Mason. In retrospect the choice is impeccable but it broke with the tradition of having Mason played by handsome leading men. Burr's portrayal of villains was remarkable but he had enacted two heroes just prior to the Perry Mason role: Steve Martin, the reporter in *Godzilla* and the DA in *A Place in the Sun* These roles appear to have aided him in securing the lead role in *Perry Mason.*

Barbara Hale portrayed Della Street, his faithful secretary, while William Hooper was Paul Drake, Perry's personal private investigator. William Talman was Hamilton Burger, whose fate it was to lose all but one case to Mason week after week. In 1963 Mason lost a case because his client was covering up for someone else. Of course, Mason ultimately discovered the real culprit and had his obdurate client released from prison.

The program combined courtroom drama with basically non-violent sleuthing. The viewer was privy to Mason's private thoughts and followed the procedural mystery in a step-by-step fashion. Any romance between Mason and Della Street was more implicitly suggested than at any time overtly displayed.

Mason, of course, was allowed far more latitude than any real lawyer would ever be permitted in a real courtroom. In fact, it often seemed that he specialized in hearings rather than actual trials. In any case, his fans loved the program and continue to love it in syndication.

Gardner wrote himself the final show, *The Case of the Final Fade-Out*, himself. Its plot involved a TV star that was accused of murdering his producer. His motive, presumably, was control of the series. Gardner appeared as a judge and everyone in the crew had a part in the show.

There were other action shows such as *77 Sunset Strip*, Hawaiian *Eye, Adventures in Paradise"* and "Surfside Six." These shows came on late in the decade and were set in Hawaii to take advantage of the introduction of color TV, limited though its use was. There were other memorable action/suspense shows: *Dragnet* (1955), ´ *Alfred Hitchcock Presents* (1956), *The Twilight Zone*, and a whole series of "adult westerns," including *Gunsmoke* (1955-1975), *Wagon Train* (1957-1965), and *Bonanza* (1959-1973), which focus on the settling of the Western United States.

Dramas

There were many dramatic presentations on television in the fifties. Many had come over from radio, such as *Lux Presents Hollywood*. Others developed to fit the need for programming. Fortunately, there were talented young writers eager to experiment for the new medium. Rod Serling, Paddy Chayefsky, Stephen Sondheim and many other now famous playwrights honed their skills on television.

Playhouse Ninety, The US Steel Hour, and the *Philco Playhouse* were only the more famous of the regular programs. The general quality of the live programs is remarkable in its consistency. Many of the scripts were later used for movies, such as *Marty*, Champion, and *The Days of Wine and Roses*. These dramatic presentations gave young actors a means for developing their own talent. James Dean and Paul Newman were among the many future stars that appeared on early television shows. The term "Golden Age of Television" is often reserved for these dramatic programs.

There were also the seemingly inevitable "soaps, " or soap operas so-called because they tended to be sponsored by soap and detergent products. Irma Phillips is the creator of the soaps. She began to develop these shows in the 1920s. The invention of the soap opera is credited to Irna Phillips, who began developing such programs for local radio broadcast in Chicago 20s for a Chicago radio station. Many of these radio soaps made the move to television. Among her shows are *The Brighter Day* (1954-1962), *The Guiding Light* (1952-), and *The Edge of Night* (1956-1984).

The Game (Quiz) Shows

There were quiz shows, or game shows, on radio, of course, before they came to television. The grand prize on radio, however, was at most $64. On TV it became $64,000, and then it increased, as the programs became increasingly popular. Their popularity seemingly knew no bounds in the late 1950s as people sweated, sighed, rolled their eyes, and otherwise expressed pain as they strove to answer abstruse questions on esoteric topics.

The number of quiz shows reached 22 by 1958. Then the bottom dropped out of the boom as the naiveté of the viewers turned to cynicism. The news of the shows' rigging spread quickly once Herbert Stempel, a disgruntled game show loser blew the whistle after he agreed to lose to Charles Van Doren.

Van Doren was the favorite of the American public. He was a Columbia University instructor from a distinguished family. His father was Mark Van Doren and his uncle Carl Van Doren, both famous poets and scholars. To discover that this fair-haired boy was privy to the fixing of the games stunned the audience. The lies of television executives further upset the public. Finally, the industry's defense was simply that no laws had been broken and that no one had been hurt. It was just entertainment and scripting entertainment was no different for quiz shows than for any other program.

Congressional hearings further gave TV a black eye. No laws were violated but the public stayed away from quiz shows until their return at the end of the 20th century when, ironically, many of the old shows reappeared. *Twenty-One*, the game show on which Van Doren disgraced himself is back as is *The 64,000 Question*, the old Sunday night winner.

Dr. Joyce Brothers, preselected to lose, actually beat the odds and went all the way. She needed the money and spent three months preparing for the contest, becoming an expert on prize fighting. No matter how many answers her opponents may have received. Dr.

Brothers kept winning. She went on to become a TV icon in her own right as one of the early TV psychologists.

Broadcast Journalism

One of the earliest uses of broadcasting was the spread of maritime weather conditions. From that early spreading of weather news, broadcasting went into communicating other information. Ham radio operators and early experimental broadcasters spread the word about election results, entertainment, sports, and gossip. Radio offered live coverage of the news. As with virtually everything else on TV, TV simply added pictures to a form radio had developed.

There were news programs in the early 1950s. By later standards of the decade, they were rather amateurish. John Cameron Swayze had his admirers but NBC's *The Huntley-Brinkley Report* (1956) was appreciably better than what had preceded it. Chet Huntley and David Brinkley covered the 1952 and 1956 conventions for NBC. They worked well together as a team and in 1956 NBC teamed them. Their "Goodnight, Chet" and "Goodnight, David" signoff became famous. The program began as a fifteen minute national telecast presented in the early evening and soon all three networks had film, later videotaped, highlights of the day's events. Walter Cronkite, although present on CBS news programs, did not become a TV anchor until 1962 Walter, "the most trusted man in America," covered various special events and carried over his "You Are There" historical program from radio to TV. By the 1960s TV became most peoples source of news, replacing newspapers and magazines.

At the beginning of the decade, if people wanted to see the news, they relied on Movietone News or some other similar movie filming, shown before the feature film at a double feature at the local movie house. Soon TV offered serious competition. The networks produced hour-long documentary programs during the 1950s, such as *CBS Reports*, a job now virtually the preserve of public television. In 1951 Edward R. Murrow became the reporter for "See It Now." Viewers of the first program saw both the Golden Gate and Brooklyn Bridges. TV spanned the continental United States in one moment. The cigarette chain smoking Murrow, showed Americans the world on TV. When no one else in the television news business was brave enough to take on tail gunner Senator Joseph McCarthy, Murrow did. Eventually, he became too controversial for CBS.

The longest running TV show began in 1947. Lawrence E. Spivak 's *Meet the Press* is still on the air today. TV also covered the 1952 and 1956 National Conventions as well as Eisenhower's two inaugurations. In 1952 Dave Garroway was *The Today Show's* first host, along with Frank Blair on the news desk. The chimp, J. Fred

Muggs was a regular. Garroways signoff was "Peace," said with an upraised hand, palm outward. Sigourney Weaver's father Sylvester "Pat" Weaver conceived of the program.

The McCarthy-Army Hearings

Edward R. Murrow who decided to take on Senator Joseph McCarthy, however, best demonstrated the power of TV. Murrow who had built CBS's news department and fashioned it during World War II decided that it was time to expose the Communist hunter who was exerting such power over the dark side of the American character. Interestingly, Murrow let TV bring down McCarthy through literally showing him at his worst.

The time was certainly ripe for Murrow's expose. McCarthy had overstepped himself by stating that the Army was "coddling Communists. A charge President Dwight D. Eisenhower criticized as "just damn tommyrot." The Chairman of his own Republican party warned McCarthy, and McCarthy's handling of witnesses, including the Secretary of Defense, at his Army hearings drew outraged comments from many Americans. Senator McCarthy discovered that it was one thing to attack Democrats for being soft on Communism; it was quite another matter, however, to attack his own party for the same thing.

The Republicans simply wanted to keep the old tail-gunner off the front pages. That was the perfect opportunity for Edward R. Murrow to use his live program, See *It Now* on CBS-TV to attack McCarthy. On March 9, 1954, Murrow drew a distinction between "investigating and persecuting," saying that the Senator from Wisconsin had repeatedly ignored the line between the two. Murrow showed film clips of McCarthy's speeches demonstrating the Senator's lack of discernment. Television's visual muscle showed McCarthy striking various poses. One commentator noted that McCarthy assumed attitude, various poses, including "laughing or chuckling with an almost fiendish expression." as one writer put it.

Murrow showed that he still knew how to use words as well as image. "His primary achievement," Murrow said, "has been in confusing the public mind as between the internal and the external threat of Communism." The public loved it, including Margaret Truman, President Harry Truman's daughter, who sent congratulations. In fairness, Murrow granted the Senator time to reply, something TV networks had refused him after Eisenhower's criticism.

McCarthy did not deviate from his script. Senator McCarthy stated that Murrow "followed the Communist line." Moreover, the Senator said, Murrow was linked to a Moscow revolutionary school and had spread Communist propaganda. McCarthy's near hysterical behavior fueled by his increasing isolation and heavy drinking further alienated the American people who, thanks to TV, saw him self-destruct.

Murrow's show was his greatest moment on TV. News commentator Elmer Davis said the program "taught everyone who works in television that the medium can show up a man's character and his record . . . by putting on the screen his own actions and words." It did not take the Senator long to show the truth of Davis's words. The Army-McCarthy hearings, televised in full in 1954, allowed McCarthy to destroy his own image. In December, on a 67-22 vote, the Senate voted to "condemn" McCarthy, effectively ending his career. Three years later he was dead.

Children's Television

The first children's TV show was "Howdy Doody, created by "Buffalo" Bob Smith. Like so many early television stars, Smith began in radio. ."I started out professionally in radio when I was 15," Smith recalled. "I was doing everything you could possibly imagine. I was a musician and singer primarily (and) did whatever they needed." Smith' was good enough to sing with a successful professional group, the Hi Hatters, who toured with Kate Smith.

At 17 he not only was hired as a staff pianist on a Buffalo radio station, hut NBC Radio put him opposite the enormously popular New York-based Arthur Godfrey. When Godfrey moved on to other things, Smith's show became the top-rated show in New York. This success prompted NBC to ask him to put together a children's radio program. Smith did so and his friend Elmer became the forerunner of Howdy Doody. Elmer first used the signature Howdy Doody lines that became a later television trademark.

In 1947 NBC wanted a children's television program. They asked Smith to create a program. They gave him all from Tuesday until Saturday. Smith managed to put the program together, but for the first three shows no one saw Howdy Doody because he was in the desk drawer until a puppet could be made. Smith's radio experience and musical experience filled in the gaps for this live show.

The first Howdy Doody puppet was similar to the one that Smith later used for his thirteen year, 2500 episode run. Eventually< he introduced the shows other characters: Flub-a-Dub, Princess Winterspring Summerfall, Clarabell, Phineas T. Bluster, Dilly Dally and Chief Thunderthud were added. Smith also incorporated live kids in the show, using a "Peanut Gallery" that seated 40 kids, plus "Buffalo Bob."

"Howdy Doody" was literally the first show on television, since until that time there was only a test pattern. At 5:30 p. m., hundreds of thousands of kids plunked themselves in front of the TV set to hear Buffalo Bob asking, "Hey kids —what time is it?" Kids in the Peanut Gallery and at home shouted together, "It's Howdy Doody time!"

The program was so enormously popular that there were five kids watching. Per TV set. The show was sold out to sponsors for the 13 years of its reign. Wonder Bread, Campbell Soup, Twinkies and other sponsors who were new to the television medium profited from the show's success, inducing others to enter the lucrative medium. Buffalo Bob took care to sell things that pleased parents as well. He reminded kids to eat vegetables, not eat candy or sugar before meals, cross the streets safely, be kind to others, and other bits of parental advice. Many kids felt closer to him than to their own busy fathers.

"Howdy Doody" had many firsts. It not only opened up each day's lineup at 5:30 p.m.; it was also the first show on the air in color. It was also the first program with live music. It was the first real network TV kid's show and Howdy Doody and his promotional materials demonstrated how lucrative TV aimed at kids could be.

One of the regulars on "Howdy Doody," Bob Keeshan, created a show that was designed to be gentler and with less violence than "Howdy Doody." "Captain Kangaroo" was a network children's staple from October 30, 1955 to December 8, 1984. It contained a mixture of cartoons, stories, songs, and sketches, over which Bob Keeshan, its creator and star, presided.

Keeshan, born in Lynbrook, New York, began his career at sixteen as an after school NBC page. Upon graduating from high school, he entered the Marines and served from June 1945 to September 1946. After being discharged he returned to NBC and became its Fourth Floor Receptionist at Radio City. Keeshan attended pre-law classes at Fordham University. All plans of becoming a lawyer were dropped, however, when he became an assistant to Buffalo Bob Smith, architect of the *Howdy Doody Show*.

One day, he decided to dress as a clown and bring some props on the set. The audience howled with appreciation. For five years after that incident, Keeshan played Clarabell the Clown (1947-1952), a character he created for Howdy Doody. This early exposure nurtured his flair for entertaining youngsters.   On October 3, 1955, Keeshan began *Captain Kangaroo* and that became the focus of his creative attention for the next twenty-nine years, making Keeshan portrayer of the longest running series character in television history. The program featured regular characters; such as, Mr. Green Jeans, Mr.

Moose, Bunny Rabbit, Dancing Bear, Debra, and others.   One commentator has called it "a sit-com for the very young". Although the show appears formless to an adult, Keeshan was aware of the relatively short attention span of his audience and varied his fare accordingly. The program was aimed at six to eight year olds but his audience was comprised of three to nine year olds, and their parents.

Keeshan retained the right to accept sponsors or not and to monitor their method of presentation. This stand left the show under subscribed for much of the early period of its run. By the early 1960s, however, the program brought in millions of dollars in revenue. Basically, parents trusted what the Captain sold.

In common with Fred Rogers, who also took a low-key approach to children, Keeshan emphasized what today is called "values education." He advised kids to "share what you have to share." The books he chose to read on the program were those that addressed the curiosity of young children while being entertaining: *Mike Mulligan*, *Stone Soup*, *The Little Lighthouse*, and others. Libraries reported that circulation rose after the Captain read one of these books.

The fifties saw many other shows specifically aimed at kids. Most were of mediocre quality even by fifties standards for kids shows. Some of the more popular shows were Kukla, Fran and Ollie, a show that began in 1952 and originated in Chicago. Burr Tillstrom was the show's creator. Kukla was the star puppet, and Ollie was a dragon puppet, while Fran Allison was the human of the trio. The program was very low-key and subtle and gave way to more boisterous and action packed programs.

Among the "educational" programs for kids the most popular was Miss Francis's "Ding Dong School, "with "Romper Room," a close second. Interestingly, "Romper Room" was a local show with a national format, for it had local hostess/teachers in each city. In essence, it was a franchised program. There was an identical format in each city. The notion of good doo-bees and bad don't-bees had to be on each program. Before his game show fame, Jack Barry was the host on the children's TV shows "Winky Dink," a rather inane program starring a star.

There were the inevitable animal hero programs, Fury and Flicka, cornered the horse market, except for those trick horses of the cowboy shows like Roy Rogers's Trigger and Gene Autrey's Champion, not to mention the Lone Ranger's Silver. Lassie, of course, had the dog hero market cornered. She, played by a canine female impersonator, took care of each of the five families who owned her.

` Appropriately, Walt Disney decided to put his formidable talents to use on TV. Interestingly, he did so to promote his other venture, especially his new Amusement Park, Disneyland. Both premiered in the same year, 1955. The amusement park in Anaheim, California has kept its original name. The TV show, however, has had six; including "Walt Disney Presents "(1958), and "Walt Disney's Wonderful World of Color" (1961) among them.

Disney, the wise promoter, used the theme parks sections as segments on his TV broadcast. Thus, there were Tomorrowland, Adventureland, Frontierland, and Fantasyland. The seemingly omnipresent Davy Crockett, in fact, first appeared on a Frontierland segment. Disney celebrated the opening of Disneyland on his program with a group of kids who also had a spin-off of their own, the Mousketeers, featuring of course every prepubescent young boy's dream, Annette. The "Mickey Mouse Club" had its own long series to launch.

Yet another show that had its origins on radio had a successful TV run. Froggy the Gremlin moved easily from radio to TV as part of "Andy's Gang," featuring every cowboy's sidekick, Andy Devine. (1955-1960). Devine had been the sidekick on Guy Madison's "Wild Bill Hickock" TV program.

Teens

There were very few programs specifically aimed at a teen audience. In 1956, however, Dick Clark demonstrated to advertisers the power of teens with his successful American Bandstand. The program began as a local Philadelphia show. Soon it went national and the kids on the show became trendsetters. Their dances caught on, their clothes set the style, and their choice of music influenced record sales. Clark also began to integrate performers and audience, quietly demonstrating that Black and White could be together.

Clark helped launch many careers and gave a boost to others. Among those entertainers who profited from his program were Bill Halley and the Comets, Connie Francis, Buddy Holly, Fabian, Booby Darrin, and Ritchie Valens From 1957, when it went national, until the early 1960s when Clark became too busy, "American Bandstand" was on the air each weekday afternoon, giving it a powerful hold among America's teens.

There were Clark imitations but few of the shows reached his audience in the fifties. Sixties shows were more successful and "Soultrain," "Hullabaloo," and others would not have been possible without "Bandstand's" success and proving that there was plenty of disposable income among teens.

Conclusion

Television came of age in the fifties. It had been around in some form as long as radio, and it first it was just radio with little pictures. But by the end of the fifties, those pictures weren't so tiny, and they were in living color. If everything wasn't golden in its Golden Age, enough of it was to make those who were there feel great nostalgia and to make others wish they had been there.

In a short ten-year period, the American public had turned to the little box with pictures as its primary form of entertainment. That revolution affected sports, the movies, the music industry, and clubs. With a flick of the knob, viewers could see the World Series, college football, top entertainers, dramas, and movies. There were no parking fees, no need to dress up, and TV dinners made it possible to eat comfortably in front of the set.

TV at its best could have the viewer "See It Now" with Edward R. Murrow. Space shots would be covered live as would elections, conventions, the Olympics, tragedies and triumphs. Interestingly, the limited number of channels meant that TV helped create, for a brief moment, a common popular culture in the country. Everybody knew the same programs and actors and players. It helped tie regions together through making them more familiar. The same fads – mouse ears, coonskin caps, and hula hoops- advertised products, and way of life was exhibited every day for just about all to see.

Suggested Readings and Works Cited

Aaker, Everett. *Television Western Players of the Fifties: A Biographical Encyclopedia of All Regular Cast Members in Western Series, 1949-1959.* Jefferson, North Carolina: McFarland & Company; 1997.

Anderson, Christopher. *Hollywood TV: The Studio System in the Fifties (Texas Film Studies).* Austin: University of Texas Press, 1994.

Boddy, William. *Fifties Television: The Industry and Its Critics (Illinois Studies in Communication).* Champagne: University of Illinois Press, 1992.

Marling, Karal Ann Marling. *As Seen on TV: The Visual Culture of Everyday Life in the 1950s* Cambridge: Harvard, 1994.

Stone, Joseph and Tim Yohn. *Prime Time and Misdemeanors: Investigating the 1950s TV Quiz Scandal-A D.A.'s Account.* New Brunswick: Rutgers, 1994.

APPENDIX A

Average Prices for Selected Items in 1955

House		$22,000.00
Ford Car		1,606-2,944.00
Steak		.95
Milk/gallon		.86
Average Income		4137.00
Burgers	5 for	1.00
Gas	per gallon	.23
Postage Stamps		.03
Coca Cola	6 for	.37
Women's Jacket		4.95
Men's Rayon Shirt		3.99
Bread	per loaf	.18
TV dinner		.75
House		22,000.00
Ford car		1,600-2, 944.00
Eggs	dozen	.75
Concert Ticket		2.00
Movie Ticket		.75
Record Album		1.00
Black and White TV		476.00
Paperback book		.25
Plane Ticket	NY- LA	200.00
Minimum Wage		.75
Magazine		.25
Baseball Ticket		1.00

APPENDIX B

Time Line of Popular Culture

1950
- Rodgers and Hammerstein win a Pulitzer for Broadway favorite *South Pacific*.; Frank Loesser's *Guys and Dolls* opens on Broadway.
- Favorite songs include "Rudolph, the Red-Nosed Reindeer" and "The Tennessee Waltz".
- Leiber meets Stoller in Los Angeles. Still only teenagers, they begin writing songs that very afternoon!
- Regular color television transmission.
- :Vidicon camera tube improves television picture.
- Changeable typewriter typefaces in use.
- :A.C. Nielsen's Audimeters track viewer watching.
- Marilyn Monroe appears in *The Asphalt Jungle ; All About Eve* wins 8 Oscars.
- Ray Bradbury's *The Martian Chronicles* published
- Levittown expands quickly
- Smokey the Bear introduced by the National Forestry Service
- Nat "King" Cole's "Mona Lisa"

1951
- College basketball point-shaving scandal
- NBA holds its first All Star game
- Joe DiMaggio retires
- *I Love Lucy's* first episode on CBS
- First LaCoste "Alligator" shirt exported to America
- New Jersey Turnpike opens
- *The African Queen*; *A Streetcar Named Desire*
- Walt Disney's *Cinderella* opens in theaters
- J. D. Salinger's *The Catcher in the Rye* published
- Peanuts debuts
- Club Med Opens
- Diners Club offers the first credit card

1952
- FBI's 10 Most Wanted List

- Marilyn Monroe brings back the Sweater Girl look, which Lana Turner had popularized in the forties
- Sony offers a miniature transistor radio.
- *American Bandstand* begins as a local dance show in Philadelphia
- *High Noon* in theaters
- The first 3-D movie released
- First Holiday Inn opens
- Rocky Marciano wins heavyweight championship
- Ernest Hemingway's *The Old Man and the Sea*
- E. B. White's *Charlotte's Web*
- John Steinbeck's *East of Eden*

1953

- *Playboy* debuts, featuring Janet Pilgrim as its first Playmate
- Patti Page's "How Much Is Tat Doggie in the Window"
- Les Paul and Mary Ford's "Vaya con Dios (May God Be with You)"
- Joe DiMaggio marries Marilyn Monroe
- *Roman Holiday*; *From Here to Eternity*
- William Inge's *Picnic* and Arthur Miller's *The Crucible* open on Broadway
- NFL's Dallas Texans become the Baltimore Colts; Boston Braves move to Milwaukee; St. Louis Browns become the Baltimore Orioles
- Bermuda shorts for men become popular
- The Kinsey Report published
- Corvette introduced

1954

- Sporting events are broadcast live in color.
- Transistor radios are sold.
- Regular color TV broadcasts begin
- *On the Waterfront*; Hitchcock's *Rear Window* and *Dial 'M' for Murder* are in movie theaters. *Dial 'M' for Murder* is originally released as in 3-D
- The Chordettes "Mr. Sandman;" Frank Sinatra's "Young at Heart"
- Seamless nylon stockings produced
- Swanson introduces frozen dinners
- Major League Baseball Players Association, first significant profession sports union, formed

- First Newport Jazz Festival

1955

- Music is recorded on tape in stereo.
- *The Seven Year Itch*; *East of Eden*; *Mister Roberts* are hit films
- Sloan Wilson's *The Man in the Gray Flannel Suit* is a major novel
- Ford produces the Thunderbird
- Philadelphia Athletics move to Kansas City
- Allen Ginsberg gives his first reading of "Howl"
- Bill Hayes, "The Ballad of Davy Crockett"; Bill Haley and His Comets, "Rock Around the Clock"; Chuck Berry, "Maybelline"
- Tennessee Williams's *Cat on a Hot Tin Roof* opens on Broadway
- *Mad* magazine debuts, featuring Alfred E. Newman and his "What, Me Worry?" slogan
- Ann Landers begins her advice column
- James Dean dies in an auto accident
- Disneyland opens; "The Mickey Mouse Club" appears on television

1956

- Construction begins on the Guggenheim Museum
- Jackson Pollock dies in an automobile accident
- *The King and I*; *Giant*; *Around the World in Eighty Days* are in movie theaters
- Grace Metalious's *Peyton Place* published
- Elvis Presley's "Heartbreak Hotel", "Blue Suede Shoes", "Love Me Tender", The Platters' "The Great Pretender", Perry Como's "Hot Diggity", and Doris Day's "Que Sera Sera" are top songs.
- Mike Stoller survives the wreck of the Andrea Doria to be met on the dock by his partner, Jerry Leiber, with the news that Elvis Presley has recorded "Hound Dog". The song soon tops both Billboard and Cashbox charts. Many to be the high-water mark of rock & roll history look this upon.

1957

- Disneyland's "House of Tomorrow opens.
- Elvis makes his first movie, *Love Me Tender*

- *American Bandstand* moves to ABC and reaches a national audience
- *The Bridge on the River Kwai, The Three Faces of Eve, Twelve Angry Men* open in movie theaters
- *Leave It to Beaver* debuts
- Frisbee and Hula Hoop introduced
- *West Side Story* opens on Broadway
- Blue jeans and the "Beatnik" look gain popularity
- Elvis stars in *Jailhouse Rock*
- Johnny Mathis has a hit with "Chances Are"; Sam Cooke with "You Send Me"; and Elvis with "Jailhouse Rock"
- Jack Kerouac, *On the Road* ; Dr. Seuss's *Cat in the Hat* published
- NFL's Player's Association becomes a labor unit; NY Giants move to San Francisco; Dodgers move from Brooklyn to Los Angeles
- The sack dress debuts

1958

- Elvis is drafted
- *The Donna Reed Show* debuts
- *Gigi, Cat on a Hot Tin Roof,* open in movie houses
- Truman Capote writes *Breakfast at Tiffany's*
- First Grammy award presented
- Paul Anka become an overnight sensation
- Danny and the Juniors, "At the Hop"; Silhouettes "Get a Job"; Everly Brothers, "All I Have To Do Is Dream"; Laurie London, "He's Got the Whole World in His Hands"
- Arnold Palmer wins his first major golf tournament
- First Pizza Hut opens

1959

- Buddy Holly, The Big Bopper, and Ritchie Valens die in a plane crash
- Ricky Nelson appears in *Rio Bravo* with John Wayne; *Ben Hur; The Diary of Anne Frank* are also hits
- The Barbie dolls appears for the first time and is photographed with the first Polaroid camera
- The microchip is invented.
- Xerox manufactures a plain paper copier.

- Bell Labs experiments with artificial intelligence
- Guggenheim Museum opens
- Lorraine Hansberry's *A Raisin in the Sun* opens on Broadway; Richard Rodgers and Oscar Hammerstein's *The Sound of Music* with Julie Andrews is a major Broadway hit
- Tops songs include Bobby Darin's "Mack the Knife", and The Platters' "Smoke Gets in Your Eyes",
- Shirley Jackson publishes *The Haunting of Hill House*; Philip Roth's *Goodbye, Columbus* is published

APPENDIX C

Political Events

- 1950 President Harry Truman) approves production of the hydrogen bomb and Sends air force and navy to Korea in June
- 1952 Death of Josef Stalin, Premier of the Soviet Union.
- 1953 Fighting ends in Korea
- 1953 U.S. and North Korea sign armistice at Panmunjon. The 38th parallel is established as boundary between North and South Korea.
- 1953 Leftist government of Premier Mohammed Mossadegh in Iran is ousted and replaced with regime loyal to Shah Pahlevi.
- 1953 Eisenhower delivers his "Atoms for Peace" speech at the United Nations proposing an international atomic energy agency and peaceful development of nuclear energy.
- 1953 Geneva Conference on Indochina results in Geneva Accords partitioning Vietnarn at the 17th Parallel and provides for unifying elections in two years.
- May 7, 1954 French garrison at Dien Bien Phu surrenders to the Viet Minh.
- Eisenhower attends the Geneva Four Power Conference and submits his "Open Skies" proposal allowing mutual air reconnaissance over military installations.
- Oct.-Nov. 1956 Suez Canal Crisis. Israel invades Gaza Strip and the Sinai Peninsula, and British and French forces attack Egyptian bases around the Suez Canal.

- Oct.-Nov. 1956 Armed revolt in Budapest, Hungary is crushed by Russian armed forces.
- Oct. 4, 1957 Soviet Union launches first earth satellite, Sputnik, into orbit.
- Jan. 1, 1959 Fidel Castro's guerilla forces overthrow the Batista regime in Cuba.
- May 1, 1960 A U-2 reconnaissance plane piloted by Francis Gary Powers is shot down over the U.S.S.R.
- May 16, 1960 The Paris Summit meeting collapses when Khrushchev demands an apology from President Eisenhower for the U-2 flights.
- 1960 The Congo (Zaire) becomes independent from Belgium on June 30, 1960 and widespread violence leads to intervention by U.N. troops.

Author's Biography

Frank A. Salamone was born in Rochester, NY, in 1939. He received a B.A. in history from St. John Fisher College in Rochester, an MA in History from the University of Rochester, and a Ph.D. in anthropology from SUNY- Buffalo. He has felt at home in both fields of study ever since. Writing this book was a labor of love, for it brought to life for him a happy period of his life, one in which he grew up surrounded by his parents, sister, and loving relatives and friends. Salamone is married to Virginia Ann O'Sullivan Salamone and they have two children, Frank Charles and Catherine Ann-Frances. He has published over 150 articles, over 10 books and delivered many papers at international and national conferences. He is a Professor of Anthropology at Iona College in New Rochelle, NY, and Secretary of the American Italian Historical Association.